WHITE ON BLACK

WHITE ON BLACK

Contemporary Literature
about Africa

John Cullen Gruesser

UNIVERSITY OF ILLINOIS PRESS
Urbana and Chicago

This book is printed on acid-free paper.

Library of Congress Cataloging-in-Publication Data

Gruesser, John Cullen, 1959–
    White on Black : contemporary literature about Africa / John Cullen
Gruesser.
        p.   cm.
    Includes bibliographical references and index.
    ISBN 0-252-01916-4 (cloth : alk. paper)
    1. English literature—20th century—History and criticism.
2. Africa in literature.   3. American literature—White authors—
History and criticism.   4. American literature—20th century—
History and criticism.   5. Americans—Travel—Africa—History—20th
century.   6. British—Travel—Africa—History—20th century.
7. Blacks—Africa—Historiography.   8. Blacks in literature.
9. Africa in literature.   I. Title.
PR149.A37G78   1992
820.9'326—dc20   91-41357
                                                                CIP

To Susan and Jack

Contents

Acknowledgments

This project began as a dissertation at the University of Wisconsin-Madison and would never have been written without the advice and assistance of a number of professors and fellow students there in the English, Afro-American studies, and African studies departments. Discussions with Jan Vansina, Nellie McKay, Betsy Draine, and Tilottama Rajan proved especially valuable. Hours of patient editorial help, invaluable advice, and constant encouragement came from Craig Werner and John Lyons, whom I can never hope to repay for their generosity. I certainly cannot forget the people I worked with during and since my time at Madison, including Kelly Anspaugh, Steve Bernstein, Tom Curtis, Sylvan Esh, Bradley Hughes, John Carlisle, Richard Katz, and especially Eli Goldblatt. Eric J. Sundquist and Aldon Nielson assisted me greatly in preparing my revisions. I would like to thank Kean College for giving me a course reduction to prepare the final version of the manuscript. In addition, longtime friends Phil Johnson, Mike Herrmann, Joe Murphy, and Tim Ungs deserve special mention. I am also indebted to my editors at the University of Illinois Press, Ann Lowry and Rita Disroe, for their advice, patience, and support. Finally, I must thank my parents, my sister, and, most important of all, my wife, Susan, whose patience and love are what really made this book possible.

Preface

Africa? A book one thumbs
Listlessly, till slumber comes.
—Countee Cullen, "Heritage"

In organizing this five-chapter study on fiction and travel literature about Africa by non-black writers since 1945 it has been necessary to perpetuate one pervasive Africanist myth. Because the majority of these writers have accepted the arbitrary distinctions isolating North Africa, southern Africa, and sub-Saharan or black Africa, I limit myself to the final, imaginary category.[1] Given this study's focus on outsiders who depict Africa, the reason for the exclusion of writers such as Chinua Achebe and Nadine Gordimer should be clear.

Less obvious is the distinction between such figures as Elspeth Huxley, Isak Dinesen, and Doris Lessing, on the one hand, and the late Maria Thomas, William Duggan, and William Boyd, on the other. Why do Lessing's twenty-five years in Rhodesia disqualify her while Duggan and Thomas, despite extensive work and living experience in Africa, and Boyd, who spent the first decade and a half of his life in Ghana and Nigeria, are included? First, while Zimbabwe is today clearly a "black African" nation, having acquired majority rule in 1980, when Lessing lived in what was then Rhodesia the country was part of the southern African apartheid world. Second, in the late 1940s when Lessing wrote *The Grass Is Singing*, she was an African writer, living in Africa, and the daughter of a settler. In contrast, Thomas and Duggan were and wrote as Americans in Africa. And Boyd, while he grew up in West Africa, left there for secondary school and university in the United Kingdom and Europe, eventually moving to England permanently. Thus, in the early 1980s when he published *A Good Man in Africa* and *An Ice-Cream War*, he was an outside writer. This study omits Lessing for the same reason it does not deal with Isak Dinesen or Elspeth Huxley. Despite the many significant differences among them, all three of these writers were permanent residents, settlers in colonial Africa, whose writing about the continent resulted from that unique and now largely obsolete perspective.

Rather than writing a genealogy in the strictest Nietzschean and Foucauldian sense, I structured this project to argue that, at least in their works about Africa, creative writers—like their counterparts in philosophy, social science, and literary and cultural criticism—have recently become increasingly aware of discursive formations and have begun to seek methods of circumventing their stultifying and hegemonic influences.[2] To this end, after defining and illustrating Africanist discourse and reviewing the dominant traditions of writing about Africa, I look at contemporary non-black literature about Africa in terms of three postwar generations that descend from the established traditions and a fourth category that deliberately avoids the traditions and consists of attempts to write suppressed history and provide an outlet for silenced voices.

The first postwar generation includes books written between 1945 and and the early 1960s by authors who wholly or largely ignore political changes occurring in Africa during the years just before and just after the first African nations received their independence from the European colonial powers. Although writing as much as sixty years later, these authors exhibit little or no deviation from three firmly entrenched ways of portraying Africa that reached their acme at the beginning of the twentieth century: the expatriate (or going-native) tradition, the political assessment tradition, and the fantasy tradition.

Predominantly composed of works from the 1970s, the second postwar generation contrasts with its predecessor by being much more openly political. However, while these works scrutinize the political realities of postcolonial Africa, they do so within the confines of Africanist discourse and rely on the established traditions of writing about Africa. Thus, in the second generation we find some of the most brutal condemnations of Africa and Africans. Independent Africa is often represented as the worst of two worlds: it is the product of African "primitivism" (a common Africanist theme), and failed European colonialism. This second generation amounts to Africanist adjustments to postcolonial conditions.

By the time we reach the 1980s and the third generation of writing about Africa since 1945, a major shift has taken place. While authors still rely on the political assessment, expatriate, and fantasy traditions, they consciously work to subvert them and often are politically engaged in a way that outsiders writing about Africa have not been previously. Moreover, their sympathies are no longer so clearly and automatically tied to the West and its interests. As a whole this generation reflects a metaconsciousness of Africanist discourse; that is, it understands that the Africa of previous writers exists more in the imagination than in actuality.

The writers of the fourth category, also comprised of works from the 1980s, go even further than those in the third generation by completely abandoning the established traditions. At this point, genealogy in a Nietzschean and Foucauldian sense actually takes place. The non-black depictions of Africa in this last category evince not only the metaconsciousness of the third generation but also a recognition of the need to rewrite history in order to render Africa more accurately.

NOTES

1. Recent African historians, most notably Ali Mazrui, have argued against dividing up Africa into three different sections and stressed the continent's "Triple Heritage": Indigenous African culture, Islamic culture, and Western Christian culture. Nevertheless, these divisions are still widely accepted. In the first chapter of *The African Image*, when Ezekiel Mphahlele uses the word "Africa," he refers to independent "Black Africa," which excludes Southern Africa. Throughout the book he distinguishes between Africa south of the Zambesi and Africa north of the Zambesi. See Ezekiel Mphahlele, *The African Image*, rev. ed., New York: Praeger, 1974.

2. In addition to Michel Foucault and Edward Said, who will be dealt with in the first chapter, see Johannes Fabian's *Time and the Other*, New York: Columbia University Press, 1983, which discusses how the language and methods of anthropology work to negate the "coevalness" of the Knower and the Known.

WHITE ON BLACK

1

An Introduction to Africanist Discourse

My imaginary idea of this country was so lively (I mean that I had imagined
it so vividly) that I wonder whether, in the future, this false image will not
be stronger than my memory of the reality and whether I shall see Bangui,
for instance, in my mind's eye as it is really, or as I first imagined it would be.
                                        —Andre Gide, *Travels in the Congo*

Definition of Africanist Discourse

From the time of Homer to the present, Westerners have reached out
to the least-known part of the world and brought it back as language,
in the process revealing more about themselves and their culture
than about Africans and theirs. "Africanist discourse," a term recently coined by Christopher Miller, refers to a discourse at odds
with itself, projecting the West's desires on the perceived blank slate
of Africa and depicting the continent alternately as a dream or a
nightmare. In this first chapter, I define Africanist discourse and
closely examine Winston Churchill's *My African Journey* to illustrate specific conventions of Africanist discourse. Here, I delineate
Africanist writing more or less in its pure form so that later literature
about Africa can be compared. In order to isolate three ways of writing about the continent that will be reflected in some manner in
many of the later depictions by non-black authors, I discuss, along
with Churchill's book, two other germinal texts, Joseph Conrad's
Heart of Darkness and Edgar Rice Burroughs's *Tarzan of the Apes*.
These three means of depicting the continent are as follows: Africa
as imperialist possession, the political assessment tradition; Africa
as metaphor, the expatriate tradition; and Africa as fantasy world,
the fantasy tradition.

Christopher Miller's *Blank Darkness: Africanist Discourse in
French* supplies a useful theoretical framework for understanding
works about Africa by Western writers. Miller builds on Michel
Foucault's analyses of discursive systems, an approach that Foucault describes in detail in *The Archaeology of Knowledge*, and on

Edward Said's *Orientalism*. Foucault defines discourse as "the group of statements that belong to a single system of formation," and goes on to explain, "thus I shall be able to speak of clinical discourse, economic discourse, the discourse of natural history, psychiatric discourse."[1] Foucault stresses the connection between power and discursive systems. These systems restrict people to seeing and talking about a subject in pre-established ways; exceptions are explained away or ignored because there is no way to talk about them. In other words, discursive systems are at heart violent: "We must conceive discourse as a violence that we do to things, or, at all events, as a practice we impose upon them; it is in this practice that the events of discourse find the principle of their regularity" (229).

Inspired by Foucault, Said, in *Orientalism*, examines the West's depiction of the Orient, particularly the Arab world, as its own reverse image. From the early 1800s through the present, "orientals" have not been allowed to represent themselves; rather, only the Orientalists have had the knowledge and "objectivity" to represent them. The results of as well as the purpose behind Orientalist discourse are hegemonic: "My contention is that Orientalism is fundamentally a political doctrine willed over the Orient because the Orient was weaker than the West, which elided the Orient's difference with its weakness."[2] Said's underlying thesis corresponds with Foucault's: all scholarship and all representations are political, objectivity is a myth, truths are opinions that have become accepted. Although Said believes that all representations "are embedded first in the language and then in the culture, institutions, and political ambience of the representer" (272), he refuses to dismiss the entire endeavor as pointless: "I certainly do not believe the limited proposition that only a black can write about blacks, a Muslim about Muslims, and so forth" (322). Therefore, we must continually question our methods and conclusions, particularly when we are writing about "Other" people(s).

In his introduction, " 'Telle figure que l'on veut': Deriving a Discourse," Miller cites an array of Western and Eastern accounts of Africa from the *Iliad* through Leo Africanus and beyond to support his assertion that "Africa is conceived of as a void and unformed prior to its investment with shape and being by the Christian or Islamic outside."[3] Building on Said, Miller goes on to claim that if the Orient is a reverse image in the mind of Europe, then Africa, as a third term in the equation, is nothing, less real than either the West or the East, and thus filled with a myriad of fantasies by the European imagination:

The two interlocking profiles of Europe and the Orient leave no room for a third element, endowed with a shape of its own; as on a sheet of paper, both of whose sides have been claimed, the third entry tends to be associated with one side or the other or to be nullified by the lack of an available spot in our intellectual apparatus. It is Africa that was always labeled the "third part of the world," and Africanist discourse reads as the struggle with the problems inherent in that figure. Africanist writing projects out from itself an object that refuses to conform to the demands placed upon it. (16)

Consequently, Africanist discourse regards Africa ambivalently. Miller explains in his conclusion, "The blank slate of Africa, with no past or future, can be made to fulfill the desires of your own present. From there it is only one step to the fulfillment of your nightmares as well. . . . Ambivalence is the controlling force of Africanist discourse" (248). Thus, Africanist writing produces both favorable and unfavorable depictions of Africa: "The positively valorized instances of Africanist discourse could thus be defined as wishing for something one cannot have. . . . The negative versions would be having something one does not wish for—provided that having is understood as that dubious end-product of a wish, hallucination" (248–49). In other words, Africanist writing depicts the continent as either a dream or a nightmare, and often as a combination of the two—a dream that becomes a nightmare.

Three major conventions of Africanist discourse are found in English: binary oppositions, image projection, and evolutionary language. The oppositions are a manifestation of the West's ambivalence toward Africa. First, the continent is either dreamlike or nightmarish or both; or the West is one thing—good, reasonable, bright, and so on—while Africa is its opposite—evil, irrational, dark. Drawing on the work of Frantz Fanon, Abdul JanMohammed describes these oppositions as manichean.[4] Second, regarding Africa as a blank space, Africanist writers have used many different images in describing the continent—a heart, a swamp, a question mark, and so on—no one more appropriate than the other, as each is used to mold the perceived formlessness of Africa into a shape recognizable to the Western eye. Finally, Africanist writers tend to use evolutionary language, to describe Africans and Africa as lagging behind Westerners and the West in development (Africans are children; the continent is prehistoric; the people and the land recall an era the West experienced centuries ago, etc.) Patrick Brantlinger shows how the work of Darwin and others lent credence to the belief in higher and lower races. In addition, V. G. Kiernan and Alec G. Hargreaves demonstrate how the phenomenon of the colonial mirror and the colonial belief in progress reinforced the Europeans' sense of their own superiority while projecting the worse aspects of themselves on the natives over whom they ruled.[5]

From 1885 to 1914, the age of high imperialism for Europeans in Africa prevailed. The first date corresponds with the opening of the Berlin Conference, which diplomatically regulated and legitimized the Scramble for Africa by the major European powers. After the conference, colonialism in Africa began in earnest and imperialism reached its acme. Many historians regard World War I as the event symbolically marking the death of the old order. Although the beginning of the end of colonialism in Africa did not occur until the 1950s and many assert that a form of imperialism exists today, unself-conscious high imperialism was questioned, though not dismantled, during the years between the wars. Although by no means the first examples of fiction, travel writing, and fantasy literature about Africa, *Heart of Darkness* (1899), *My African Journey* (1909), and *Tarzan of the Apes* (1912) were all written in the age of high imperialism and each became a classic in its genre. Conrad's book is based on his own journey up the Congo river as a steamship captain in 1890; Churchill's book was first published in 1908 as a series of letters in *Strand Magazine*. Burroughs had never been to Africa, but his fanciful depiction of the continent was so popular that he went on to publish twenty-four Tarzan books that inspired a number of movies, and he became one of the most popular authors in history.

"Sunshine and Nightshade":
Illustration of Africanist Discourse

To understand how the relationship between Africans and Europeans changed in those one hundred years, one need only compare Churchill's early twentieth-century account of his trip through what are now Kenya, Uganda, the Sudan, and Egypt (beginning in Mombasa and ending in Cairo) with Mungo Park's record of his travels in West Africa in search of the mouth of the Niger in 1795 and 1805. Park advanced eastward from Gambia largely because of the generosity of peasants who fed him and often only at the pleasure of African rulers (although sometimes at their displeasure: on his first trip he was held prisoner for months and on his second he was killed at Boussa).[6] In contrast, Churchill, because of his position in the British government, came as a ruler of East Africa, with the power to decide the fate of Africans.

Winston Churchill's *My African Journey* is the quintessential high-imperialist travel book. As a representative of the British government, Churchill solicits public support for England's actions in East Africa, tries to recruit "earnest and intelligent youth" to come to help govern the region, and makes practical proposals to accelerate the exploitation of Britain's African possessions. Three topics dominate the book's eleven short chapters—politics, "science," and hunting. Shouldering the white man's burden of uplifting and civilizing the Africans, Britain must govern responsibly. East Africa should be exploited for the benefit of the British Empire rather than solely for the aggrandizement of English settlers in the region, and race relations among black, white, and "brown" (Asiatic) people must be carefully managed. Fortunately, the British have a great tool at their disposal to enable them to achieve these goals: "science," which for Churchill encompasses everything from trains to medicine. Last, although the British colonizers in East Africa hunt obsessively and Churchill himself spends a substantial portion of his time shooting at and killing a wide variety of animals, his feelings about hunting are ambivalent; he prefers using arms in service of the empire rather than for personal pleasure.

In the first chapter, entitled "The Uganda Railway" after the route from Mombasa to the border of Uganda, Churchill describes the train line as not only a political but, to the surprise of many, an economic success. Yet the railway serves another purpose as well: it brings European technology, customs, and perspectives to the Africans. It is "one slender thread of scientific civilization, of order, authority, and arrangement, drawn across the primeval chaos of the world."[7] And the railroad has an additional purpose, that of hunting. Churchill explains that trolleying up and down the line is the best way of shooting big game.

Throughout the book, Churchill relies on oppositions that isolate Europe and Africa from one another, either by stressing their lack of spatial connection or, more frequently, using evolutionary language to assert a temporal separation between the two continents. European customs are described as "civilized" and valorized over all things African that find no analogue in Europe. Descriptions of animals contribute to Churchill's Africanist writing. In the first chapter, a rhinoceros is used to stress the opposition between Europe and Africa. Churchill calls the beast a "grim straggler from the stone age" that is "not a twentieth century animal at all"; and, when the dome of Mount Kilimanjaro can be seen in the distance behind the rhino, this is all that is needed "to complete a scene unaltered since the dawn of the world" (14). Africa contrasts with time-obsessed Europe by becoming the land that time forgot.

Moreover, as the second chapter reveals, if the animals and landscape are throwbacks, it follows that the people are not culturally equal to Europeans. Not only does "a veritable abyss of knowledge and science separat[e] the ruler and the ruled" (24), but because the British are so superior, in the area around Mount Kenya two colonial officers manage to govern "seventy-five thousand natives who have never previously known or acknowledged any law but violence or terror" (26). If the barrier between the two kinds of people cannot be easily or rapidly lifted, the way to make Africans serve imperialist ends is simple: by adopting the rulers' customs, such as "a taste for European attire," the East Africans' life "will gradually be made more complicated, more varied, less crudely animal, and [they themselves will] gradually be raised to a higher level of economic utility" (23–24).

In chapters five and six, two of the most interesting sections of *My African Journey*, Churchill describes the Kingdom of Uganda and the administrative capital of Kampala. In contrast to the regions Churchill has traveled through to get to it, the Baganda nation is "a fairy tale": "there is discipline, there is industry, there is culture, there is peace" (56). All this, however, is in Churchill's words "a glittering mask" because "Uganda is defeated by its insects" and is "fatal to the white man." To combat the ravages of sleeping sickness, the colonial government has begun constructing stone houses for the Baganda and "the police of science," as Churchill terms the English doctors, have started to investigate ways of preventing the spread of the disease. This grave situation in Entebbe and other parts of Uganda leads Churchill to reflect on the responsibility of the imperial government, repeat his recruiting pitch, and perhaps imply more than he intends: "What an obligation, what a sacred duty is imposed upon Great Britain to enter the lists in person and to shield this trustful, docile, intelligent Baganda race from dangers which, whatever their cause, have synchronized with our arrival in their midst!" (65).

Following this section Churchill makes his most strongly imperialist and Africanist statement: "Let us be sure that order and science will conquer and that in the end John Bull will be really master in his curious garden of sunshine and nightshade" (65). If the image of the "glittering mask" indicated that in reality Africa is not what it appears to be, the "garden of sunshine and nightshade" contains both the favorable and unfavorable sides of Africanist discourse. Africa is both beautiful and meretriciously poisonous—a dream that becomes a nightmare. Like a garden, the continent's boundaries have been staked out, but orderly cultivation has not yet begun. The word "curious" effectively conveys Africanist ambivalence.

Despite the gap between the Westerner and the African, "progress" is being made, as Churchill reports in his description of the Kingdom of Uganda in the sixth chapter. He comments approvingly on "the rapidity with which the Baganda people are leaving their past behind them. Already they laugh at their old selves" (70). The more European the Baganda and other Africans become, the better in Churchill's estimation, and thus he is favorably disposed to the house of the eleven-year-old Kabaka of Uganda, who has begun to learn European ways: "Altogether it is a pleasing spectacle to find in the heart of Africa, and amid so much barbarism, squalor, and violence, this island of gentle manners and peaceful civilization" (71).

Churchill then fuses the political and scientific strands of his narrative in a startling way. Seeing the coming wave of socialism, Churchill suggests colonial vivisection be performed on the most attractive guinea pig—Uganda: "It would be hard to find a country where conditions were more favorable than in Uganda to a practical experiment in State Socialism" (76). It is worth noting that in his proposal Churchill draws on science fiction to describe the cultural distance between the English and the Baganda: "Choosing governors is the first and perhaps the greatest difficulty which confronts the European Socialist. In Uganda, however, this difficulty does not exist. A class of rulers is provided by an outside power as remote from and, in all that constitutes fitness to direct, as superior to the Baganda as Mr. Wells's Martians would have been to us" (77). As an acute political scientist, Churchill can see great benefits resulting from such a laboratory test: "It might at any rate be worth while to make such an experiment, if only as a prelude to those more general applications of the principles of Socialism which are held in some quarters to be so necessary" (78).

Despite some misgivings, Churchill hunts all through his trip. In the tenth chapter, he makes a final comment about hunting that clarifies his ambivalent feelings toward shooting for pleasure. He finds it "perverse" that some people in Great Britain have private herds "rather than coming to the wild to shoot." It appears that while he disapproves of hunting in a "civilized" nation like England, he is more tolerant toward East African hunters because he believes they are contributing to the tending of the yet-uncultivated imperial garden by eradicating the most visible symbols of untamed nature.

Throughout the book, Churchill writes positively about what Britain has done for Africa and what use the empire can make of it in the future. In the penultimate chapter, however, the other side of the beauty and future utility Churchill has seen in Africa is revealed—like the nightshade balancing the sunshine. Churchill informs the reader that his servant, George Scrivings, died of Asiatic cholera as they were returning to Cairo. As if reminding himself of a universal truth he should have known all along, Churchill associates Africa with death: "Too soon, indeed, had I ventured to rejoice. Africa always claims its forfeits" (124).

In his final chapter, Churchill produces an imperialist tour de force. Reflecting on the trip after its completion, he states the major lesson he learned from his journey and makes a practical proposal. His message is "Concentrate on Uganda!" which he believes has the potential to be the most prosperous of England's East and Central African possessions. Next he advocates the construction of what he calls the Victoria and Albert Railway to connect the two Great Lakes and link them with the railhead at Gondokoro in the North, thus connecting Cairo and Mombasa by a combination of river and rail routes. Churchill notes that this system could then easily be joined with Cecil Rhodes's Cape to Cairo railway, which has nearly reached the southern shore of Lake Tanganyika. Once this is accomplished the whole continent will have been traversed by British transportation lines. At that point, Churchill concludes, he may make another African journey. In this final chapter, Churchill makes clear that his trip and his account of it have been political acts—mappings of the British Empire's "curious" East African garden that contribute to the mapping of England's ultimate garden, the whole of Africa.

The Precursors

Rana Kabbani asserts that the endeavor of writing travel literature implies a colonial situation.[8] This may be going a bit too far. Nevertheless, the connection between politics and travel writing is unavoidable, and failing to reflect on or announce one's political position, far from guaranteeing objectivity and neutrality, places the writer in the imperialist camp. Mary Louise Pratt examines the relationship between travel literature and ideology. Concentrating on nineteenth-century literary travelers to Africa, she analyzes two distinct methods these travelers used in their works: the informative and the sentimental or experiential. She argues that because travel writing has never become fully professionalized or "disciplined," it is "one of the most polyphonous of genres," and thus it illustrates how "ideology works through proliferation as well as containment of meaning."[9] In *My African Journey* the connection between travel writing and political motives is clear. Churchill's book is a political assessment of British East Africa written by a member of the imperial government and designed to win support for its policies there. Although the travel literature about Africa that comes after Churchill never approaches the purely propagandistic level of *My African Journey*, some form of explicit or implicit political assessment invariably takes place.

That five casebooks on *Heart of Darkness* have been published—including the third Norton Critical Edition in a twenty-five-year period—attests to the controversial nature of the novella and the enduring critical interest in it.[10] I see no need here to illustrate how Africanist discourse functions in Conrad's work. Numerous scholars, most notably Miller in *Blank Darkness* and Chinua Achebe in his condemnatory "Image of Africa,"[11] have discussed the oppositions, image projection, and evolutionary language of *Heart of Darkness*.

What has yet to be adequately established is the connection between *Heart of Darkness* and narratives about Africa that have followed it. In Conrad's work, Africa functions as a metaphor for a condition of unlimited power and lack of external restraint that tests the basic beliefs of a Westerner. In *Heart of Darkness* we have the first in-depth treatment of the European fear of "going native" as a result of exposure to the tropics. While Miller asserts that *Heart of Darkness* is a "seminal text within French and all European Africanist discourse,"[12] its clearest and most enduring impact has undoubtedly been on writers in English. Conrad's work initiates a long line of narratives in the expatriate tradition.

In *The Myth of Africa* Dorothy Hammond and Alta Jablow argue that twentieth-century literature elaborates rather than alters the image of Africa found in accounts of the continent from 1530 until the end of the nineteenth century.[13] What they refer to as "the dark labyrinth" becomes the modern extension of the myth of the dark continent, and they cite *Heart of Darkness* as the first example of it. In these works, according to Hammond and Jablow, rather than seeking answers to geographical mysteries or attempting to "civilize" Africans, Europeans come to Africa to learn about themselves as well as escape "civilization," and at the end these modern Theseuses emerge new and better people as a result of the experience with the African labyrinth. This general description corresponds fairly well with

Conrad's Marlow, but Conrad also depicts the situation of the European who fails to follow Ariadne's thread out of the maze, Kurtz, the Westerner run amok.

In *Conrad and the Nineteenth Century*, Ian Watt traces the derivation of the phrase "going native." In English the original term was "going fantee," and it arose in connection with contact between Europeans and West Africans. In French one was stricken by *la soudanete*; in German one was *tropenkollered*, "maddened by the tropics." According to Watt, "*Heart of Darkness* is unique in being the first [work] to connect the process of 'going fantee' with an even more general consequence of the colonial situation: the fact that the individual colonialist's power, combined with the lack of any effective control, was an open invitation to every kind of cruelty and abuse."[14]

Three years before *Heart of Darkness*, Conrad wrote another story set in the Congo, which many years later he considered his best. In "An Outpost of Progress," two Belgian colonial agents, Kayerts and Carlier, left with only themselves to rely on, become increasingly savage. After an argument over sugar cubes, Kayerts accidentally kills the unarmed Carlier, and, rather than face the justice, "Progress," and "civilization" back to which a steamboat whistle calls him, he hangs himself. The situations in "An Outpost of Progress" and *Heart of Darkness* differ in one essential respect. Whereas Kayerts and Carlier are simpleminded men who come to Africa solely for monetary gain, depend totally on their African underling, and degenerate because they are cut off from the crowd that has always shaped their opinions, "All Europe contributed to the making of Kurtz."[15] A painter, a poet, a journalist, a philanthropist, and a natural politician, Kurtz embodies those qualities on which Europeans pride themselves and which make them feel superior. Thus, Kurtz's fall has more significance than the comic antics of Kayerts and Carlier, the hammering of a village chief by the ordinarily gentle ana quiet Fresleven (whom Marlow replaces in *Heart of Darkness*), or the insane firing into the bush by a French ship Marlow observes near the start of his journey. As Patrick Brantlinger explains: "In one sense, going native was universal, because in Africa—or in any foreign setting—every traveler must to some extent adopt the customs of the country. . . . But Kurtz does something worse—he betrays the ideals of the civilization that he is supposedly importing from Europe. Conrad does not debunk the myth of the Dark Continent: Africa is the location of his hell on earth. But at the center of that hell is Kurtz, the would-be civilizer, the embodiment of Europe's highest and noblest values, radiating darkness."[16] Marlow describes how "in utter solitude without a policeman" Kurtz's nerves "went wrong," how he set himself up as a god, how "his soul was mad," how he knew no restraint, no faith, and no fear.

Heart of Darkness has inspired a whole tradition of narratives in which expatriates come to Africa to escape the limitations of European society and test themselves in what is regarded as more elemental conditions. Either they pass this manufactured initiation rite and take with them a newfound self-knowledge and Weltanschauung, or character flaws that could be hidden in a European environment become more obvious in the African setting and lead them to their ruin.

Like a number of those who succeed him in the fantasy tradition, Burroughs never went to Africa. Although he was by no means the first writer to depict a place he had never visited, Burroughs was clearly writing science fiction or fantasy in the Tarzan stories. Similiar to the Mars he portrayed in numerous books, Burroughs's Africa is an imaginary location. Just as the natural sciences of astronomy and physics provided inspiration for his space books, Africanist writing and Darwin's theories were the points of departure for the Tarzan books.

Erling Holtsmark reports that Burroughs read about the flora, fauna, and tribes of Africa and that he was familiar with the works of the prominent Victorian explorers of Africa.[17] Thus, the binary oppositions and images of Africa he employs in *Tarzan of the Apes* generally correspond to those found in these Africanist works as well as to those illustrated above in *My African Journey*. One area that does require elaboration, however, is the treatment of evolution in the novel. In 1899 Burroughs bought Darwin's *Descent of Man*, and its influence in the Tarzan books is clear. Holtsmark summarizes the use of Darwin's theories as follows: "Burroughs views Tarzan's personal growth and development as the recapitulation of human evolution in the form of a single individual. Tarzan is in effect turned into a paradigm for the human race and its laborious emergence from a state of dark ignorance and savagery to civilized status."[18] However, as Holtsmark admits, the "theme of evolutionary Darwinism in Burroughs entails certain ambiguities,"[19] a statement that becomes particularly true when the evolutionary aspects of *Tarzan of the Apes* are examined in the context of Africanist discourse.

In Tarzan Burroughs creates the ultimate "noble savage." Being abandoned as a babe allows Tarzan to live unfettered by "civilized" conventions and undertake all sorts of adventures unavailable to the average person. At the same time, as the scion of a noble family, Tarzan has the breeding to become king of the jungle rather than just another animal and to avoid instinctively a whole set of taboos, including nakedness, bestiality, cannibalism, and rape. Having been untainted by his jungle experiences, upon leaving Africa, Tarzan, like an English version of Kaspar Hauser, quickly masters all the customs of "civilized" living and the best of modern thought (without ultimately failing to assimilate as Hauser does), while at the same time bringing with him his superior strength and survival skills from the rain forest.

Moreover, Burroughs's treatment of apes and Africans features an egregiously racist version of Africanist discourse. Burroughs assigns all of the positive attributes of African tribespeople, all of their conventionally noble and dreamlike qualities, to the apes who raise Tarzan. As big as gorillas but somehow distinct from them, the great apes possess drum rituals, have a language and an oral tradition, follow the logic of the law of the jungle, and do not eat their own kind. Tarzan's black neighbors, King Mbonga's people, on the other hand, possess all the savage and nightmarish characteristics traditional Africanist discourse attributes to Africans. They are so superstitious that through a few tricks Tarzan has them responding to him as though he were a deity. They wantonly attack the French search party that goes into the jungle in search of Jane Porter (and as a result all the men in the tribe are massacred when the French return in greater numbers). And, unlike the great apes, King Mbonga's people are cannibals and torturers.

Finally, in *Tarzan of the Apes* we have the best, while at the same time the most unconscious, depiction of the effect that Africanist discourse has on a non-African. Despite having been raised by apes and having no human contact for over a decade and a half, the foundling Lord Greystoke, relying solely on the meager supply of adult and children's books left in a cabin by his deceased parents and the image of himself, which he has seen in a river, learns his place in the world. Through picture books he discovers that he is a man and not an ape: "No longer did he feel shame for his hairless body or his human features, for now his reason told him that he was of a different race from his wild and hairy companions. He was a M-A-N, they were A-P-E-S."[20] Eventually he teaches himself to read and write (so well, in fact, that his very first written message includes a properly placed apostrophe). His reading also assists him when he encounters his first person, one of the blacks who have migrated close to him: "Tarzan looked with wonder upon the strange creature beneath him—so like him in form yet so different in face and color. His books had portrayed the Negro, but how different had been the dull, dead print to this sleek thing of ebony pulsing with life" (68). Tarzan's reading has taught him that blacks may be human beings, but they are a different category of human beings from himself.

Even though King Mbonga's people with their poisoned arrows have a method of hunting that is superior to his own, having seen pictures of and read about the ships and cities white people have built, Tarzan knows he is superior to his black neighbors. Thus, while he is immediately attracted to the white people he subsequently encounters and throwing a spear to disarm the most barbarous of white mutineers is the most violent act he will commit against one of his own kind in *Tarzan of the Apes,* Tarzan has no scruples about stealing from, murdering, and terrorizing his black neighbors. Discourse alone educates Tarzan in his role as an imperialist.

In Burroughs we see primarily a fantasy or science fiction writer, an author oblivious of the very discourse he is encoding into his text. Like his Mars books, his Tarzan novels were aimed at a popular audience looking for a means of escape. But Tarzan was far and away his most popular creation and the books about him have sold an unprecedented number of copies, making Burroughs perhaps the most widely read author in history. His ability to market his fantastic Africa attests to the pervasiveness of Africanist discourse among the general public.

In Churchill, Conrad, and Burroughs we have the quintessential examples of the political assessment, the expatriate, and the fantasy traditions—three ways of writing about Africa that, as subsequent chapters will show, continued virtually unchanged into the 1960s and only began to be significantly altered or abandoned in the 1980s.

NOTES

1. Michel Foucault, *The Archaeology of Knowledge,* Trans. A. M. Sheridan Smith, New York: Pantheon, 1972, 107–8. Subsequent references are to this edition.

2. Edward Said, *Orientalism,* New York: Vintage, 1979, 204. Subsequent references are to this edition.

3. Christopher Miller, *Blank Darkness,* Chicago: University of Chicago Press, 1985, 13. Subsequent references are to this edition.

4. See Abdul JanMohamed, *Manichean Aesthetics*, Amherst: University of Massachusetts Press, 1983, and "The Economy of Manichean Allegory: The Function of Racial Difference in Colonialist Literature," *Critical Inquiry* 12 (Autumn 1985): 59–87.

5. See Patrick Brantlinger, *Rule of Darkness*, Ithaca: Cornell University Press, 1988; Alec G. Hargreaves, "European Identity and the Colonial Frontier," *Journal of European Studies* 12 (1982): 167–79; and V. G. Kiernan, "Europe in the Colonial Mirror," *History of European Ideas* 1 (1980): 39–59.

6. See pp. 141–47 below.

7. Winston Churchill, *My African Journey*, in *The Collected Works of Winston Churchill*, vol. 1, Centenary Limited Edition, London: Library of Imperial History, 1973, 11. Subsequent references are to this edition.

8. Rana Kabbani, *Europe's Myths of Orient*, Bloomington: University of Indiana Press, 1986, 10.

9. Mary Louise Pratt, "Scratches on the Face of the Country; Or, What Mr. Barrow Saw in the Land of the Bushmen," in *"Race," Writing, and Difference*, ed. Henry Louis Gates, Jr., Chicago: University of Chicago Press, 1986, 160.

10. Joseph Conrad, *Heart of Darkness*, 3d ed., ed. Robert Kimbrough, New York: Norton, 1987.

11. Chinua Achebe, "Image of Africa," *Massachusetts Review* 18 (Winter 1977): 782–94.

12. Miller, *Blank Darkness*, 182.

13. Dorothy Hammond and Alta Jablow, *The Myth of Africa*, New York: Library of Social Science, 1977.

14. Ian Watt, *Conrad in the Nineteenth Century*, Berkeley: University of California Press, 1979, 145.

15. Joseph Conrad, *Heart of Darkness*, in *Heart of Darkness and the Secret Sharer*, ed. Albert J. Guerard, New York: New American Library, 1983, 122–23.

16. Brantlinger, *Rule of Darkness*, 193.

17. Erling Holtsmark, *Edgar Rice Burroughs*, Boston: Twayne, 1986.

18. Erling Holtsmark, *Tarzan and Tradition*, Westport, Conn: Greenwood, 1981, 145.

19. Ibid., 147.

20. Edgar Rice Burroughs, *Tarzan of the Apes*, New York: Ballantine, 1977, 50. Subsequent references are to this edition.

2

First-Generation Postwar Writers: Ignoring Political Realities

... Africa will always be the Africa of the Victorian atlas, the blank unexplored continent the shape of the human heart.
—Graham Greene, "Convoy to West Africa"

Although fifty years separate the first generation of outsiders writing about Africa following the Second World War from their early twentieth-century precursors, the ideological gap between these two groups is not very great. Like Churchill, who said that he did not become Prime Minister to oversee the dismantling of the English Empire, Evelyn Waugh, Graham Greene, Saul Bellow, and other members of this first generation either find it impossible to adjust to the political realities in Africa following the war or refuse to do so. Not only do the political assessment, expatriate, and fantasy traditions survive intact, but there is little indication in the first-generation works that African independence is desirable, imminent, or even feasible. The prospect of a noncolonial Africa poses a threat to the assumptions that underlie Africanist discourse: if Africans create countries of their own, there will no longer be a blank space onto which the West can project its fantasies. Thus, operating within the established traditions of Africanist discourse, first-generation writers either openly or implicitly rebel against the idea of an independent Africa.

In many instances the first-generation works are rooted in the liberalism of entre les guerres travel writing, which, although it questioned some aspects of the imperial endeavor in Africa, never suggested that colonialism could or should be abolished in the foreseeable future. Evelyn Waugh and Graham Greene are cases in point. During the 1930s Waugh wrote four books about Africa: two travel accounts, Remote People (1931) and Waugh in Abyssinia (1935), which inspired two novels, Black Mischief (1932) and Scoop (1938). His fifth and final book about the continent, A Tourist in Africa, is an admittedly nostalgic attempt to write a between-the-wars travel book in 1960. Waugh's use of this outmoded subgenre underscores his refusal to deal with the political realities of Africa on the eve of independence.

To his credit, Greene exhibits a metaconsciousness about the endeavor of writing about Africa that is absent in Waugh; nevertheless, he continues to depend on the conventions of Africanist discourse, tacitly approves of the colonial and missionary effort, and chooses an African setting not for the sake of exploring its political complexities but rather to avoid politics altogether. Greene has acknowledged the powerful influence of Conrad's *Heart of Darkness* as well as his own "African fixation," which may explain why he has written about Africa at regular intervals. In *Journey without Maps* (1936), Greene describes his trek on foot through Liberia; in the novel *The Heart of the Matter* (1948), he draws on his work in Nigeria and Sierra Leone during the war; and in *A Burnt-Out Case* (1961), another novel, he is inspired in part by his 1959 trip to the Congo "in search of a character." As a number of critics have pointed out, the putatively apolitical *Journey without Maps*, in which Africa is largely metaphorical, holds the key to much of Greene's later writing, particularly his two African novels.[1]

In *Abroad* Paul Fussell argues that the period between the two world wars—in which both Waugh and Greene's writing about Africa is rooted—was the height of English literary travel, and he outlines the major conventions of the travel books produced during this time. After the First World War, shortages of food and other products, dreary English weather, and laws restricting personal freedoms caused many British to seek delicacies, sunshine, and expanded horizons in foreign countries. One way in which a number of between-the-wars travelers supported themselves was through the travel book. Typically, a work of this sort includes five parts: it begins with what Fussell calls the I-hate-it-here motif; laments the bother of securing proper travel documents; describes the voyage out; relates the sights and the writer's impressions of the foreign country; and concludes with an account of the author's return home.

Fussell distinguishes the traveler from the explorer and the tourist:

All three make journeys, but the explorer seeks the undiscovered, the traveler that which has been discovered by the mind working in history, the tourist that which has been discovered by entrepreneurship and prepared for him by the arts of mass publicity. The genuine traveler is, or used to be, in the middle between the two extremes. If the explorer moves from the risk of the formless and the unknown, the tourist moves toward the security of pure cliché. It is between these two poles that the traveler mediates, retaining all he can of the excitement of the unpredictable attaching to exploration, and fusing that with the pleasure of "knowing where one is" belonging to tourism.[2]

However, because of the pervasiveness of Africanist discourse, for the outsider writing about Africa the poles Fussell talks about do not really exist. For explorer, traveler, and tourist alike, Africa is still a blank space that needs to be defined, and new images are coined for this purpose. Because Africanist discourse has become fully engrained in the Western mind, writers readily fall back on oppositions between Europe and Africa and on evolutionary language. The books written about Africa during the period between the wars and by the first generation of writers after the Second World War are not so much about going to Africa, as one goes to Paris or Florence, but rather attempts to escape aspects of the West that disturb their authors. For this reason, although they may question certain Western assumptions during the course of the journeys, these books ultimately reaffirm imperialism. Their depictions of Africa combine favorable and unfavorable impressions of the continent and its people based less on African realities than on how the supposedly exotic continent contrasts with the West. Ironically, the Africanist opposition separating the West and Africa was so automatically accepted by writers such as Evelyn Waugh that they often overlooked instructive parallels between events in Africa and Europe.

Evelyn Waugh

Waugh himself acknowledged the escapist character of between-the-wars traveling. After World War II, he compiled *When the Going Was Good*, which was to "comprise all that I wish to preserve of the four travel books I wrote between the years 1929 and 1935."[3] The preface to that book both describes and eulogizes the phenomenon of between-the-wars traveling. Although from 1928 to 1937 Waugh "had no fixed home and no possessions which would not conveniently go on a porter's barrow" and traveled "continuously in England and abroad" during that period, he describes himself as unremarkable for his generation: "I never aspired to being a great traveller. I was simply a young man, typical of my age; we travelled as a matter of course" (9). He explains that traveling was a rite of youth, "an ordeal, an initiation, a test of manhood." Europe, Waugh felt, could be visited at his leisure when he was older and lacked the strength to journey elsewhere. Like other literary travelers he did not suspect that change would quickly come to Europe, a continent seemingly so rigid that they sought temporarily to escape it: "We turned our backs on civilization. Had we known, we might have lingered with 'Palinurus'; had we known that all that seeming-solid, patiently built, gorgeously ornamented structure of Western life was to melt overnight like an ice-castle leaving only a puddle of mud; had we known man was even then leaving his post. Instead, we set off on various stern roads; I to the Tropics and the Arctic, with the belief that barbarism was a dodo to be stalked with a pinch of salt" (8). Written in 1946, his lamentation for the death of European civilization indicates that *entre les guerres* travel writers went abroad to escape politics rather than report on them.

In addition, Waugh went to Africa for economic reasons. In 1930 he was employed by *The Graphic* to cover the coronation of Haile Selassie in Ethiopia and decided to traverse the African continent east to west afterward and write a book about the entire trip. Following the coronation Waugh went to Aden, Zanzibar, and what are now Kenya, Uganda and Zaire, but he didn't make it to the west coast; with his money and enthusiasm running low, he headed south through Rhodesia and South Africa in order to speed his return to England. These experiences and Waugh's reactions to them make up *Remote People* (1930). Two years later he set *Black Mischief* in Azania, a fictional island off the coast of East Africa that serves as a microcosm for the continent geographically, historically, and politically; many incidents in the novel recall the events recorded in the travel book.

In 1935 Waugh returned to Ethiopia as a war correspondent. His duties, he remarks in the preface to *When the Going Was Good,* made him no longer a free traveler, but rather placed him "in the livery of a new age." The much anticipated battles between the Ethiopians and the Italians did not materialize as quickly as European news organizations expected and even when fighting eventually began correspondents were not allowed to go to the front. Waugh was recalled, and he reports at the end of *Waugh in Abyssinia* that "like the rest of the world" he "began to forget about Abyssinia."[4] Three years later Waugh again transformed his African experiences into a satirical novel, *Scoop,* in which the *Daily Beast* sends nature writer John Boot to cover the war in the African republic of Ishmaelia.

Despite scattered criticism of the West in these four books about Africa, Waugh displays no consciousness of Africanist discourse and never takes a stand against imperialism. In *Remote People,* although he criticizes certain British policies in East and Central Africa, Waugh never questions England's right to be there. Moreover, his own ultimately abandoned project to bisect the continent latitudinally recalls Churchill's imperialist mapping of East Africa. In *Black Mischief*, Waugh makes it clear that he thinks African self-rule is impossible. And even though Waugh has seen and noted the changes resulting from the Italian invasion of one of only two independent black nations in Africa, he never condemns it in *Waugh in Abyssinia*. This is perhaps the greatest irony of Waugh's travels in Africa in the 1930s. His two trips to Ethiopia gave him an opportunity to see the effects of fascism before it was unleashed on Europe, but imperialism and Africanist discourse were so deeply etched in his mind that he failed to make the connection between Africans besieged by foreign oppressors and Europeans threatened by the same forces. Waugh's inability to see a link between actual fascism in Africa and impending fascism in Europe is nowhere more clear than in the final section of *Waugh in Abyssinia*, where he praises the roads the Italians are building for their newly conquered African colony. Above all else, writes Waugh with complete seriousness, these roads will bring the Ethiopians "the inestimable gifts of fine workmanship and clear judgment—the two determining qualities of the human spirit, by which alone, under God, man grows and flourishes."[5]

A Tourist in Africa

Over twenty years after *Waugh in Abyssinia*, the author's basic approach to Africa had not changed. Although he had announced in the preface to *When the Going Was Good* that his traveling days were over, in 1959 he returned to Africa at the age of fifty-five and wrote another book about the continent, *A Tourist in Africa*, which is short and filled with a lot of tensions. These spring from Waugh's attempt to write an apolitical, 1930s travel book at a time when colonialism in Africa was dying and change was apparent everywhere. The work follows the generic lines of between-the-wars travel books as the chapter titles reveal: "Departure" (Ennui in England), "Voyage," "Voyage Continued" (Kenya), "Tanganyika," "Tanganyika Continued," "The Rhodesias," "The Rhodesias Continued," and "Return." Despite the volatile political climate in the countries through which he travels, Waugh attempts to ignore politics. Although he fails to keep this up throughout the book, he also fails to pursue the political implications of his material. In fact, Waugh's most frequent target is the shorts worn by white people in East and Central Africa; they are a symbol for what he terms "the craven preference for comfort over dignity,"[6] which Waugh suggests may be responsible for the decline of the British Empire in Africa—rather than an African desire for self-determination and political independence. Both his nonpolitical and infrequent political comments reflect Waugh's Africanist and procolonial disposition. Waugh attempts to go to Africa "with eyes reopened to the exotic"—in other words to focus on the otherness of Africa, the way it contrasts with Europe. But this proves difficult: "It is not so easy as it was thirty years ago to find a retreat. Tourism and politics have laid waste everywhere" (7). He tries to limit himself to observations about people and places, but even on these subjects, he remains surprisingly reticent. Waugh spends much of his time visiting remnants of past African cultures rather than examining what is happening to present ones. Even in these episodes he curtails his descriptions of what he sees and fails to pursue luminous images because he doesn't feel the reader will care. Although he enjoys crumbling mosques and goes out of his way to see them, he assumes that most of his readers can't tell one from another, so he doesn't bother to portray them.

In discussing one ruin, the stone edifice of Great Zimbabwe, both Waugh's penchant for the exotic and his paternalism become apparent. In a statement that ironically and unintentionally reflects on his own discourse, he comments on the inability of Europeans to comprehend purely African creations: " 'the Temple' at Zimbabwe leaves the visitor without any comparison. It is an example of what so often moved G. K. Chesterton to revulsion. It is the Wrong Shape. Something utterly alien" (122–23). Then in attempting to defend the position that Bantu built Great Zimbabwe, Waugh in his liberalism slights what he wishes to champion, the Bantu themselves. Waugh's attitude ostensibly contrasts with that of White Rhodesians who have hailed carbon dating results that indicate the wood in Zimbabwe is seven hundred years old, a date that these whites feel would make it impossible for Africans to have erected the fortress. Waugh cites the presence of Tudor wood in modern villas to argue for a later Bantu construction date. However, historians have since proved that Bantu did indeed build Great Zimbabwe about seven centuries ago. Thus, like the colonial effort to shield Africans from their detractors, Waugh's defense of the Bantu serves to keep them in an inferior position.

Ultimately, Waugh cannot avoid acknowledging the reality of independence movements, but he does so without altering his Africanist and imperialist stance. At the end of the book he declares, "From Algeria to Cape Town the whole African continent is afflicted by political activities which it is fatuous to ignore and as fatuous to dub complacently an 'awakening' " (157). Although Waugh criticizes some colonial practices and recognizes implicitly that colonialism is moribund, he stops short of rejecting the imperial endeavor. His time in Rhodesia enables him to condemn the attitudes of the whites there and in South Africa without attacking the English colonizers in East and Central Africa. Discussing racism in Rhodesia, Waugh distinguishes between the white pioneers at the turn of the century and their grandchildren: "The Afrikaan conception of 'apartheid' would have been alien and (I think) outrageous to most of the early adventurers" (142). Later he claims, "In Rhodesia there is an infection from the south of racial insanity" (158). As elsewhere in *A Tourist in Africa*, without acknowledging his own Africanist stance, Waugh nevertheless provides the ammunition for an attack on the very perspective from which he writes. Yet while Waugh believes that colonial ideals have degenerated into apartheid, he also sees no hope in the nationalist movements. Of Tanganyikan nationhood he writes, "For someone as unpolitical as myself it is difficult to guess what is meant by "a nation" of people as dissimilar as the Chagga, the Masai, the Gogo, the Arabs of Pagani, the fishermen of Kilwa, the Greek and Indian magnates of Dar-es-Salaam, whose frontiers were arbitrarily drawn in Europe by politicians who never set foot in Africa" (98).

While Waugh demonstrates less consciousness of Africanist discourse than Greene, his sketchy assessment of the political situation in Africa and his comments on the abuse of language in the continent foreshadow the wholesale condemnations of postcolonial Africa to be found in the political assessments of second-generation postwar writers, which will be discussed in chapter three. In effect, these writers update Africanist discourse to fit the postcolonial situation. Taking a step that Waugh demurs, second-generation writers often lump together the colonial endeavor and the continued white dominance in southern Africa as one greedy, poorly conceived project. Then, they dismiss contemporary Africa because it is a combination of failed and flawed colonialism and primitive and unfeasible African nationalism. Second-generation writers also use a familiar theme of Waugh's to illustrate the hopelessness of the continent following independence: the corruption of language in Africa. In both *Remote People* and *Waugh in Abyssinia* the author comments on the abuse of language in Africa, especially by journalists and the merchants who cater to them. The following passage is only one example Waugh gives of the problem in *A Tourist in Africa*:

The oddest manipulation of vocabulary [in Rhodesia] is the one by which a white American is classified as a European and a black American as an "alien native." "Native," surely the most honourable appellation for white or black, is never used of whites, and some blacks resent it. "Nigger" (except as a term of affection used among niggers) and "Kaffir" have long been thought offensive. "Bantu" is held to be inexact by anthropologists. "African" is clearly too vague for use. . . . In my lifetime I have seen "Anglo-Indian," which I still use to describe my mother's family, come to mean Eurasian. Goanese for some mysterious reason are huffy if they are not called Goans. There is no end to the flood of gentilisms that are eroding the language. (133–34)

Like the second-generation writers who echo him, Waugh blames Africans themselves for the abuse of language in the continent rather than pointing the finger at Africanist discourse or the colonial powers, which imposed their languages on the Africans.

Waugh refuses to predict the future in his final chapter, but what he has written suggests a grim outlook. One sentence does indicate his point of view: "The foundations of Empire are often occasions of woe, their dismemberment, always" (157). This statement adumbrates many of the political assessments of second-generation writers who rarely refrain from proclaiming how disastrous the future of postcolonial Africa will be. Waugh occupies a significant transitional position in the genealogy of Africanist writing. His politics differ only slightly from Churchill's and like his precursor he displays no consciousness of Africanist discourse. Ironically, however, because of the time in which it was written, *A Tourist in Africa* amounts to a rather taciturn dirge to the high imperialism that *My African Journey* loudly trumpets. And although, in contrast to Waugh, many second-generation authors acknowledge Africanist thinking to some degree, their assessments of postcolonial Africa continue to echo that of *A Tourist in Africa* as well as its observations about the degeneration of the colonial mission, the dangers of African nationalism, and the misuse of language in the continent.

Graham Greene

By avoiding the political realities of Africa on the eve of independence, Graham Greene's writing about Africa after 1945 resembles Evelyn Waugh's; however, it differs from Waugh's in two important respects: first, Greene has a nascent consciousness of Africanist discourse; and second, he uses the expatriate tradition in both *The Heart of the Matter* and *A Burnt-Out Case*. Before examining these two novels, I will look briefly at Greene's obsession with both Africa and Conrad's *Heart of Darkness* and then discuss his between-the-wars travel book about the continent, *Journey without Maps.*

Greene acknowledged what he has called an "odd African fixation,"[7] which ultimately stemmed from the powerful influence of Africanist writing in general and Conrad's *Heart of Darkness* in particular. In 1932, Greene decided that he had to abandon Conrad because his influence was too great and too disastrous.[8] Three years later, in an extreme example of the "anxiety of influence," Greene went to Liberia to undertake a "journey without maps" in part to carve out his own Africa rather than having to rely on Conrad's. In 1942–43 Greene returned to West Africa to work for the British Foreign Office in Nigeria and Sierra Leone. He used a wartime West African setting in *The Heart of the Matter* (1948), which resembles *Heart of Darkness* in many respects. Written in the expatriate tradition, the novel tells the story of a Catholic colonial police officer who is gradually corrupted by sentiment. Still fixated on Africa and Conrad, in 1959 Greene went for the first time to the Belgian Congo, the setting of *Heart of Darkness*. Keeping a "Congo Journal" reminiscent of Conrad's "Congo Diary," he went "in search of a character," the hero of his sketchily outlined book set in a Congolese leper colony. This second African novel about going native, *A Burnt-Out Case* (1961), also has clear links to Conrad. In this novel a dissipated European architect tries, ultimately unsuccessfully, to isolate himself among the lepers in a remote Congolese village.

A number of critics have stressed the pivotal position of *Journey without Maps* in Greene's *ouevre* because of its connection with Conrad and reliance on a metaphorical Africa.[9] Unlike other *entre les guerres* travel books about Africa, *Journey without Maps* indicates an incipient consciousness of Africanist discourse. But rather than viewing it in terms of violence and hegemony as Miller does in *Blank Darkness,* Greene is fascinated by Africa's metaphorical possibilities. Both in person and in his writing, Greene sets out to explore not the realities of Africa in the 1930s but instead the Africa of Africanist discourse.

Although Greene went to Africa for personal rather than the commercial or scholarly reasons that prompted the high imperialists, his impetus is more abstract and metaphysical than the standard between-the-wars desire to escape from Europe. Ostensibly, *Journey without Maps* records Greene's 350-mile trek with his cousin Barbara from the Sierra Leone–Liberian border through northwest and central Liberia and a part of French Guinea to the black republic's small seaport of Grand Bassa. Literally a journey without maps (no accurate ones existed when Greene went), it also represents a psychological journey back to Greene's uncharted childhood.

Greene does not go to Africa to find out about the continent and its people but to learn about the West. Something has gone wrong with the modern world and the author believes that by going to Africa he will be returning to a common human past, a stage from which the modern world has evolved. Greene, however, has no desire to return permanently to the stage that Africa represents; rather, he wants to learn about the present by experiencing the past. But Greene's journey turns out to be less of a psychoanalysis of the modern world than self-therapy, with Greene returning to his own remote past and comparing the primal emotions of his childhood to what he witnesses among the Liberians. In *Journey without Maps* Greene uses standard Africanist oppositions but always valorizes the African side of the dichotomy. Instead of representing death as it did for Churchill, for example, Africa symbolizes life for Greene. Brought close to death by fever, he finds a will to live in Africa. Moreover, the journey has a rejuvenating effect on Greene's psyche, increasing his ability to come to terms with modern life.

Throughout *Journey without Maps* Greene demonstrates an awareness of Africanist discourse and a conscious desire to exploit its metaphoric potential. He immediately connects his project to the notion of blankness through an epigraph from Oliver Wendell Holmes: "The life of an individual is in many respects like a child's dissected map. . . . With every decade I find some new pieces coming into place. Blanks which have been left in former years find their complement among undisturbed fragments. If I could look back on the whole, as we look at the child's map when it is put together, I feel that I should have my whole life intelligently laid out before me."[10] While still young, parts of one's life seem like empty spaces in the scheme of one's lifetime, but with age comes understanding and an ability to see shapes in what were previously formless spaces. For Greene the blanks in the epigraph refer to childhood, and in the course of the book he repeatedly equates childhood itself with Africa.

After introducing the idea of blankness in the epigraph, Greene makes clear early in *Journey* that the reality of Africa is less significant to him than its symbolic value: "when I say that to me Africa has always seemed an important image, I suppose that is what I mean, that it has represented more than I could say" (20). Greene explains that even when he was fourteen Africa had been a symbol for him, and he proceeds to mold an image for the favorable Africa he wishes to depict in the book—one that looks back to Conrad and ahead to his own African novels—"I thought for some reason even then of Africa, not as a particular place, but a shape, a strangeness, a wanting to know. The unconscious mind is often sentimental; I have written 'a shape', and the shape, of course, is roughly that of the human heart" (37).

At the end of the book Greene again indicates his consciousness of Africanist discourse. The West, according to Greene, already comprises Africa; the wail of a child in an English tenement "was as far back as one needed to go, was Africa" (250). For this reason, "Africa had never really been strange."; "the 'heart of darkness' was common to both Africa and Europe" (248). In addition, Greene specifically links Freud's explorations into the human mind with journeys to the interior of Africa: "Mungo Park, Livingstone, Stanley, Rimbaud, Conrad represented only another method to Freud's, a more costly, less easy method, calling for physical as well as mental strength. The writers, Rimbaud and Conrad [like Greene himself], were conscious of this purpose, but one is not certain how far the explorers knew the nature of the fascination which worked on them in the dirt, the disease, the barbarity and the familiarity of Africa" (248). In *Journey without Maps* Greene simultaneously denies and reaffirms the separation between Africa and Europe. Everything that one can find in Africa can be discovered in the West, and it is experienced by each Westerner during childhood. But Europe has evolved beyond Africa and mature Europeans have outgrown their African stage.

Like Conrad, Greene uses Africa as an elaborate metaphor to portray the alienation of modern Western life. In contrast to Conrad, however, Greene lets this technique so dominate his work that *Journey without Maps*, like his later African novels, lacks the contemporary political dimension present in *Heart of Darkness*. For this reason imperialism is never really an issue in the travel book. Greene chooses independent Liberia, a place where whites had not yet reproduced the conditions of their countries, not because he finds colonialism abhorrent but because it makes a more effective metaphor.

In his two African novels, Greene consciously uses Africanist discourse to produce a metaphorical background against which he stages spiritual variations on the expatriate tradition. In *Heart of*

Darkness, against the backdrop of a metaphorical Africa, Kurtz falls morally, betraying Europe's cultural values. In *The Heart of the Matter* and *A Burnt-Out Case*, the Roman Catholic protagonists undergo tests of faith in a metaphorical African setting. Typical of the expatriate tradition, no African character plays a major role in either of Greene's novels; Africans are merely part of the setting. Like Waugh's *A Tourist in Africa* and his own *Journey without Maps*, Greene's African novels both tacitly support the colonial effort and deliberately ignore the political situation of Africa during the years between the Second World War and widespread African independence in the early 1960s. Moreover, each of Greene's African works relies on some variation of the Africanist opposition between life and death. In *Journey without Maps* Greene repeatedly associates the continent with life; in *The Heart of the Matter* Africa clearly represents decay and death. More ambiguously, in *A Burnt-Out Case* the continent appears to represent life for the protagonist, who cannot find a home elsewhere, but in the end, as in Churchill, Africa means death. The expatriate tradition dictates that outsiders who have given up their Western moral or spiritual values must not escape Africa alive so that they can return to infect Europe.

The Heart of the Matter

In *The Heart of the Matter*, Greene takes great pains to connect his metaphorical African setting with disease, decay, and death. One of the first images of the book is that of a vulture taking off from a corrugated iron roof, and throughout the novel references to rats, roaches, flying ants, pye dogs, as well as vultures, occur frequently so that the link between rot and the African environment remains clear. Greene compounds this association with putrefaction by repeatedly mentioning the "monkey house" or "zoo smell" of the police station where the protagonist, Assistant Police Commissioner Major Henry Scobie, works. Echoing *Journey without Maps*, early in the novel Scobie reveals that he loves the West African colony precisely because it is more elemental than Europe: "Why, he wondered, swerving the car to avoid a dead pye-dog, do I love this place so much? Is it because here human nature hasn't had time to disguise itself? Nobody here could ever talk about a heaven on earth."[11] As with his wife Louise whom he loves only when she is pathetically pitiable, Scobie loves Africa for its ugliness.

Within this environment of physical corruption, Scobie succumbs to moral and spiritual corruption; he goes native. Several passages in the book refer to colonials who have gone native in the conventional sense of the phrase. Early in the novel Scobie thinks to himself, "Be careful. This isn't the climate for emotion. It's a climate for meanness, malice, snobbery, but anything like hate or love drives a man off his head. He remembered Bowers sent home for punching the Governor's A.D.C. at a party, Makin the missionary who ended in an asylum at Chislehurst" (31). Later Scobie recalls police officers who suffered nervous breakdowns and struck witnesses while trying to establish the truth. Moreover, Scobie goes to investigate the death of Pemberton, a young colonial administrator gone native in the remote area of Bamba, who has committed suicide because of money he owed to Yusef, a wealthy Syrian merchant.

Greene, a Roman Catholic convert who often examines the role of faith in his characters' lives, carefully draws a distinction between Scobie and the other characters in the book. Just as Kurtz's fall, monumental because all of Europe contributed to produce him, sets him apart from the tattered Russian and the likes of Kayerts and Carlier, Scobie's lapse takes on larger significance because he possesses great faith. Scobie converted to Catholicism when he married and deeply believes in God and the Church's teachings on sin and hell. He is more devout than anyone around him, including Louise and Father Rank, the local priest. The absurd scene in which the two young colonial officials, Harris and Wilson, argue over the rules of a cockroach killing contest parodies Scobie's strict adherence to canon law, underscores the difference between him and characters of their ilk, and recalls the buffoonery of Kayerts and Carlier in "An Outpost of Progress." Greene makes the spiritual distinctions between men evident when he states, in reference to Scobie, "Only the man of goodwill carries always in his heart the capacity for damnation" (60).

Africa slowly corrupts Scobie, the honest man of goodwill, eventually driving him to his death. Scobie's fall occurs in six stages: he allows himself to be corrupted by sentiment; loses his integrity by borrowing money from the devious Syrian Yusef; enters into an adulterous affair with Helen Rolt; egotistically decides to sacrifice himself in order to save his wife and his mistress; betrays his servant Ali, thereby undermining the colonial mission; and finally commits suicide, the unpardonable sin, for it involves turning one's back on God. Significantly, the most basic Africanist and colonialist relationship, that between the white administrator and his faithful servant, is the last one Scobie betrays before he takes his own life.

Scobie's dominant response to people is pity. The first step in his decline occurs when he reads and burns rather than turns in an illegal letter that he finds in a routine search of a Portuguese captain's cabin. Scobie pities the captain who appeals to the police officer's Catholicism and explains that he was merely writing to his daughter in Germany. Afterward, Scobie realizes that his sentimentality has compromised him: "Only his own heart-beats told him he was guilty—that he had joined the ranks of the corrupt police officers. . . . They had been corrupted by money, and he had been corrupted by sentiment. Sentiment was the more dangerous, because you couldn't name its price. A man open to bribes was to be relied upon below a certain figure, but sentiment might uncoil in the heart at a name, a photograph, even a smell remembered" (55). Having thus tarnished himself, Scobie has less reluctance to borrowing money from the unscrupulous Yusef to pay for Louise's passage to South Africa, thereby completely sacrificing his integrity. Having been passed over for promotion but refusing to leave the colonial African environment he loves, Scobie blames himself for his wife's unhappiness. When Louise expresses a desire to go to South Africa to escape the colony, Scobie promises to find a way to pay for this even though he doesn't have the money.

Throughout *The Heart of the Matter* Greene openly or implicitly supports the colonial endeavor. Africans appear only as servants, and Yusef, the only major non-European character, is Syrian not African. Epitomized by Scobie, whose job it is to maintain law and order, colonials clearly represent forces of good striving against African chaos. The image used to describe Scobie's actions and attitudes towards Louise unmistakably recalls the iconography of turn-of-the-century white man's burden propaganda. In it Scobie portrays a saintly white man assisting an African porter (Louise) who can no longer shoulder his load. After Scobie reassures the restless Louise that he will find some way of sending her to South Africa, "He was surprised how quickly she went to sleep: she was like a tired carrier who has slipped his load. She was asleep before he had finished his sentence, clutching one of his fingers like a child, breathing as easily. The load lay beside him now, and he prepared to lift it" (44). This image establishes the connection between the egotism inherent in Scobie's behavior toward the unattractive and pitiable women in the novel and the colonial sense of superiority over African subjects.

Further complicating his own situation, Scobie falls in love with another unattractive and unhappy woman out of pity. Married for just a few months, Helen Rolt loses her husband in a submarine attack and survives forty days on the open seas. Scobie sees her first when she is brought on shore and later she moves into a house close to his. Helen attracts him, just as Louise and the colony do, because of her ugliness: "He had no sense of responsibility towards the beautiful and the graceful and the intelligent. They could find their own way. It was the face for which nobody would go out of his way, the face that would never catch the covert look, the face which would soon be used to rebuffs and indifference that demanded his allegiance. The word 'pity' is used as loosely as the word 'love': the terrible promiscuous passion which so few experience" (159). Soon afterward Greene explicitly links the physical corruption of the environment with Scobie's moral and spiritual decline through the word "decay": "Pity smouldered like decay at his heart" (178). Hereafter the two kinds of corruption become indistinguishable.

Scobie's situation becomes even more desperate when Louise returns and suicide is the only solution he can see that will release him from his problems, put an end to his corruption, and spare Louise and Helen from pain. Egotistically Scobie begins to view his life as a contest against God. Unable to break off the affair with Helen, he questions God's wisdom by wondering how a person can love God at the expense of another person. Moreover, he tries to rationalize suicide by describing the Crucifixion as a suicide. Scobie assumes that his sins are so great that they cannot be forgiven, declaring, "O God, I offer up my damnation to you. Take it. Use it for [Louise and Helen]" (225). When late in the book he learns that he has in fact received the promotion to Commissioner, he views it as proof that he belongs to "the devil's party." Rather than ending his relationship with either Helen or Louise, Scobie blasphemously believes that he is more important to his mistress and his wife than he is to God: "O God. I can't leave her. Or Louise. You don't need me as they need me" (233). Later Scobie himself links the notion of a battle between himself and God to the motif of decay: "It seemed to him that he had rotted so far that it was useless to make any effort. God was lodged in his body and his body was corrupting outwards from that seed" (244).

In the penultimate stage of Scobie's fall he betrays not only his servant of fifteen years but by extension the colonial relationship between colonizer and colonized. Made distrustful by his own untrustworthiness, Scobie no longer feels he can rely on Ali and ironically turns to Yusef for help. The Syrian had used a letter Scobie wrote to Helen to blackmail him into passing a small package, presumably of diamonds, over to the same Portuguese captain during another inspection. Ali has seen Yusef's boy deliver a small diamond to Scobie as a gesture of thanks for his services, and now having something to hide Scobie begins to believe the conventional colonial wisdom that no black can be trusted. Yusef asks Scobie for some personal item that will prove to Ali that his master wishes him to come to Yusef's dangerously located office late at night. With heavy symbolism, Scobie uses his broken rosary to betray Ali, whose throat is slashed, probably on Yusef's orders, right outside the Syrian's office. Scobie feels that he himself has killed Ali, who becomes a symbol for God to him: "Oh God, he thought, I've killed you; you've served me all these years and I've killed you at the end of them. God lay there under the petrol drums and Scobie felt the tears in his mouth, salt in the cracks of his lips. You served me and I did this to you. You were faithful to me, and I wouldn't trust you" (247–48). Having allowed Ali to die because of his own insecurities about his position as a colonial administrator, Scobie in this passage further objectifies Ali as a representation of his infidelity to God.

More important, Scobie's betrayal of Ali occurs at a strategic point in the protagonist's decline. It clearly is presented as the most serious of Scobie's failings and represents the point of no return for him. What makes Scobie's betrayal of Ali so unforgivable, the novel implicitly argues, is that, like Kurtz, he has undermined the colonial relationship. According to the colonial rhetoric, Europeans will take care of Africans and bring order out of chaos so long as the Africans respect and serve their European masters. In fact, Ali is the one character in the book with whom Scobie experiences true peace. Scobie's dream of perfect happiness and freedom described early in the book involves walking through a cool meadow with Ali walking silently at his heels. Moreover, while waiting for Ali to come to Yusef's office, Scobie recalls his servant's fifteen years of faithful service: "He remembered the long trek beside the border: innumerable lunches in the forest shade, with Ali cooking in an old sardine-tin, and again that last drive to Bamba came to mind—the long wait at the ferry, the fever coming down on him, and Ali always at hand" (245). By indirectly causing Ali's death, Scobie has given the lie to the colonial mission, and the expatriate tradition dictates that he must pay for this with his own life.

Believing his life to be one crime against God after another, equating himself with vermin to be exterminated (and thus the nightmare side of Africanist discourse), and seeing no other way of sparing Louise and Helen pain, with careful premeditation Scobie commits suicide after shamming angina. Both Scobie's life and the book itself end ambiguously. Scobie dies saying "Dear God I love . . . ," leaving it uncertain whether his last thoughts are of Louise, Helen, himself,

Ali, or God. And while Louise and Father Rank agree that Scobie loved God and no one else, the priest contrasts the church's teaching which damns Scobie for killing himself with God's mercy: "The Church knows all the rules. But it doesn't know what goes on in a single human heart" (272). Such ambiguity is typical of Africanist discourse and Greene. Africa gradually corrupts Scobie, the man of great faith, propelling him to his demise. The meaning of this death remains ambiguous, however, just like the metaphorical continent itself and the human heart, Greene's favorite image for it.

A Burnt-Out Case
In *A Burnt-Out Case* Greene blends elements from *Journey without Maps* and *The Heart of the Matter* to produce one of his most ambiguous and controversial works. Critics who argue that Greene is a major twentieth-century novelist view his second African novel as one of his best. Other commentators who have reservations about Greene's importance use *A Burnt-Out Case* to illustrate the author's deficiencies.[12] In the book, Greene again displays a consciousness of Africanist discourse and creates a metaphorical Africa. He also performs a moral and spiritual test on a Catholic protagonist, and relies on the Africanist opposition that associates Africa with either life or death. In contrast to Scobie who is corrupted by sentiment in *The Heart of the Matter*, Querry, the protagonist of *A Burnt-Out Case*, feels none at all. He comes to a leproserie in Africa to escape the modern world as Greene himself did in *Journey without Maps*. Eventually he is cured of his world-weariness, learning once again how to laugh, feel happy, and experience pain. However, like a burnt-out case, a leper whose disease has been arrested, after being cured Querry doesn't want to return to the modern world. His desire to remain buried in Africa, to not think anymore, is another way of going native. Like the conventional fallen hero of the expatriate tradition, Querry ultimately dies in his African refuge.

In the dedication to *A Burnt-Out Case*, Greene explicitly presents the African setting as a metaphorical testing ground purged of contemporary political realities: "This is not a *roman a clef*, but an attempt to give dramatic expression to various types of belief, half-belief, and non-belief, in the kind of setting, removed from world politics and household preoccupations, where such differences are felt acutely and find expression. This Congo is a region of the mind, and the reader will find no place called Luc on any map."[13] Making use of the Africanist concept of blankness, the novel repeatedly stresses the isolation and emptiness of the leper colony. Although some topical political references are included and Dr. Colin makes a few anticolonial statements, Greene's desire to construct a "Congo of the mind" lessens any impact such contemporary references might have and again excludes any African character from a role more significant than that of a servant or an unspecified leper patient.

Querry's arrival in Luc by riverboat, the initial consonant sound of his name, his superior intellect, and his uncertain though clearly European nationality all suggest a connection with Kurtz. Seeking an isolated and empty refuge, Querry stops at Luc because "the boat goes no farther." Querry tells Dr. Colin that coming to Africa to die was in his mind, but more than anything else he was looking for desolation: "chiefly I wanted to be in an empty place, where no building or woman would remind me that there was a time when I was alive, with a vocation and a capacity to love—if it was love" (46). Echoing *Journey without Maps*, Greene emphasizes barrenness and otherness rather than the romantic qualities of the African landscape presented by other Africanist writers: "There was little in the forest to appeal to the romantic. It was completely empty. It had never been humanized, like the woods of Europe, with witches and charcoal-burners and cottages of marzipan; no one had ever walked under these trees lamenting lost love, nor had anyone listened to the silence and communed like a lake-poet with his heart" (54). In fact, Greene attributes the presence in Africa of Querry and other disillusioned Westerners to the continent's blankness rather than to colonialism, which had always provided a dumping ground for Europeans who couldn't conform to the dictates of the "modern" world. "It is characteristic of Africa," Greene begins part five, "the way people come and go, as though the space and emptiness of an underdeveloped continent encourage drift; the high tide deposits the flotsam on the edge of the shore and sweeps it away in its withdrawal, to leave elsewhere" (119).

Although isolated and empty, Greene's Africa again contains physical corruption. In contrast to *The Heart of the Matter*, where animals are used to stress decay, in *A Burnt-Out Case* human beings rot with leprosy. Throughout the novel Greene uses an extended metaphor linking the Africans' physical disease and treatment and Querry's spiritual illness and recovery. Just as lepers cannot experience pain in the places where they have been infected, Querry arrives in Luc unable to feel any emotions. Early in the book he calls himself mutilated, able to perceive nothing stronger than discomfort. Dr. Colin eventually diagnoses him as a burnt-out case. Querry admits being drawn to Africa because of the pain and fear present there, expressing a wish to learn how to suffer again. An analogy is also made between pain and faith, something else that Querry can no longer experience. Telling a parable based on his own experience with faith, Querry links his state of unbelief with the idea of vacancy. He believes God has punished him with unbelief because he has broken God's rules.

Even though Greene sets his book just before Belgium's departure from what is now Zaire, contemporary political references are infrequent. When they do occur, Greene's longing for a metaphorical Africa makes them inconsequential. *A Burnt-Out Case* contains significantly fewer comments on the political situation in the Congo than does Greene's much shorter "Congo Journal," written during his trip to research the book.[14] Rioting in Leopoldville is mentioned four times in the novel but described as "hundreds of miles away" and thus without effect on the isolated community at Luc. Greene stops short of openly asserting the positive influence of European missionaries on Africans, as he does in *Journey without Maps*, but his portrait of the priests at Luc is generally favorable, and he never questions their presence. The biggest concession Greene makes to the changing political climate in Africa is the inclusion of the liberal Dr. Colin, who blames whites for Africa's problems. The doctor cites Hola Camp, Sharpeville, and Algiers to argue that Africans' belief in European cruelty is justified; he claims that European-inspired hope is the latest and most fatal disease Africans suffer from; and, although he does not support African independence, he believes Europeans have taught Africans how to desire liberty at the expense of someone else's freedom. However, Greene's metaphorical Africa vitiates the impact of Colin's sentiments. Having emphasized the barrenness and isolation of the leproserie, Greene allows Colin's statements no more relevance than words uttered in a vacuum. Moreover, the doctor never questions his own presence in Luc and he works harmoniously with the priests in the leper colony. The "trouble-makers," Africans who arrive in Luc from the Lower Congo, are given a chance to express themselves in a mere seven lines of a song; however, the local Africans cannot understand their language and it is left to Colin and Querry to interpret the meaning.

In contrast to Scobie whom Africa corrupts, Querry comes to the continent to be rejuvenated, to escape the corruption of Europe as Greene did in *Journey without Maps*. Again, the basic Africanist opposition between life and death has not been altered. The test in *A Burnt-Out Case* is not whether Querry will lose his faith but whether he will regain it. Slowly Querry succeeds in getting his feeling back. After establishing himself in the community and working on constructing a new hospital, he admits to Dr. Colin that he is happy. The real test of Querry comes when he is confronted with losing his refuge in the leper colony. When outsiders begin to threaten the life that Querry has established for himself in Luc, he shows how much he has begun to care again, declaring at one point "I'm fighting for my life" (135). Querry repeats this thought with even more conviction when he realizes that Marie Rycker's false claim that he is the father of her unborn child will cost him the situation he has created for himself with the priests. He tells her, "You've burned the only home I have" (184). By the end of the novel both Dr. Colin and Querry himself believe that he has been cured. Querry acknowledges that instead of feeling only discomfort he can suffer again, and he concurs with Colin's assessment of his condition when he says that he is "pretty well cured of everything" (193).

As the dedication indicates, Greene dramatizes different types of belief in his metaphorical Congo. Most of the priests are calmly secure in their faith, just as Dr. Colin feels content with his atheism. In contrast to these characters are those who lack certainty about their faith and loudly assert either their belief or lack of it. Rycker, who runs a palm oil factory in between the closest town and the leproserie, worries far more about the fine points of Catholic doctrine than the priests do, preaches hypocritically to his young wife about the virtues of a Christian marriage, and welcomes Querry as an important Catholic intellectual with whom he can discuss his faith. Likewise, the significantly named Father Thomas unsuccessfully tries to camouflage his doubts about his faith by chiding his fellow priests for their lack of piety. He too champions Querry as a kindred spirit. Meanwhile, Querry loudly and frequently declares his lack of faith. But his actions while in Luc and, as Colin points out, his obsession with his unbelief belie this avowal. By the conclusion of the novel, Querry recovers both his ability to feel emotion and his belief in God.

Although Africa appears to represent life for most of *A Burnt-Out Case*, in the end it means death for Querry. In addition to manipulating the Africanist opposition associating the continent with life or death, through Querry's demise Greene reinforces the conventions of the expatriate tradition. Querry does not go native in the sense that Kurtz and Scobie do; however, his decision to stay in Africa after having gotten his feeling back represents another form of going native. Dr. Colin's explanation of what often happens to lepers who have been cured applies equally well to Querry himself: "You see they become attached to their hut and their patch of land, and of course for the burnt-out cases life outside isn't easy. They carry the stigma of leprosy. People are apt to think once a leper, always a leper" (123). Querry's servant, Deo Gratias, is one of the burnt-out cases; early in the novel he is pronounced cured but he asks to be allowed to remain in the colony and is eventually assigned to Querry. Just before Marie Rycker's lie robs him of his position in Luc, Querry clearly expresses his desire not to return to the modern world. He tells Colin, "I am happy listening, saying nothing. The house is not on fire, there's no burglar lurking in the next room: I don't want to understand or believe. I would have to think if I believed. I don't want to think anymore. I can build all the rabbit-hutches you need without thought" (175). However, the state of arrested development for which Querry argues here is neither acceptable to the expatriate tradition nor compatible with Greene's investigation of different types of faith. The expatriate tradition demands that the character either extricate himself from the African labyrinth and bring the knowledge gained from the experience back with him or suffer the punishment for staying too long in the maze, death. Greene's purposes, too, require that Querry make some more substantial decision about his faith. A sentence from Greene's "Congo Journal" illuminates this tension. Talking about the novel he is still sorting out in his head and referring to the protagonist who later became Querry as X, Greene feels compelled to kill off his main character in order to achieve a Conradian sense of inscrutability: "Yet I feel that X must die because an element of insoluble mystery in his character has to remain."[15] Thus, Querry's death as a falsely accused adulterer at the hands of Rycker cannot be avoided. As with Scobie, Querry fails to complete his dying sentence, which contributes to the ambiguity of his character. Greene refuses to state unequivocally whether Querry regains his belief, but presumably the word left out of his final line, "this is absurd or else . . . ," is "just," which would indicate that he accepts God's will.

The similarities between *Heart of Darkness* and *A Burnt-Out Case* are clear, but Greene's novel also closely resembles *Lord Jim,* another Conrad work about going native. Both protagonists travel to the ends of the earth to escape notoriety—Querry fame, Jim infamy—but neither succeeds in getting away from his past. Brown stumbles upon Jim in Patusan and reminds him of the Patna incident; discovering Querry by chance in the Congo, Parkinson refuses to let him forget his past and assists in sending him to Pendele, the paradise for which he and Deo Gratias long. Both characters die ironically and ambiguously. Jim the erstwhile coward faces death courageously, if meaninglessly, while Querry the former roué meets his fate as an innocent adulterer.

Jim and Querry differ in one important respect. Whereas Jim is a simple man placed in complex circumstances, Querry is a complex man who finds himself in an empty and isolated environment. Just as Scobie's heart is associated with Africa's ambiguity at the end of *The Heart of the Matter*, Querry, the question mark, possesses the same blankness as Greene's metaphorical Africa. Father Joseph's assessment of Querry at the end of the novel, "he was an ambiguous man" (196), echoes Greene's statement about the continent at the beginning of part three: "Inexplicable objects were the fingerprints of Africa" (61). Querry becomes a blank space onto which the discontented European characters project their fantasies: The schlock journalist Parkinson turns Querry into a saint to sell newspapers; Rycker invents an idea of Querry as a Catholic intellectual to satisfy his own self-importance; Father Thomas treats Querry as a kind of St. John of the Cross who can understand his own spiritual problems; and Marie Rycker fantasizes that Querry has fathered her child to satisfy her school girl romanticism, endure making love to her unappealing husband, and escape from an intolerable marriage. Although each of these false projections in some way contributes to Querry's death, it is Rycker and Father Thomas, the two characters insecure in their faith, who turn on Querry the instant he fails to live up to their fantasies about him. In this respect, they resemble Africanist writers who reject Africa when the continent appears to contradict the expectations they have for it.

Like Conrad before him, Greene is aware of the metaphorical possibilities of Africa and he exploits them without hesitation. In contrast to Conrad, Greene deliberately omits a contemporary political dimension in his African works. Moreover, he adapts the conventions of the expatriate tradition to his interests in various states of belief in God. Greene occupies a significant position in the genealogy of Africanist writing. He is the last major author to use the expatriate tradition before widespread African independence and also the last author to deny changes in the African political climate without resorting to the fantasy tradition.

Works by the second generation of outsiders writing about Africa after World War II differ from Greene's by relying heavily on politics and including more developed African characters, but they do so in an Africanist context. Third-generation writers and writers in the fourth category who subvert or totally abandon the political assessment, expatriate, and fantasy traditions expand on Greene's consciousness of Africanist discourse. However, unlike Greene these authors recognize the violence inherent in Africanist discourse and often create major African characters.

Saul Bellow

Henderson the Rain King

In *Henderson the Rain King*, Saul Bellow, like Greene, consciously exploits Africanist discourse; he does so, however, not to create a work in the expatriate tradition but rather one in the fantasy tradition. Just as Burroughs uses Africa as a fantasy world to illustrate the superior intellect and morality of British nobility, so Bellow manufactures a fantastic Africa to make observations about the United States in the late 1950s. Neither author had firsthand experience of the continent when he wrote his work; each relied instead on Africanist discourse and his imagination.

Although it could be argued that Henderson undergoes trials in Arnewiland and Waririland and that he appears to go native when he becomes Sungo and roars like a lion, unlike Kurtz or Scobie, Henderson is never in any danger of betraying Western values or damning himself. As Henderson himself observes, his Africa is so much a reflection of himself that at no time is there a sense that he is being tested as a representative of his culture.[16] Moreover, rather than being a more elemental environment where he either can be more easily tested (in the way that Kurtz is in the Congo and Scobie is in West Africa) or escape the oppressiveness of the modern world (like Greene in Liberia), in his Africa Henderson finds himself face to face with the two things that caused him to leave his New England home—alienation and death. In fact, throughout his African experiences, Henderson encounters situations that resemble events from his past.

Emphasizing Bellow's background in anthropology, Jonathan Wilson suggests that Bellow uses the superstitions of the Arnewi and the Wariri to parallel the arbitrary rituals that govern modern American life and implicitly to argue that "societies' rules and conventions are onerous and potentially deadly, but if you break them, chaos is certain to follow."[17] The association between Africans and superstition goes back to Burroughs, but Bellow has updated it to point out the arbitrariness of modern life in the West. In producing his Africa, Bellow draws not only on anthropology in depicting tribal life but also on the philosophy of William Reich, the psychology of William James, alienation and death (two of the most important themes of American literature), and Africanist discourse.[18] As a result, a fantastic Africa emerges, characterized by blankness, binary oppositions, and arrested development, an Africa bearing almost no resemblance to the rapidly changing continent on the eve of independence.

Eusebio L. Rodrigues has shown the extent to which Bellow borrowed from Africanist texts in writing *Henderson*, particularly his former Northwestern professor Melville J. Herskovits's *The Cattle Complex in East Africa* and Sir Richard Burton's *A Mission to Gelele the King of Dahomey*.[19] Rodrigues argues that the "realistic particulars" Bellow took from these Africanist texts anchor the novel and refuse "to allow it to become pure fantasy" (255). In other words, Bellow relies on Africanist discourse to lend his Africa more legitimacy than a purely fantastic setting would have possessed. However, as Miller has shown in *Blank Darkness*, Africanist writing frequently has little to do with either reality or legitimacy. What has yet to be established is the way in which Bellow constructs his Africa along conventional Africanist lines.

After he arrives by plane in Cairo, the particulars drop out of Henderson's description of his journey. For a time he stays with his boyhood friend Charlie and his wife, who are photographing "the Africans and the animals," but then Henderson sets off with his guide Romilayu "to see some places off of the beaten track." The world they enter, the plateau of Hinchagara, is one of blankness and retarded development. Upon entering this territory, which "has never been well mapped," Henderson feels he is "entering the past—the real past, no history or junk like that. The prehuman past."[20] Similarly, when he later approaches Arnewiland, Henderson declares "Hell, it looks like the original place. It must be older than the city of Ur" (183).

Bellow's Africa not only lacks history, development, and a specific location, but it is a world of oppositions. Although it differs from the West by possessing such fantastic elements as Amazons, skull tossing games, and lion cults, Bellow's Africa is organized around the oppositions between the two peoples Henderson encounters: the Arnewi and the Wariri. As Rodrigues shows, the cattle herding Arnewi derive from Herskovits's writing on East Africa and the Wariri are based on Burton's travels in West Africa. Dahfu, the king of the Wariri, explains to Henderson that the two peoples were once united: "A legend exists that we were once the same and one, a single tribe, but separated over the luck question. The word for them in our language is nibai. This may be translated 'unlucky'. . . . We claim ourselves to be the contrary. The saying is, Wariri ibai. Put in other words, Lucky Wariri" (297). Thus, linguistically as well as literally, the Arnewi are not-Wariri.

Nearly all the properties associated with the favorable or dream side of Africanist discourse are attributed to the Arnewi. An ordered, matriarchal society living an Edenic existence in a kind of prehistorical golden age, the Arnewi are innocent people. Willatale and Mtaba are the two women of "Bittahness," elders who have reached a stage where they can transcend sexual difference. In typical Africanist fashion, "Bittahness" means precisely the opposite of what it sounds like, bitterness. In nightmarish contrast to the Arnewi, the patriarchal Wariri belong to a chaotic, fallen world that is filled with fear, death, and deceit.

What Henderson's Africa really presents him with is another version of the things that drove him from America. Judie Newman points out that Henderson's African experiences work as "a refraction and exaggeration of elements which are only hinted at, or alluded to, in the prologue [chapters one through four, which are set in the United States]."[21] For example, Bellow's fantastic African mirror transforms a cat that Henderson tries to kill on his Connecticut estate into the lioness Atti, with which the terrified Henderson passes long hours in Waririland.

Henderson spends all of the prologue and much of the rest of the book trying to explain just why he made his trip to Africa, although the answer can actually be found in the very first chapter. Henderson feels alienated from his life as a wealthy, Ivy League–educated scion of a famous New England family, and he suffers from a Hemingwayesque obsession with death, as his initials and various aspects of his biography indicate. In Arnewiland, Henderson experiences the same kind of alienation he felt at home in Connecticut, being unable to live by the Arnewi's taboos and eventually ostracizing himself by wrecking their cistern. Similarly, in Waririland, Henderson, who fears death but flirts with it constantly, finds himself among people who are more obsessed with death than he is and he narrowly escapes from them with his life.

Bellow clearly recognizes and exploits the novelistic opportunities with which Africanist discourse provides him. On the one hand, because it views the continent as a blank space, Africanist discourse enables Bellow to make Africa into anything he desires, that is, a place at once the opposite of the United States while at the same time identical with it. On the other hand, because of its pseudoscientific pretensions, Africanist discourse offers Bellow a certain degree of legitimacy that would be unavailable to him if he turned Henderson into a modern-day Gulliver traveling through a totally fictitious continent or if he opted for science fiction by setting the novel on another planet.[22] Bellow shows no interest in contemporary Africa; he makes only one vague reference to the changes taking place in the continent. The Africa of Africanist discourse, however, provides him with a fantasy he cannot pass up: the opportunity to write a book about America without having either to set the book in the United States or ground it in the political and social realities of another country.

Despite his suppression of contemporary political events and reliance on allegory, Bellow foreshadows later writing about Africa in one significant respect. By depicting Henderson comically, as a buffoon instead of an intellectually or morally superior hero like Kurtz or Scobie, Bellow resembles second-generation postwar authors who frequently portray whites and other outsiders in the continent as clownish, incompetent, or powerless. Moreover, like Greene but to a lesser extent, Bellow exhibits a consciousness of Africanist discourse, but he chooses to exploit it for his novelistic purposes, either failing to see or deliberately overlooking its underlying violence. This conscious use of Africanist discourse approaches a form of schizophrenia among the second-generation authors who write about Africa after independence. Often these writers criticize colonial, white expatriate, and at times African adherence to Africanist ways of thinking while at the same time they themselves continue to observe, think, and write about the continent from the same Africanist perspective.

The Gradual Move toward Political Engagement

Although the first generation of outsiders writing about Africa largely ignores the political realities of the continent in the years between the Second World War and the advent of widespread independence in Africa, a number of writers could not overlook one significant historical event—the Mau Mau uprising in British East Africa. The Mau Mau revolt shook the European settler population from its complacency because of its attacks on whites and blacks loyal to them. In October 1952, a State of Emergency was declared and a four-year campaign against the rebels began, which eventually resulted in the death of eleven thousand revolutionaries, one hundred Europeans, two thousand African loyalists and the detention of another twenty thousand Kikuyu. Although the repressive measures finally put down the revolt, the Mau Mau uprising triggered the Kenyan independence movement. In December 1963, Jomo Kenyatta, who had been imprisoned from 1953 to 1959 for his participation in the rebellion, became the first prime minister of independent Kenya.

Either explicitly, as in Robert Ruark's *Something of Value* (1955), or implicitly, in works such as David Karp's *The Day of the Monkey* (1955) and Nicholas Monsarrat's *The Tribe That Lost Its Head* (1956), white authors from England and the United States felt compelled to respond to the Kikuyu rebellion. Echoing and expanding the sensationalism of colonial and British accounts of the revolt, Ruark writes a novel that closely resembles Victorian adolescent fiction about Africa, which pitted brave, morally superior English heroes against cowardly African savages.[23] Inspired by and as reactionary as Waugh's books about Africa in the 1930s yet totally lacking their grace and wit, Monsarrat's novel does suggest that some kind of a political change is needed in the aftermath of a revolt by members of the more barbaric of the two tribes that compose the indigenous population of the island of Pharamaul. At the end of the book, a younger, more liberal colonial administrator takes over the post previously held by a senior, less-enlightened member of the old school.[24] By far the most interesting and progressive of these three novels, *The Day of the Monkey* deals openly with nationalism and independence and includes at least one admirable and fully realized African character, Dr. Luba, the Gandhi-like founder of the nationalist movement and the friend of the colony's governor. The book, however, works to minimize the importance of these factors: there are almost no specific references to contemporary Africa; beyond Luba no real independence movement exists; even before the rioting, the British had already decided to give the Protectorate its freedom, not because it is prepared for self-rule but because it has little strategic significance and has become too costly; and instead of local and regional politics, the cold war dominates.[25]

Taken as a whole, these Mau Mau–inspired novels divert attention from the real issue: Africans not only desired but were ready to fight for their freedom. Instead, these works focus on other concerns—African barbarity, African superstition, Communism—but the solution for each of these is largely the same: continued Western domination. These novels occupy a transitional position between writers of the first generation such as Waugh, Greene, and Bellow, who almost totally avoid making reference to contemporary African political realities and the writers of the second generation, who are often obsessed with the politics of postcolonial Africa. Because they were written during the time of colonialism and implicitly support it, the fictional responses to the Mau Mau revolt properly fall within the category of first-generation writings. Nevertheless, the way in which these works utilize Africanist techniques and divert attention from the real issues allies them closely with the writings of second generation authors, who often criticize independent Africa for its "primitivism" and political extremism.

A more important figure linking the first and second generations is the Canadian writer Margaret Laurence. Appearing a year before Greene's apolitical *A Burnt-Out Case*, Laurence's often-overlooked first novel, *This Side Jordan*, set on the eve of Ghanaian independence, takes African nationalism as a major theme and contains a number of fully drawn African characters, most notably Nathaniel Amegbe and Victor Edusei.[26] In contrast to Waugh and many second-generation writers, Laurence predicts a bright future for Africa, envisioning blacks and whites overcoming their prejudices and working together harmoniously. In fact, the novel ends with Nathaniel declaring, "Cross Jordan, Joshua," as he lifts up his newborn son, which suggests that during the next generation Africans will find their promised land.

Having spent seven years in Africa before writing *This Side Jordan* and following it up with a collection of stories and a travel book about the continent as well as a critical work on Nigerian authors, in the late 1960s, Laurence, however, distanced herself from the sanguine prognosis for the New Africa found in her first novel: "[When I wrote the book] Jordan the mythical could be crossed; the dream-goal of the promised land could be achieved, if not in Nathaniel's lifetime, then in his son's. This was the prevailing spirit, not only of myself but of Africa at the time. Things have shifted considerably since then."[27] Appearing around the time that second-generation writers began producing their works about Africa, this statement by Laurence more closely resembles their often dire predictions for the continent.

NOTES

1. See Gwen R. Boardman, *Graham Greene: The Aesthetics of Exploration*, Gainesville: University of Florida Press, 1971; and M. M. Mahood, *The Colonial Encounter*, Totowa, N.J.: Rowman, 1977.

2. Paul Fussell, *Abroad*, New York: Oxford University Press, 1980, 39.

3. Evelyn Waugh, *When the Going Was Good*, London: Duckworth, 1946, 7. Subsequent references are to this edition.

4. Waugh, *When the Going Was Good*, 298. This passage recalls Edward Gibbon's statement about Ethiopia between the sixth and the sixteenth centuries: "Encompassed on all sides by the enemies of their religion, the Ethiopians slept near a thousand years, forgetful of the world, by whom they were forgotten." *The Decline and Fall of the Roman Empire*, vol. 2, Chicago: Encyclopedia Britannica, 1952, 159–60.

5. Evelyn Waugh, *Waugh in Abyssinia*, qtd. in Paul Fussell, *Abroad*, 198.

6. Evelyn Waugh, *A Tourist in Africa*, Boston: Little, Brown, 1986, 60. Subsequent references are to this edition.

7. Graham Greene, *The Lost Childhood*, 14, qtd. in Gwen R. Boardman, *Graham Greene: The Aesthetics of Exploration*, 131.

8. Graham Greene, *In Search of a Character*, New York: Penguin, 1968, 42.

9. See Boardman, *Graham Greene*, and M. M. Mahood, *The Colonial Encounter*.

10. Graham Greene, *Journey without Maps*, New York: Penguin, 1978, 7. Subsequent references are to this edition.

11. Graham Greene, *The Heart of the Matter*, New York: Penguin, 1978, 35–36. Subsequent references are to this edition.

12. On the positive side, see Grahame Smith, *The Achievement of Graham Greene*, Totowa, N.J.: Barnes,1986. On the negative side, see Frank Kermode, "Mr. Greene's Eggs and Crosses," first published in *Encounter* April 1961 and reprinted in Harold Bloom, ed., *Graham Greene: A Collection of Critical Essays*, New York: Chelsea, 1987, 33–42.

13. Graham Greene, *A Burnt-Out Case*, New York: Penguin, 1977, 5. Subsequent references are to this edition.

14. In a footnote to the "Congo Journal," Greene seems genuinely annoyed by reporters who attribute his presence in the Congo to the riots in Leopoldville that occurred two weeks before his arrival (*In Search of a Character*, 14). But although politics play a larger role in the journal than in the novel, Greene still stresses the isolation of Africa and makes a reference to science fiction to do so: "In the evening [I] heard over the radio news of the disturbances in Brazzaville: one feels that European Africa is rapidly disintegrating. To hear such news three hundred miles within the bush surrounded by Africans is a little like one of the science fiction stories of Ray Bradbury" (56).

15. *In Search of a Character*, 49. Greene reread *Heart of Darkness* during his trip to the Congo and refers to it often in the "Congo Journal."

16. John Jacob Clayton points out that in Henderson's departure from Arnewiland a parallel with *Lord Jim* is suggested and then withdrawn. After ruining their cistern with his improvised bomb in an attempt to rid the water of the frogs that are polluting it, Henderson offers his life to Prince Itelo, the most prominent male among the Arnewi. Itelo, however, refuses to strike

Henderson and his travels continue. In contrast to the laughable, almost picaresque Henderson, characters in the expatriate tradition receive no second chances. See *Saul Bellow: In Defense of Man*, 2d ed., Bloomington: Indiana University Press, 1979.

17. Jonathan Wilson, *On Bellow's Planet*, Rutherford, N.J.: Farleigh Dickinson University Press, 1985, 122.

18. For a detailed discussion of Bellow's use of Reich, James, and William Blake in *Henderson the Rain King*, see Eusebio L. Rodrigues, *Quest for the Human: An Exploration of Saul Bellow's Fiction*, Lewisburg, Pa.: Bucknell University Press, 1981.

19. Eusebio L. Rodrigues, "Bellow's Africa," *American Literature* 43 (May 1971): 242–56. Subsequent references to this article are given in the text.

20. Saul Bellow, *Henderson the Rain King*, in *The Portable Saul Bellow*, New York: Penguin, 1977, 182. Subsequent references are to this edition.

21. Judie Newman, *Saul Bellow and History*, New York: St Martin's, 1984, 75.

22. I don't mean to imply that any depiction of a mythical continent or of another planet automatically disqualifies it from any connection with the real world. Jim Crace's *Continent* (New York: Harper and Row, 1987) illustrates how, through a careful crafting of authentic details, emotions, and situations, an imaginary location can become palpable.

23. Robert Ruark, *Something of Value*, Garden City, N.Y.: Doubleday, 1955.

24. Nicholas Monsarrat, *The Tribe That Lost Its Head*, New York: Sloane, 1956.

25. David Karp, *The Day of the Monkey*, New York: Vanguard, 1955.

26. Margaret Laurence, *This Side Jordan*, New York: St. Martin's, 1960. The book is not without its problems, including Nathaniel's interior monologues and its quick resolution to all the major conflicts, which some critics have derided; nevertheless, the novel's treatment of independence and depiction of African characters make it an "event," to use Foucault's term, in the genealogy of the writing about Africa by outsiders. See pp. 135–36 below.

27. Maragaret Laurence, "Ten Years' Sentences," *The Canadian Novel in the Twentieth Century*, ed. George Woodcock, Toronto: McClelland, 1975, 237.

3

Second-Generation Postwar Writers: Africanist Adjustments to Postcolonial Conditions

In part as a response to the new freedoms and responsibilities that came with independence, the 1960s were a tremendously productive for time African authors. Curiously, during this decade comparatively few outsiders wrote about the continent. Second-generation postwar writers, the first group of outside authors to depict Africa following independence, wrote most of their works ten or more years after the demise of colonialism, when Western authors could no longer ignore political realities as Waugh, Greene, and Bellow had done. Just as Africanist discourse existed long before colonialism, it survived independence: second-generation postwar writing amounts to Africanist adjustments to postcolonial conditions.

Like Western governments, Western authors gave the newly independent African states roughly ten years to build unified countries within the arbitrary boundaries inherited from colonialism; to provide adequate education, health care, and other services; and to create diversified, competitive economies in regions that had always been the suppliers of raw materials and the dumping grounds for Western manufactured goods. When it became apparent that the African nations could not perform these miracles, Western writers began to look for someone or something to blame. Africanist discourse provided second-generation writers with a pre-existing "analysis" of postcolonial Africa's problems. According to this line of thinking, political freedom released the darkness, blankness, and nightmarish aspect of Africa that colonialism had sought but failed to control. Writers such as V. S. and Shiva Naipaul, Paul Theroux, and Martha Gellhorn concede that the colonial mission failed largely because it was motivated by greed. Generally, they view colonialism as something that is over and done with, part of Africa's past but not really part of the West's because colonialism has had no easily perceivable lasting effects on the colonizing countries. According to the second-generation writers, independent Africa has failed precisely because it is the product of nightmarish African primitivism and flawed colonialism. Just as Victorians blamed Africans for slavery after the practice was no longer economically advantageous to the English, so the second generation of outsiders writing about Africa blames independent Africa for the colonialism that had stopped being economically viable for European countries.

V. S. and Shiva Naipaul, John Updike, and Paul Theroux update Africanist discourse to suit postcolonial conditions. Paradoxically, while the writers of the second generation rely heavily on the major Africanist conventions—binary oppositions, the notion of blankness, and evolutionary language—they often possess a metaconsciousness of Africanist discourse that goes beyond that of Greene. Second-generation figures, particularly V. S. Naipaul, are aware of the existence and the negative effects of Africanist thinking on the part of white colonialists, expatriates, and earlier Western writers. At the same time, however, these second-generation writers fail to see the extent to which Africanist discourse operates in their own writing and the degree to which they themselves compound the problem.

V. S. Naipaul

Although it contains such popular mainstream authors as Updike and Theroux, V. S. Naipaul dominates the second generation of outsiders writing about Africa since 1945, having written four important works of fiction and nonfiction about the continent. Naipaul has become one of the most controversial figures in contemporary literature; his work elicits high praise from Western critics, writers, and audiences, while receiving deeply felt scorn from third-world critics and writers.[1] Naipaul's background explains some of the contradictory responses his writing has evoked. Born in Trinidad of Indian parents in 1932, Naipaul went to Oxford on a Trinidadian government scholarship and stayed on in England first as a part-time editor for the BBC's Caribbean Service and later as a novelist and book reviewer. In 1955 he married Patricia Hale, an Englishwoman. Although based in England, Naipaul has traveled frequently to third-world countries gathering information and experiences for his novels and travel accounts. He has acknowledged another exile, Joseph Conrad, whose subjects and sensibilities resemble his own, as his literary ancestor.[2]

An exile in every sense, Naipaul cultivates his position as "a man apart," someone whose allegiance is not bound to a country, a people, or a political perspective. He has launched scathing attacks on both the West and the Third World; however, most of his writing concerns West Indians, Indians, Moslems, and Africans. Only three of his books have been set in the First World. Referring to the designation "Writer," which appears on his passport, Naipaul proudly claims, "I have never had to work for hire; I made a vow at an early age never to work, never to become involved in people that way. That has given me a freedom from people, from entanglements, from rivalries, from competition. I have no enemies, no rivals, no masters; I fear no one."[3] Although Naipaul believes he has no enemies and nothing to fear from others, many view Naipaul as a frightening antagonist because of his Africanist writing.

The Naipauls as Travel Writers

Had the brothers Naipaul not existed, would we have to invent them?
—Michael Thelwell, Letter to the Editor of
the *New York Times Book Review*

V. S. and Shiva Naipaul, the major non-black authors who wrote travel literature about Africa in the 1970s and early 1980s arrive in Africa skeptical and prepared to be disillusioned. They come neither to promote imperialism as Churchill did nor to escape the West as *entre les guerres* literary travelers such as Waugh and Greene did; rather, they come to gather material for works of literature that, though still travel books, aspire to be something more, almost novels. The Naipauls's harshest critics assert that this amounts to literary imperialism: they come to Africa for a period of time, mine the continent for its most brutal and bizarre attributes, manufacture condemnatory literary works from these raw materials, and sell them to Western journals or publishers for tidy sums. Like Africanist authors from the colonial era, the Naipauls condemn that which is non-Western. In addition, however, they condemn colonialism and imperialism's effects on Africa (which were briefly questioned or partially damned by writers like Waugh, Greene, and Richard Wright).[4] The Naipauls reject nationalism and the New Africa because it mixes "tribalism" and colonialism to produce new societies differing radically from those in the West. In part because of the Mau

Mau rebellion and the British propaganda it engendered, for the Naipauls nationalism becomes synonymous with "primitivism." In the process of bashing nationalism and colonialism, they develop two themes touched on by Waugh: racism and the misuse of language in Africa.

While both writers rely on Africanist methods, the approaches of the Naipauls differ. Shiva Naipaul's *North of South* (1979) resembles Waugh's *A Tourist in Africa* because it describes his journey through a number of East and Central African countries. Unlike Waugh, who eschews politics whenever possible, Naipaul engages in political commentary that often manifests itself in sweeping generalizations and hyperbole. North and South translate into black and white ruled countries, and Naipaul wanted to remain north of southern Africa and its racial policies. In his writing, Naipaul goes beyond merely detailing the abuse of language in Africa, linking such misuse to the theme of lying in Conrad's *Heart of Darkness*. In contrast, rather than attempting to describe the whole continent, V. S. Naipaul portrays specific countries, although his nonfiction works about Africa are also politically oriented from start to finish. In "A New King for the Congo: Mobutu and the Nihilism of Africa" (1975) and "The Crocodiles of Yamoussoukro" (1983), the senior Naipaul focuses on two contemporary African nations, Zaire and the Ivory Coast, and stresses the ways in which they differ from the West. Though much subtler than his brother, the elder Naipaul relies on the oppositions his sibling employs and adds another, expatriates versus Africans. Quintessentially Africanist—using binary oppositions and evolutionary language and asserting the blankness of Africa—the two Naipauls, especially V. S., are nonetheless aware of Africanist thinking. "The Crocodiles of Yamoussoukro" concerns Africanist image-making as much as it does African image-making. What the Naipauls and other second-generation authors fail to realize is the degree to which, despite their metaconsciousness, they perpetuate Africanist thinking.

North of South

Almost twenty years after *A Tourist in Africa*, Shiva Naipaul in *North of South* provides an even more brutal assessment of many of the same places Waugh visited. Both books concern race, colonialism, nationalism, and the abuse of language, but Naipaul places even greater emphasis on binary oppositions in his writing and stresses the Africanist theme of blankness. In contrast to Waugh, the younger Naipaul evinces an awareness of Africanist thinking; how ever, he does not recognize his own participation in the process. Moreover, Naipaul seeks to distinguish himself from his predecessors in the political assessment tradition. In the preface to *North of South*, he announces his desire to produce "not . . . a straightforward travel book or a current affairs book or (God forbid!) a sociological treatise but (almost) a kind of novel, a montage of people, of places, of encounters seen and interpreted."[5]

Race is the major topic of *North of South*. Not only the opposition in the title but a number of other dichotomies in the book are racially based. When independence brought white colonialism to an end and ushered in black nationhood, Naipaul explains, this resulted in racism: "The change in their relationship is unfair to both black and white. It breeds stress. This stress nourishes the impotent and puerile racism that feeds on a cycle of tales detailing native ineptitude" (47). As their titles indicate, racial oppositions dominate chapters two, "Black and White: Old Style, Black and White: New Style," and three, "Between Master and Slave." In them, Naipaul discusses the tensions between blacks and whites as well as the racism both groups exhibit towards Asiatics, the people from the subcontinent.

Shiva Naipaul also relies on the opposition between white colonialism and black nationalism, first seen in Waugh. Together these flawed concepts have created contemporary Africa. Demonstrating a consciousness of Africanist thinking, Naipaul talks about colonial settlers in Kenya regarding Africa as a blank space on which to project their own desires. For the settlers "the Highlands provided an opportunity to reconstruct a type of existence ruined by creeping suburbia, labor unions and general elections. . . . Primitive Africa invoked dreams of overlordship. It was like going back to the beginning of the world: Africa was a clean slate on which anything could be written" (146). The flawed aristocratic vision of the colonial settlers persists in Kenya and other parts of Africa, according to Naipaul. Most of the settlers have gone but their way of thinking remains. Moreover, there is a contemporary analogue of the settler to be reckoned with as well. Naipaul asserts that a new group of nostalgic Europeans (in an ironic updating of Churchill's plans for Uganda) view Tanzania as a modern experiment in socialism: "For if the Highlands of neighboring Kenya stimulated to fresh life outmoded and frustrated aristocratic longings in a certain type of European settler, then, with much the same justice, it could be said that Independent Tanzania has stimulated the fantasies of a certain type of outmoded socialist. . . . They are different sides of the same coin" (199).

In Naipaul's estimation, nationalism fares no better, however. Because of its diversity and its past history, the East African coast, "brings home the nonsensical nature of African nationality." Resorting to generalization and exaggeration, Naipaul claims that of all the nationalist leaders in Africa, Julius Nyerere "is just about the only African head of state one can contemplate without immediate sensations of outrage or embarrassment. . . . he makes it possible to believe—if only for a little while—that Africa can be taken seriously, that Africa wants to 'liberate' itself" (197–98). The author's tone foreshadows his subsequent disillusionment with Tanzanian socialism.

In the concluding chapter, significantly titled "Into the Void," Naipaul makes his final, bombastic evaluation of the black-white situation and the condition of contemporary Africa: "Black and white deserved each other. Neither was worth the shedding of a single tear: both were rotten to the core. Each had been destroyed by contact with the other" (347).[6] He goes on to describe the two camps, in the process depicting Africa as the product of failed colonialism and farcical nationalism and relying on the primitive-civilized dichotomy: "Black Africa with its gimcrack tyrannies, its Field Marshals and Emperors, its false philosophies, its fabricated statehoods, returns to Europe its own features, but grotesquely caricatured. . . . As for Western civilization, that had aborted almost from the beginning. Civilized man, it seems, can no more cope with prolonged exposure to the primitive than the primitive can cope with exposure to him" (347).

The distortion of language Naipaul finds in Africa, which he eventually links to falsehood and *Heart of Darkness,* is the last major topic of *North of South.* "Words . . . words . . . words. Africa is swathed in words," Naipaul exclaims in the first chapter. Later he decries the religious reverence that Africans show for the printed word and derisively notes that mud huts, seminude dancing, and the *kokoi,* a form of dress worn by the Swahili for centuries, have been outlawed in some parts of Africa for being "colonial." Language itself becomes the central topic of the penultimate chapter. "Words," we are told in a statement that unwittingly comments on Naipaul's use of Africanist discourse, "when handled promiscuously, gradually begin to take the place of reality. They can, in the course of time, become a complete substitute for it" (284). Naipaul finds this especially true in Tanzania, where he constantly seeks a definition for *ujamaa* but never receives one he considers satisfactory.

In the final pages, Naipaul gives yet another gloomy appraisal of contemporary Africa. Racial problems, the legacy of colonialism, the impossibility of nationalism, and the instability of language have created a world of falsehood: "Hopeless, doomed continent! Only lies flourish here. Africa is swaddled in lies—the lies of aborted European civilization; the lies of liberation. Nothing but lies" (348). Just previous to this statement, Naipaul mentions Conrad's Kurtz, terming the whites of southern Africa "his suburban heirs." By juxtaposition, Naipaul suggests that the theme of lying in *Heart of Darkness* applies to the situation in Africa today. But whereas Conrad designates Europe as the origin of the falsehood, in a manner typical of second-generation postwar writers, Naipaul lays the blame for the pervasive prevarication he discovers in contemporary Africa on the continent itself.

"A New King for the Congo"

V. S. Naipaul's travel works about Africa echo many of the arguments in *North of South*, but whereas in his rhetorical approach Shiva Naipaul often opts for a buzz saw, his brother uses a scalpel. The works "A New King for the Congo," originally published in the *New York Review of Books* and reprinted in *The Return of Eva Peron* (1981), and "The Crocodiles of Yamoussoukro," first published in *Vanity Fair* and later forming one half of *Finding the Center* (1984), are about power—the way African divine kingship has been translated into political power in contemporary Africa. In both texts V. S. Naipaul uses a bewildering array of binary oppositions, but they all boil down to one: the primitive versus the civilized. These two forces have combined to produce the modern African state, an entity quite alien to a Westerner. For outsiders, like Naipaul and his readers, the world of present-day Africa is often a nightmare, but for expatriates, both black and white, it can be a dream world of their own making. The ungrounded nature of language in Africa and the Africanist concept of the void figure prominently in Naipaul's treatment of contemporary Africa. More than in any other Africanist texts, oppositions dominate in these two travel works; Naipaul and his reader struggle to "find the center" in a profusion of dichotomies.

Naipaul claims that the president of Zaire's power, his personality cult, and his nihilism result from contradictions stemming from the conglomeration of various dichotomies. Mobutu Sese Seko combines the old and the new, Henry Morton Stanley and an unknown tribesman; he has become the new Leopold II. But both the colonial and the modern are flawed, as Naipaul's description of the gaps in past and present education in Zaire indicates: "In colonial days, a headmaster told me, the school histories of the Congo began with the late fifteenth century Portuguese navigators, and then jumped to the nineteenth century, to the missionaries and the Arabs and the Belgians. African history, as it is now written, restores Africans to Africa, but is no less opaque. . . . the official *Profils du Zaire* . . . jumps from the brief mention of mostly undated African kingdoms to the establishment of the Congo Free State."[7]

The flawed civilization Naipaul writes about is an "outpost civilization." Drawing on Conrad's "An Outpost of Progress," in which the whites sent to Africa "were too simple for an outpost of progress, people who were part of the crowd at home, and dependent on that crowd" (206), Naipaul argues that an outpost civilization still exists in Zaire today. The distortions of language in the country are an example of what happens when "primitivism" and outpost civilization mix. The indigenous becomes "colonial," Mobutu's reforms become "authenticity," and the former Joseph Mobutu has now become Mobutu Sese Seko Kuku Wa Za Banga. Another example Naipaul gives of the melding of old and new is "the bad art of modern Africa," which is "a double mimicry: African art imitating African inspired Western art" (206).

The two major results of the contradictions of contemporary Zaire are nihilism and Mobutu's power. Although both are there "only for the money," expatriates do the work and Africans are "adrift and nervous in this unreal world of imitation" (208). Eventually Africans turn to nihilism, which Naipaul defines as "the rage of primitive men coming to themselves and finding they have been fooled and affronted" (208). Idi Amin was such a nihilist, so was Pierre Mlule, whose 1960 rebellion in Eastern Zaire allegedly resulted in nine thousand deaths. Naipaul views Mlule's going-native story as the reverse of Kurtz's; the African "had been maddened not by contact with wilderness and primitivism, but with . . . civilization" (209–10).

Mobutu's kingship also results from the clash of primitivism and civilization: "Mobutu embodies these African contradictions and by the grandeur of his kingship, appears to ennoble them. He is, for all his stylishness, the great African nihilist, though his way is not the way of blood" (210).[8] For his country Mobutu becomes the "prophet," the "way out," and the "substitution": "It has been Mobutu's brilliant idea to give the people of Zaire what they have not had and what they have long needed: an African king. The king expresses all the dignity of the people; to possess a king is to share in the king's dignity. The individual's responsibility—a possible source of despair in the abjectness of Africa—is lessened. All that is required is obedience, and obedience is easy" (217). But according to Naipaul, Mobutu's kingship is sterile, an end in itself. Modern Africa and the minds of Africans, asserts Naipaul, have become blank spaces. Thus, the Africanist concept of the void comes full circle. Early in the century, imperialists projected their desires on the formlessness they saw in Africa; Naipaul sees contemporary Africa returning to formlessness because it is flawed civilization grafted upon flawed primitivism. In his final paragraph Naipaul underscores his own particular notion of blankness: "To arrive at this sense of a country trapped and static, eternally vulnerable, is to begin to have something of the African sense of the void" (219).

"The Crocodiles of Yamoussoukro"

Given his admiration for Conrad, as well as Zaire's economic rise and fall and the country's easily documentable corruption, the nation that was once the Belgian Congo provided an obvious focus for Naipaul's attention. His second choice, however, contrasts with Zaire and almost every other African nation. The Ivory Coast has enjoyed political stability and, at least until recently, national harmony and economic prosperity since it gained independence in 1960. Naipaul claims he picked the Ivory Coast for his second African travel work because of its success and its ties to France. However, rather than detailing and analyzing Ivorian improvement since independence in electrification, education, and transportation, Naipaul devotes his attention to the bizarre, to the ways in which this African nation is at odds with the West.

Although Naipaul describes and questions the Africanist thinking of expatriates in the Ivory Coast in "The Crocodiles of Yamoussoukro," he never acknowledges the similarities between their way of looking at the continent and his own. Ironically, Naipaul himself provides the proof for this. Echoing his brother, Naipaul claims to be writing more than a travel book: "when I travel, I can only move according to what I find, I also live as it were, in a novel of my own making, moving from not knowing to knowing."[9] This statement aptly describes Africanists' approach to the continent, privileging their own experiences and perceptions (as well as beliefs and desires) over those of Africans.

Like "A New King for the Congo," "The Crocodiles of Yamoussoukro" examines power and relies heavily on Africanist oppositions. Yamoussoukro is President Houphouët-Boigny's "native" village, which has been transformed into an ultramodern city and the country's capital. The crocodiles serve as a symbol of the president's power; each day they are fed live chickens as a kind of ritual sacrifice in a public ceremony. Naipaul contrasts the new world typified in skyscraper-studded Abidjan, the country's largest city and former capital, with the Old World represented in magical occurrences that have been reported near Kilometer 17 on the road between Abidjan and Yamoussoukro. Rather than finding that the modern is real and the supernatural is false, Naipaul comes to realize that the former has reality for the expatriates who have come to offer their skills while the latter has reality for the Africans. While Naipaul recognizes the existence of two worlds, he does not remain neutral toward them. One is the "day" or "workaday" world, which the author knows; the other is the "night" or "spirit" world, which scares him. Yamoussoukro and Houphouët-Boigny's power stand at the intersection of these two worlds. Thus, despite its success, the Ivory Coast, like Zaire, is built on contradictions.

This combination of two worlds is subversive and nightmarish. The modern city of Yamoussoukro, says Naipaul, "belonged to the world of the day, the world of doing and development," but "The crocodile ritual—speaking of a power issuing to the president from the earth itself—was part of the night, ceaselessly undoing the reality of the day. One idea worked against the other. So, in spite of the expense, the labor, the ambition, there was a contradiction in the modern pharaonic dream" (150). The contradiction literally gives Naipaul a nightmare. He dreams he is on a roof that has begun to disintegrate. The next morning even the concrete and steel buildings of Abidjan seem magical creations to him.

Naipaul also discovers that expatriates in the Ivory Coast live in their own dream world; their way of thinking about their new country is Africanist (although Naipaul does not use the word). People were called to Africa for different reasons, but Naipaul finds that "Everyone who went and stayed had his own Africa" (155). Africa has a strange effect on people; those who come to convert Africa to the modern world are sometimes converted to the magic world, which Naipaul views as an ironic but also an unsettling phenomenon. Apparently meant to be regarded as the contemporary equivalent of the European colonist gone native, Arlette, an expatriate from Martinique, talks to Naipaul about the upper material world and the inner spiritual world and asserts that the latter is more important. Naipaul asks her whether it would matter if Abidjan fell into ruins. She replies, "No. It wouldn't matter. Men would continue to live in their own way." Naipaul responds, "Arlette, you make me feel that the world is unstable. You make me feel everything we live by is built on sand" (174–75). It is built on sand, Arlette claims, going on to declare that her parents, who feel superior to Africans, actually live in a dream world.

The dream-nightmare opposition pervades "The Crocodiles of Yamoussoukro." "Primitive" Africa threatens the achievements of Western men and women, converts expatriates to magic, and turns the dreams of an outsider like Naipaul into nightmares. Although over seventy years separate "The Crocodiles of Yamoussoukro" and Churchill's *My African Journey*, the basic Africanist gesture of condemning the continent has not changed. John Bull no longer has a garden to cultivate, but the nightshade Churchill describes can be seen in Naipaul's depiction of the magical side of modern Africa.

"The Crocodiles of Yamoussoukro" may be the most sinister of Naipaul's books on Africa. Rather than merely reveling at the sight of one of independent Africa's greatest failures as "A New King for the Congo" does, "The Crocodiles of Yamoussoukro" uses the machinations of Africanist discourse to deny Africa one of its greatest successes. The Ivory Coast may appear to have achieved many things, Naipaul argues, but the true character of Africa and Africans makes Ivoirian accomplishments illusory and ultimately threatens all of the modern world.

V. S. Naipaul's African Fiction

History has disappeared. Even the Belgian colonial past. And no one, African, Asian, European, has heard of Conrad or *Heart of Darkness*.

—V. S. Naipaul, *A Congo Diary*

V. S. Naipaul's two African works in the expatriate tradition echo many of the Africanist assessments of his travel accounts. *In a Free State* (1971) comprises five parts: two journal entries open and close the book, describing trips to Egypt from Europe; two lengthy short stories depict people from the Third World (India and Trinidad) coming to the First World (the United States and England); and the title story, a novella, concerns two white expatriates driving from the Northern capital of a recently independent East African country to their homes in the South during a time of political upheaval. *A Bend in the River* (1979), a popular success regarded by many as Naipaul's best novel, focuses on an African-Indian shopkeeper in the city at "the bend in the river"—modeled on Kisangani on the Zaire or Congo—from soon after the country has achieved independence until he is forced to leave a decade later because his shop has been nationalized and the region is in political turmoil. With its Zairian setting, the book, which Christopher Miller has dubbed "the strongest Africanist narration since *Heart of Darkness*,"[10] repeats many of the events and attitudes expressed in "A New King for the Congo."

Although the expatriate tradition continues through the second-generation writers and beyond, African independence causes the tradition to alter significantly. The Naipauls' political assessment of contemporary Africa as flawed colonialism grafted upon African primitivism excludes the presence of a monumental white figure who betrays the colonial mission. Having lost Africa because of either a lack of conviction in the colonial mission or its sheer falsity, outsiders no longer have a place in Africa. There are no more Kurtzes or Scobies to fall morally, just unimportant, obsolete outsiders who have become part of the problem. However, the Africanist approach to Africa does not change: Africa and Africans are still the seat and source of corruption; the continent is still riddled with contradictions; and, with the departure of the Europeans, Africa reverts to its former state of absolute blankness, lacking history, a past, and a future. Thus, while Naipaul's choice of Salim, a native African (though still an outsider), rather than a white character as his protagonist in *A Bend in the River*, represents an advance within the expatriate tradition, the author continues to rely heavily on the conventions of Africanist discourse.

In Africanist works written before the end of colonialism, the absence of restraints and the almost unlimited sense of power available to colonialists in Africa produced an environment conducive to going native. *In a Free State* and *A Bend in the River* also utilize settings where allegiances and responsibilities are unclear. In Naipaul's first work of fiction on Africa, being "in a free state" clearly means both obtaining personal or national independence and existing in a condition of flux, occupying a position between two different places or states of mind. The themes of independence, dependence, and "dangling" between two worlds play important roles in *A Bend in the River* as well.

Three of the five parts of *In a Free State* involve Africa and relate to the theme of going native. The first piece, a "Prologue, from a Journal" entitled "The Tramp at Piraeus," describes a two-day crossing from Greece to Alexandria on a steamer during which apparently civilized people go native. An English vagabond attracts Naipaul's attention and the author meticulously describes the tramp's appearance and self-conscious actions. He also records the conversation of two Lebanese businessmen with whom he sits at lunch as well as the childish scene the tramp makes after dinner by ripping up a magazine in the smoking room.

The following morning at breakfast one of the Lebanese announces his intention "to kill" the tramp for his antics during the night in the cabin they shared with the other Lebanese and a muscular Austrian, Hans. Together these three conspire to get back at the tramp: "It was to be like a tiger-hunt, where bait is laid out and the hunter and spectators watch from the security of a platform. The bait was the tramp's own rucksack."[11] When the tramp finally enters the cabin, the Austrian blocks the door and the two Lebanese harangue him for his behavior. Throughout the rest of the day, whenever the tramp appears one of the Lebanese yells "Hans!" as if the three are going to accost the tramp again. In retaliation, the tramp locks the trio out of the cabin and threatens to set it afire if they attempt to enter it, forcing them to sleep elsewhere. In the morning the boat has arrived at Alexandria and the people separate themselves according to nationality to await the immigration officials. The tramp appears and queues up nervously, but his antagonists either fail or refuse to see him. "That passion was over," for them, writes Naipaul; they have turned their attention to the purposes that caused them to make the trip.

In a companion piece, an "Epilogue, from a Journal," called "The Circus at Luxor," Naipaul again travels from Europe to Africa, by plane from Milan to Cairo. This time, however, he not only observes non-Africans going native, he also becomes embroiled in the process himself. The title ostensibly arises from Naipaul's observation of the same members of a circus from China he saw tipping waiters at a restaurant in Milan tipping Egyptian waiters at a drab eating place in the desert near Luxor. This coincidence leads him to reflect on the number of empires that have met in that ancient location. The bulk of the piece, however, concerns events that transpired the previous day.

At a rest house, desert children beg for food from tourists. A man with a camel-whip chases them away, striking the sand with his whip. Throwing apples to make the children run far and getting them to come quite close in pursuit of sandwich fragments, a group of middle-aged Italians turn the whole thing into a game. Soon, however, the game reaches a point that Naipaul finds intolerable: "A tall Italian in a cerise jersey stood up and took out his camera. He laid out food just below the terrace and the children came running. But this time, as though it had to be real for the camera, the camel-whip fell not on sand but on their backs, with louder, quicker camel-shouts" (243). None of the other guests seems disturbed by this scene, but Naipaul cannot stand it anymore and makes a move to stop it, in the process nearly losing his own self-control: "Lucidity, and anxiety, came to me only when I was almost on the man with the camel-whip. I was shouting. I took the whip away, threw it on the sand" (243). Afterward, realizing the game will soon begin again, Naipaul feels "exposed" and "futile," and he leaves promptly. The next day he decides to go to the drab eating place rather than return to the rest house.

In both of these journal pieces, the environment causes people to abandon their normal behavior. While most of the action in "The Tramp at Piraeus" takes place at sea rather than in Africa, if only by juxtaposition both locations are associated with flux, places where people lose their heads and become violent, places where people go native. Similarly, in "The Circus at Luxor" Africa represents a location where people's behavior changes, where they treat one another like animals. Moreover, when Naipaul tries to put a stop to the madness, his efforts prove ineffectual and he is caught up in the mayhem.

Situated between these two journal pieces, the long title story of *In a Free State* continues Naipaul's exploration of freedom and flux, this time in an unnamed, newly independent East African country based on Uganda. "In a Free State" contains many of the same Africanist assessments of postcolonial Africa found in the nonfiction of both Naipauls. It is also another second-generation version of the expatriate tradition. Driving through an unstable political environment, the petty white protagonists verbally assault one another inside the car as physical violence erupts around them. Africa, a place in continuous flux where, according to Naipaul, things have little or no meaning, provides the crisis conditions that reveal the shallowness of the main characters, Bobby and Linda.

Although "In a Free State" contains many specific events and observations reminiscent of the Naipauls' travel works on Africa, other things remain vague, giving the fictitious country a dreamlike quality (which can readily become nightmarish). The novella begins like a fairy tale; one can almost hear the phrase "Once upon a time" leading into the first sentence, "In this country in Africa there was a president and also a king" (103). Stressing the distinction between what is colonial and what is African and suggesting the shortcomings of both, Naipaul starts the action in the capital, "an English-

Indian creation in the African wilderness. It owed nothing to African skill; it required none. . . . Africa here was decor. Glamour for the white visitor and expatriate; glamour too for the African, the man flushed out from the bush, to whom, in the city, with independence, civilization appeared to have been granted complete" (103–4). This passage contains a typically Naipaulian condemnation of independent Africa: the hand-me-down colonial civilization is meretriciously flawed, and, rather than actually possessing it, the Africans only "appear" to have inherited it.

Misuse of language, anti-Indian prejudice, and blankness, Naipaul implicitly argues, indicate the true condition of this independent African nation. Nomenclature in the country has no connection with reality. Africans in the capital wear their hair in the "English style," that is, "parted low on the left and piled up on the right." Some whites like Bobby, on the other hand, sport " 'native shirts' " that are "designed and woven in Holland." While colonialism has ended, racism has not. At a hotel in the capital, blacks and whites can mingle but Asiatics are excluded. Likewise, "The Union Club had been founded by some Indians in colonial days as a multiracial club; it was the only club in the capital that admitted Africans. After independence the Indians had been deported, the club seized and turned into a hotel for tourists" (111). Away from the Indian-English capital, emptiness dominates. Naipaul terms it "an unfinished landscape, a scratching in the continent" (144) and argues that this vacancy extends to the Africans themselves. At one point he coins an adjective to express this, describing the face of an employee of a hotel-resort in the bush as "African-blank."

As Bobby and Linda drive the length of the country, from the capital in the North where they have attended a conference to the expatriate compound in the Southern Collectorate where they live, they encounter and argue about the beauty and decay of the country. The Western-backed president, whose tribe is dominant in the North, has ordered the arrest of the king, whose rival tribal base is in the South, putting any member of the king's tribe in jeopardy. After passing a group of "blank-faced" Africans early in the trip, Linda attributes Mau Mau–type activities to them: "They are going to swear their oaths of hate. You know what that means, don't you? You know the filthy things they are going to do? The filth they are going to eat? The blood, the excrement, the dirt?" (122).

Similarly, after describing the runaround she received trying to find out whether any of her houseboy's relatives were casualties of an earthquake a few years previously, Linda suggests that "Perhaps in a place like this there isn't any news" (143). Later in a statement reminiscent of *North of South*, Linda argues that falsehood pervades the country: "You go out driving with Sammy Kisenyi, making educated conversation, and you see a naked savage with a penis one foot long. You pretend you've seen nothing. You see two naked boys painted white running about the public highway, and you don't talk about it. Sammy Kisenyi reads a paper on broadcasting at the conference. He's lifted whole paragraphs from T. S. Eliot, of all people. You say nothing about it. Outside you encourage and encourage. In the compound you talk and talk. Everybody just lies and lies and lies" (218).

While Linda asserts her superiority through these comments, aggravating the liberal Bobby, the physical corruption and brutality of Africa closes in on them. When they stop at a gas station, an African attendant "fill[s] the car with his smell." Like Greene, Naipaul often writes about the odor of Africa and Africans and may also mean to link this with the theme of decay. Bobby and Linda later come face to face with violence when they pass what at first appears to be a road accident that has attracted many other vehicles, including a number of army trucks. As they leave the scene, Linda realizes what they have actually been looking at: "That wasn't an accident. . . . That was the king. They've killed him" (214).

Although in contrast to Kurtz and Scobie these whites are purposeless and of no consequence, they nevertheless go native. While corruption and violence impinge upon them from outside, Bobby and Linda become increasingly irritable within the car. Linda, a has-been BBC broadcaster's wife, has decided to leave the country, presumably for Southern Africa. A mentally unstable homosexual more at home in Africa than in England, Bobby loves the country and regards it as home. Like the resort in which they spend the night, neither of these people has any function in the New Africa: "The resort hadn't been built for tourists in Africa; it had been created by people who thought they had come to Africa to stay, and looked on the resort for a version of the things of home: a park, a pier, a waterside promenade. Now, after the troubles across the lake, after independence and the property scare, after the army mutiny, after the white exodus South and the Asian deportations, after all these deaths, the resort no longer had a function" (171).

The corrupt, violent environment of Africa causes these obsolete whites to degenerate. In a scene that foreshadows later developments, Bobby and Linda take a walk through the village surrounding the resort and soon find themselves in the midst of a pack of dogs. Even after the pair turn back, the number of animals grows, provoking Linda to cry, "Oh my God, these dogs don't have any owners. They've gone wild" (188). Bobby, who was attacked by a dog as a child, temporarily loses control: "Rage overcame Bobby. 'I'll kill them. I'm wearing these steel-tipped shoes. I'll kill the first one that attacks me. I'll kick its skull in. I'll kill it' " (189).

Throughout the trip, Linda's anti-African rhetoric and Bobby's ready defense of all things African have made things tense. After leaving the resort and passing the site of the king's murder, Bobby and Linda's verbal attacks turn personal. Driven on by his insecurity, Bobby eventually declares, "You're nothing. You're nothing but a rotting cunt. There are millions like you, millions, and there will be millions more" (219). Soon after this Linda demands that Bobby stop the car and she walks back toward the last village they passed. While Bobby's assertion of Linda's insignificance is just, Naipaul indicates that it applies equally to himself.

The final scenes of the novella make it clear that there is no place in the country for Bobby, despite his liberal attitude toward Africans. Driving South together again after a reconciliation, Bobby and Linda have wasted enough time to cause them to be in violation of a four P.M. curfew. At the entrance to the king's territory, coming upon presumably the same army trucks they passed earlier, Bobby decides to stop and inquire about the curfew even though there is no roadblock. He and Linda can see prisoners, some of whom appear dead, but the soldier they speak to cannot answer their question about the curfew. Bobby enters a nearby building and, after refusing to surrender his watch, is severely beaten and kicked by a group of soldiers. He decides to "play dead" and eventually succeeds in returning to the car. After they arrive in the expatriate compound without further incident, Bobby feels protected once more. However, upon seeing his bruises, Bobby's houseboy Luke cannot suppress a laugh, causing Bobby to reflect, "I will have to leave. But the compound was safe; the soldiers guarded the gate. Bobby thought: I will have to sack Luke" (238). Naipaul makes it clear that both Bobby's pro-African attitude and his very presence in Africa have been compromised.

As in Greene, the African environment in "In a Free State," devoid of restraints and filled with corruption and violence, brings about the decline of whites. The difference, however, is that Bobby and Linda lack the stature of such characters as Scobie and Querry.

Consistent with the second postwar generation's approach to independent Africa, which condemns both African "primitivism" and flawed European civilization, these white expatriates have become inconsequential and part of the problem.

A Bend in the River possesses a substantiality and unity exceeding that of *In a Free State*. Moreover, because of its popularity, critical acclaim, and craftsmanship, the book is the most important second-generation work about Africa. It follows the basic pattern of narratives in the expatriate tradition: prolonged exposure to a corrupt African environment results in the moral decline of an outsider. Naipaul, however, brings one significant innovation to the tradition. Instead of a white going native, Naipaul's protagonist is a man with divided loyalties, born and raised in Africa but of Indian descent. Thus, Salim is both an insider and an outsider, a person whose fate is inextricably linked with the continent's but who has a foreign, that is, an Africanist, perspective on the events he narrates. His position in between two worlds as he himself sees it, makes him "a man apart," so that even near the end of the book when he is imprisoned and hears the screams of Africans who are his fellow prisoners, a barrier exists between them and him.

In *A Bend in the River*, the second-generation assessment of independent Africa as flawed colonialism combined with African primitivism receives its fullest treatment. Setting the book in an unnamed country clearly modeled on Zaire, Naipaul draws heavily on the events and opinions he recorded in "A New King for the Congo."[12] The unidentified town at the "bend in the river" is Kisangani, formerly Stanleyville, the location of Kurtz's Inner Station in *Heart of Darkness*. Salim comes to Zaire in the early to middle 1960s—just a few years after the Belgians abruptly pulled out and about the same time that Mobutu, here the "Big Man," seized power in a military coup. He leaves the country roughly ten years later when his shop has been nationalized, the region is in turmoil, and he has just been released from prison, where he was held for smuggling.

Salim has a qualified respect for European civilization because it produced the history books in which Salim learned about his people's past; without the introduction of a Western perspective he doubts whether this past would be remembered or even exist at all. However, history books and a sense of the past also enable Salim to look in a detached way at familiar things, including the Indian community in East Africa. This has uncomfortable consequences: "It was from this habit of looking that the idea came to me that as a community we had fallen behind. And that was the beginning of my insecurity."[13]

Adopting this evolutionary point of view, Salim ranks Africans and their accomplishments far below those of his Indian community. Even more remote from the historical perspective of Europe than Salim's Indian community, Africans had no past or history of their own until the Europeans came. When the outsiders left, history left with them and Africa began to revert to what it was before they arrived, bush and primitive people. Thus it has no future as well. This argument echoes Naipaul's assessment of Zaire and Africa in "A New King for the Congo"—the continent is once more becoming a blank space. Salim often reflects on Nazruddin's assessment of property in a ruined suburb outside of Kisangani, an assessment that applies to all of the New Africa, "This isn't property. This is just bush. This has always been bush" (23).

Despite his admiration for Europeans, Salim recognizes the flaws in their civilization. Not content with simple greed, Europeans lied to themselves about their motivations. Echoing Conrad, Salim feels that, in addition to history, falsehood is the legacy Europe bequeathed to Africa, and he succinctly identifies the hypocrisy towards Africa that resulted from the contradictory impulses inherent in European civilization: "The Europeans wanted gold and slaves, like everybody else; but at the same time they wanted statues put up to themselves as people who had done good things for the slaves. Being an intelligent and energetic people, and at the peak of their powers, they could express both sides of their civilization; and they got both the slaves and the statues" (17).

When the Europeans departed at independence, Africans not only took over political power but they also inherited the capacity to lie from their former rulers. As the New Africa takes shape, this fact terrifies Salim: "I feared the lies—black men assuming the lies of white men" (16). The creation and operation of the Zairian state, particularly Mobutu's efforts to erect modern cities in the jungle and turn children from the bush into individuals capable of functioning in the contemporary world, are an example of the falsehood that characterizes independent Africa. Salim's description of the construction of the New Domain outside of Kisangani, which begins to deteriorate soon after it is completed, conveys this sense of falsehood. Similarly, the image that Mobutu has created for himself in photographs hung in every shop in the country is untrue. Zabeth, a *marchande* from a bush village who comes to Salim's shop to purchase her goods, informs him that the elaborately carved stick the Big Man carries, supposedly a powerful fetish, is a sham: "that isn't a fetish he's got there. It's nothing" (224).

In addition to being riddled with falsehood, Naipaul's Zaire teems with violence. Arriving in the country just after the civil war following independence has ended, Salim lives through the "Second Rebellion," which dominates the first section of the book, and leaves in the midst of another battle. Salim's comment early in the novel on the killing in the forest of people from one tribe by members of another is presented as an emblem of the whole continent: "Africa was big. The bush muffled the sound of murder, and the muddy rivers and lakes washed the blood away" (53).

Instead of Salim, one of the New Africans presents Naipaul's final assessment of the flawed civilization and reemergent primitivism of independent Africa. Zabeth's son Ferdinand, a child from the bush who goes through the country's educational system, eventually becomes a member of the government. It is he who releases Salim from prison at the end of the novel, but unlike Salim, Ferdinand has no place to which he can escape. Decrying the present state of the country and renouncing his education and accomplishments, Ferdinand, the New African, has become an Africanist. He explains that his education has robbed him of the one thing that was truly his (and for Naipaul the only thing truly African), the simple life in the bush: "Everything that was given to me was given to me to destroy me. I began to think I wanted to be a child again, to forget books and everything connected with books. The bush runs itself. But there is no place to go to. I've been on tour in the villages. It's a nightmare. All these airfields the man has built, the foreign companies have built—nowhere is safe now" (272).

In this world without a past or future, full of lies and violence—where everyone, African, Indian, and white, is left dangling, and from which there is no escape—the position of an outsider becomes especially tenuous. In an echo of the lesson learned by Bobby and Linda in "In a Free State," the white headmaster of the lycee and an amateur anthropologist, Father Huismans, is murdered while traveling through a remote region collecting artifacts. The death takes on great significance because like Salim, Huismans is "a man apart." He also translates and provides Salim with the source of a Latin motto carved on a ruined monument near the docks. *Miscerique probat populos et foedera jungi*, "He approves of the mingling of the peoples and their bonds of union," deliberately alters a line from the *Aeneid*. In the original when Aeneas comes to Africa and the affair with Dido jeopardizes his mission to found Rome, the gods intervene, declaring their disapproval of the mingling of Africans and Romans. In Naipaul's novel, however, the owners of a steamship company changed the line to assert that relations between Europeans and Africans are approved. This revelation shocks Salim: "I was staggered. Twisting two-thousand-year-old words to celebrate sixty years of the steamer service from the capital! Rome was Rome. What was this place? To carve the words on a monument beside this African river was surely to invite the destruction of the town. Wasn't there some little anxiety, as in the original line in the poem?" (63).

Salim certainly believes in the veracity of Virgil's line and *A Bend in the River* works hard to confirm it. That the European Father Huismans, the key who unlocks this mystery for Salim and a great believer in the future of Africa, dies at the hands of Africans is surely meant to prove that the "gods" do not approve of the mingling of Africans and Europeans at the "bend in the river." Salim himself attributes Huismans's death to the incompatibility between the priest's civilization and the African environment: "The idea Father Huismans had of his civilization had made him live his particular kind of dedicated life. It had sent him looking, inquiring; it had made him find human richness where the rest of us saw bush or had stopped seeing anything at all. But his idea of civilization was also like his vanity. It had made him read too much in the mingling of peoples by our river, and he had paid for it" (82).

In "Past and Present Darkness: Sources for V. S. Naipaul's *A Bend in the River*," which focuses on the similarities between Naipaul's novel and *Heart of Darkness*, Lynda Prescott argues that, as a representative of European civilization who dies because of his fascination with African customs, Father Huismans plays a role in Naipaul's book similar to that of Kurtz in Conrad's novella.[14] However, it is Salim who bears a greater resemblance than Huismans to Kurtz and other characters who succumb to the corruption of Africa in the expatriate tradition.[15]

On the one hand, insecurity, insignificance, and powerlessness—attributes typical of outsiders in postcolonial depictions of Africa—differentiate Salim from colonial protagonists in the expatriate tradition such as Scobie and Kurtz. On the other hand, similar to his predecessors, Salim brings traditions and principles with him when he comes to Kisangani, and he is aware of his decay as he chronicles his drift into licentiousness, self-deception, violence, criminality, and betrayal.

Salim has no place to go back to, no life to fall back on, as he once thought he would. Not long after he arrives in Zaire, Salim receives word that African independence on the coast has destroyed his family's position and forced most of the Indian community to emigrate. Thus, Salim has been permanently severed from the restraints he knew as a child: "[Life in Zaire] was the opposite of the life of our family on the coast. That life was full of rules. Too many rules; it was a prepacked kind of life. Here I had stripped myself of all the rules. . . . I had also discovered that I had stripped myself of the support the rules gave" (191). Salim does inherit one thing from his family, the responsibility for a family servant. Known as Ali on the Coast, he soon gets the name Metty because of his mixed racial background. When he arrives he tells Salim of the violence directed against the Indian community, which he witnessed. Thus, Metty's presence in Kisangani is a reminder that, with the destruction of his past life, "the world is what it is" for Salim; his fortunes are now tied to those of the town at the bend in the river.

At first, Salim delights in the "sexual casualness" of this part of Africa, but it later grows to perturb him. He comes to agree with Mahesh, an Indian living with his wife in the town, who views this casualness as "part of the chaos and corruption of the place." Metty's presence forces Salim to avoid being seen with African women so that word will not get back to members of his family. As a result, a reversal of the master-servant relationship begins to take place between Salim and Metty. While Metty can openly pick up women in front of his employer, Salim must conceal his sexual behavior.

Like the Africans and many of the expatriates around him, Salim is also gradually seduced by the lies of the Big Man. Responding to an economic boom that follows the chaos of the Second Rebellion, Salim begins to abandon his Africanist perspective on the newly independent country, regarding the bush as more than just blank space and believing in the future: "We felt that there was treasure around us, waiting to be picked up. It was the bush that gave us this feeling. During the empty, idle time, we had been indifferent to the bush; during the days of rebellion it had depressed us. Now it excited us— the unused earth, with the promise of the unused. We forgot that others had been here before us, and had felt like us" (95). Viewing the town as ordinary rather than unreal is, from Naipaul's Africanist perspective, Salim's mistake. He succumbs to the lure of the New Domain, the university town built on the ruins of a colonial suburb on the outskirts of the town, more than any other aspect of the president's attempt to build modern Africa in the bush. There Salim meets a wide variety of interesting people unavailable to him in the town. As he becomes dependent on the excitement that the Domain offers him, Salim feels "tenderness" for the Big Man and forgets the "vainglory" of the Latin motto Father Huismans translated for him. Through the people in the Domain, Salim feels "bound more closely with the fact of the President's power" and therefore more dependent upon him (184). Thus, in contrast to visiting foreigners who laugh at the Big Man's promotion of the "African madonna," Salim has invested too heavily in the president's impossible dream to scoff at any part of it. Salim eventually recognizes the falsity of the Big Man's endeavors but not before it costs him financially and emotionally.

The main reason Salim becomes so enmeshed in the life of the Domain is his affair with Yvette, which he recognizes as corrupting and which ends in physical violence. From the time he sees her at a party in a European blouse, Salim becomes obsessed. Although they meet often and couple intensely, Salim derives little satisfaction from their affair; rather, he experiences only a void, a need to be fulfilled, and feels his manhood has been reduced by his obsession with giving Yvette pleasure. As a result of their relationship, Salim grows increasingly concerned about his own corruption. After closing his shop for three hours to meet Yvette at his flat on a Friday, and thus missing a great deal of business, Salim links his decline to the concept of going native: "I had my first alarm about myself, the beginning of the decay of the man I had known myself to be. I had visions of beggary and decrepitude: the man not of Africa lost in Africa, no longer with the strength or purpose to hold his own" (179). Realizing that adultery has become a way of life for him, Salim thinks how "sly and dishonourable and weak-willed" such behavior would seem if he were still living on the coast. That past, however, is gone. Salim attributes the affair to the unreal African environment: "In no other place would it be just like this; and perhaps in no other place would our relationship be possible" (202).

Eventually their affair becomes routine and their assignations less frequent. When Yvette behaves mechanically with Salim, he interprets this as a rebuff, responding with a shocking display of violence: "She was hit so hard and so often about the face, even through raised, protecting arms, that she staggered back and allowed herself to fall on the floor. I used my foot on her then, doing that for the sake of the beauty of her shoes, her ankles, the skirt I had watched her raise, the hump of her hip" (219). Naipaul implies that just as the affair could only take place in Africa, the violence of the continent alone drives the once principled Salim to such savagery.

Salim links the tension caused by the impending political crisis to corruption and considers fleeing the country. He returns from a trip abroad to find the political situation explosive. In his absence, Salim's shop has been nationalized and placed in the hands of an incompetent, comic book reading alcoholic named Citizen Theotime. Having lost his business, Salim turns to smuggling gold and ivory. Seeking to exchange his money for foreign currency, he goes to the Domain. At the mercy of those with whom he trades, Salim loses any illusions he might have had about the Domain and its inhabitants.

Reminiscent of Scobie's disloyalty to Ali in *The Heart of the Matter*, the most significant step in the degeneration of Greene's protagonist, the final stage of Salim's decline is his symbolic betrayal of Metty. Salim's ties to Metty are the last vestige of his past life that exists in the New Africa. Demoted to shop manager, Salim tries but can do nothing to stop Theotime from mistreating Metty. As a result, Metty believes Salim has failed him. Salim concurs: "So the old contract between Metty and myself, which was the contract between his family and mine, came to an end" (264). When Salim refuses to give him money to go away, Metty stops bringing Salim his morning coffee and reveals his master's hiding place for smuggled goods to the police. After Salim has been released and amidst rumors of imminent Khmer Rouge–type killings, Metty begs Salim to take him along. But Salim no longer acknowledges a link between them, asserting that he can only take care of himself.

Naipaul clearly intends Salim's fate as a commentary on Kurtz. Now that (symbolically at least) all the whites have gone, Salim represents the last person possessing any kind of moral compunctions in Zaire, and by extension the whole continent. When Salim returns to Africa from England, he duplicates the route taken by Marlow to reach Kurtz, journeying from London to Kisangani via Brussels and Kinshasa. More important, his departure by steamboat, down the same river Kurtz and Marlow sailed up, and from Kisangani, the location of Kurtz's Inner Station, is meant by Naipaul to close a chapter of history. Salim narrowly escapes from a collapsing Africa that is returning to the same state Kurtz found it in almost ninety years previously. Naipaul suggests that Africa's encounter with civilization, and with it time and history, was doomed to fail from the beginning because that civilization was flawed and African primitivism was too strong to overcome. Naipaul thus writes off a country and a continent in a more subtle and final way in *A Bend in the River* than either he himself does in "A New King for the Congo" or his brother does with his hyperbolic pronouncements in *North of South*.[16]

Although the basic Africanist motif of going native, which entails the corruption of all things African, has not changed, the expatriate tradition alters drastically in the second postwar generation, de-emphasizing the importance of whites and even at times shifting its attention away from them to people from Africa like Salim. For Naipaul, England, the United States, and Canada may no longer be Africa's polar opposites, may no longer provide safe havens, having entered into flux and moral decline. Nevertheless, in these places, Nazruddin and presumably Salim manage to survive, hold on to some of their past, and look ahead to some kind of a future. In contrast, now that the whites have left, Africa has no past, no future, no rationality, no moral framework.

Paul Theroux

Outsiders, even the most well-intentioned in Third World countries, are nearly always meddlers.

—Paul Theroux, "Introducing *Jungle Lovers*"

In contrast to Greene's protagonists and like the main characters in "In a Free State" and *A Bend in the River*, the outsiders in the second-generation postwar novels by white authors are inconsequential and at times foolish or ignorant. In a 1967 essay entitled "Tarzan Is an Expatriate," Paul Theroux outlines his general perception of whites in Africa. Written during his five-year sojourn in the continent, the essay effectively describes characters in his own books as well as those by other second-generation white outsiders.

Drawing on his memory of comic books inspired by Burroughs's novels, Theroux associates the demeanor of Tarzan towards his surroundings with that of white expatriates in postcolonial Africa.[17] Just as Tarzan rules the animals through his attitude of superiority, so white expatriates maintain their superiority through rules of conduct designed to bolster their morale and through racial stereotypes that stress the incompetence and inferiority of Africans. Theroux lists five reasons, all of them selfish, why white expatriates come to the jungle: "an active curiosity in things strange; a vague premonition that Africa rewards her visitors; a disgust with the anonymity of the industrial setting; a wish to be special; and an unconscious desire to stop thinking and let the body take over."[18] The monolithic white community and the corrupt political climate in many African nations make it possible to realize these expatriate desires. As a result, many whites develop what Theroux calls the Tarzan Complex:

"The expatriate has been served, waited on, pandered to, pimped for and overpaid; he has fed the image of his uniqueness and his arrogance has reached full vigor" (37).

Although the fictional postcolonial expatriates go native and give in to the pleasures offered to them, their lack of real significance and heroic stature contrasts with their more famous colonial counterparts. According to Theroux, the white expatriate, "like the Tarzan of the comics, is not an objectionable man. He is not Mr. Kurtz, "Mad" Mike Hoare or Cecil Rhodes. There is very little that can be called sinister about him. There was little duplicity in his reasons for coming to Africa, but overthrowing the government by force is the furthest thing from his mind. What is most striking about him is his ordinariness; he is a very ordinary white person in an extraordinary setting. He is a white man starting to wilt, sweating profusely, among millions of black men, frangipanis, wild animals and bush foliage" (37). This description of expatriates applies not only to characters in Theroux's African novels—*Fong and the Indians* (1968), *Girls at Play* (1969), and *Jungle Lovers* (1971)—but also to the white characters, both male and female, of Martha Gellhorn's *The Weather in Africa* (1978), and to Morgan Leafy, the protagonist of William Boyd's comic novel *A Good Man in Africa* (1981).

Paul Theroux's three books derived from his five years in Africa reflect the ambiguities of being an American in Africa during the 1960s. In their writings on Africa the Naipauls accentuate their position as complete outsiders, without ties to Africans or the former colonial powers, and condemn the continent as a product of indigenous primitivism and failed civilization. In a 1986 essay, Theroux recalls the feeling of independence experienced by himself and other Peace Corps volunteers in the early 1960s. Americans in Malawi mocked the British settlers, regarded them as traitors, and would often start fights with them in bars.[19] Brimming with idealism, possessing a knowledge of the local language, and eager to help Africans any way they could, the early volunteers saw themselves as the antithesis of the white colonialists. However, this feeling of difference was an illusion. Many of these young Americans, like Theroux, joined the Peace Corps to avoid being conscripted into the Vietnam War, a conflict they equated with American imperialism.

The tone of Theroux's African novels owes much to his tumultuous experiences on the continent. In 1965, Theroux was deported from Malawi after being implicated in a plot to kill Prime Minister Hastings Banda. According to Theroux, a reluctant revolutionary to whom he had once delivered a message framed Theroux in order to clear himself. The proceedings did not catch Theroux completely by surprise. At the time he was not sure whether he was being expelled for having worked unwittingly for the German intelligence agency, co-authored an English textbook of which Prime Minister Banda disapproved, written an editorial for a Peace Corps newspaper condemning the Vietnam War, or smuggled out the car and personal effects of a minister who had broken with Banda.[20] Theroux next served as a lecturer in the department of extramural studies at Makerere University in Uganda, meeting V. S. Naipaul, who in 1966 taught writing for six months at the school. In an essay on Naipaul, Theroux stresses the influence their friendship at that time had on him as a writer, claiming that Naipaul had "woken me and made me think."[21] Theroux taught at Makerere until 1968, when he and his wife were attacked by a mob, including some of his own students, protesting Rhodesia's racial policies. He then decided to leave Africa.

Theroux's *Fong and the Indians* and *Girls at Play* were written and set in East Africa. He wrote *Jungle Lovers*, set in Malawi, while he was teaching in Singapore after leaving Uganda. Each novel, particularly the latter two, belongs to the expatriate tradition. Written before Theroux's decision to leave the continent, *Fong and the Indians*, a mixture of realism, humor, and farce, partially succeeds in addressing some of the problems of postcolonial Africa while maintaining a hopeful outlook. The first book written after Theroux and his wife were attacked, *Girls at Play* eschews the realistic analysis of contemporary Africa, focuses almost exclusively on white expatriates, and seethes with bitter irony. In *Jungle Lovers*, which he regarded as "an ambitious novel," Theroux attempts to bring together the analysis of the contemporary Africa of *Fong and the Indians* with the depiction of futile white endeavor in the continent of *Girls at Play*. Although he includes some darkly comic bits, in his final African novel Theroux's assessment of the continent remains staunchly Africanist.

In addition to recording some choice examples of Naipaul's wit, Theroux's essay credits the older writer with having shown him that "Africa was more comedy than tragedy" (93). This statement is intriguing because Naipaul's own works on the continent avoid all but the most sneering humor. With varying degrees of success, Theroux experiments with different types of comedy in *Fong and the Indians*. In *Girls at Play* he appears, like his mentor, to have lost his sense of humor. Theroux's use of irony and jokes in *Jungle Lovers* recalls Evelyn Waugh's *Black Mischief* (1932). Much of the humor in

Waugh's unsettling novel derived from what he saw as the impossibility of black self-rule and the absurdity of white attempts to aid
the endeavor.

In an essay published the same year as *Jungle Lovers*, Theroux explains his own disillusionment with Africa, alluding to Waugh's
book to make his point. During the early and middle 1960s Theroux
felt his actions were contributing to something positive: "My little
helps were consistent with the mood of that decade in Africa, of en-
gaging oneself and being available for the purpose of national development. The image of the Azania-like joke republic committing
farcical outrages upon itself was temporarily antiquated then; it was
a time when the admission to the United Nations of a country like
Gambia (which is a riverbank) or Rwanda (half a dozen volcanoes)
would not raise a smile."[22] After this brief, willful suspension of disbelief, however, white writers began to rely on Africanist thinking
once more.[23] Theroux states that by 1970 Waugh's vision of independent Africa began to ring true for him and for Africans themselves.
Moreover, he claims that in the future Africans rather than Europeans will begin to produce Africanist texts: "Azania reasserted itself
at the close of the 'sixties—not in the European mind, but, much
more significantly, in the African one. The next *Black Mischief*, if
not the next Evelyn Waugh, will be wholly African" (71).[24] With its
black humor and despairing vision of independent Africa, however,
his own *Jungle Lovers* indicated that Theroux was not yet prepared
to surrender the mantle of Africanist discourse to Africans.

Fong and the Indians

Although Theroux pokes fun at several State Department employees
in *Fong and the Indians*, he directs most of his attention to an issue
raised in Churchill's *My African Journey*, from which Theroux takes
his epigraph, and in the work of the Naipauls: the tenuous position
of Asians in contemporary Africa. Rather than focusing on an ethnic
Indian, however, Theroux chooses a Chinese immigrant, Sam Fong,
as his main character. Choosing a Chinese protagonist allows Theroux to depict the greed of Indian merchants as well as the indignities suffered by Asians at the hands of whites and blacks. Fong's
Chinese background also ushers in the absurd cold war subplot that
dominates the second half of the novel. In what appears to be an
updating of *Black Mischief*, this opera buff illustrates the insanity
of white attempts to assist Africans in the postcolonial era. Nevertheless, the novel ends ambiguously because Theroux offers two different assessments of the New Africa. The first is the standard

Africanist condemnation of the continent. The second, however, reverses the expatriate tradition: Fong the outsider adopts African customs he once strived to avoid and a hopeful outlook without experiencing the ruin of his predecessors in the expatriate tradition who succumb to the African environment.

Although he does not think in those specific terms, Fong's initial attitude towards blacks and whites echoes the Naipauls' condemnation of African primitivism and faulty European civilization. Soon after independence Fong loses his foreman's position to an African after randomly pointing him out to a white manager as the best African worker in the carpentry shop. After a month of working for his insolent former underling, Fong quits, making three resolutions: "never trust a white, never trust a black, never be a carpenter."[25] Vowing also never to be an employee, Fong decides to become a grocer. He leases a store and unwittingly signs a contract to buy all his wares from Hassanali Fakhru, an unscrupulous Ismaili. All of Fong's customers are either black or white, which makes him uncomfortable. Fong suffers harassment along with other Asians at the hands of Africans and privately thinks of the country as "Bananaland." Moreover, he lives under the constant threat that the government will take over his store. Like V. S. Naipaul in *In a Free State* and *A Bend in the River*, Fong regards freedom in Africa as at best a double-edged sword: "[Nationalization], in four years, had not happened; but the anxiety, together with the knowledge that the Africans were in power and he himself was 'free' (the image of a man splashing in a wide muddy river occurred to him), prompted another saying which he repeated incessantly to his wife: 'A man who is free to feed himself might choose poison,' and sometimes worded as 'When people are free anything is possible, even tyranny' " (20–21). Just as a series of demeaning incidents has made Fong wary of blacks, his resolution not to trust whites "was formulated not so much from a single instance of white cruelty, the demotion, the loss of his job, as from the resulting wisdom of his long accumulation of disgraceful episodes with whites" (36).

Although he knows that Fakhru consistently cheats him, Fong feels close to him because he is neither black nor white. When Fakhru can find no one else to buy a shipment of canned milk and cannot bribe a group of Africans to sabotage the milk train from Nairobi (which would increase his milk's value), he goes to Fong. He convinces the grocer that it is just a matter of days before the train derails and the owner of the tinned milk is a rich man. As a result of this transaction, Fakhru has Fong in his power because the grocer owes him money. Fong goes into debt at the same time that attacks on whites and Indians occur, forcing him and other merchants to close up their shops.

At this point Theroux diverts attention from the comparatively realistic plot concerning Asians in East Africa to a ludicrous story involving Fong that pits two State Department employees against agents for Communist China. These farcical episodes depict the futility of outsiders' efforts to establish order in postcolonial Africa. They may also have been Theroux's way of revenging himself on the State Department, which three years earlier sent home a Peace Corps official because of Theroux's anti-Vietnam editorial, did not fight to overturn his deportation order from the Malawian government, and routinely assigned people to African postings who possessed a Tarzan Complex and did not know the local language.

Two American Foreign Service officials believe Fong to be a Chinese agent fomenting the recent unrest. They hope to win Fong over to their side by showing him the virtues of capitalism. Concomitantly, agents of the Red Chinese government, a regime about which Fong (who left the country in 1930) is wholly ignorant, accuse him of disgracing his country by fraternizing with Americans and Indians. Because they can't speak Swahili and Fong's English is so poor, Fakhru is enlisted to interpret for the Americans. This arrangement proves to be very profitable for the Ismaili, who pockets the money the Americans intend to sign over to Fong to get him out of the red.

The climax of this subplot is a gala that the American Embassy throws for Fong. The grocer goes believing he will be able to sell his milk there, Fakhru sells invitations to the party that he was asked to distribute free, and a Communist Chinese agent, Chen, spies on the festivities. Meanwhile, the Americans, none of whom speak Swahili, act like complete buffoons, offering alcohol to Moslems, asserting to the motley crowd that all people are the same, and eventually mistaking Chen for Fong. While the real Fong returns to his store, the bumbling American agents whisk Chen away for a goodwill visit of the United States paid for by the American people. Chen is given special permission to take pictures at the Pentagon, observes four Onondagas flown in from Syracuse doing a Native American dance, becomes a media sensation, and stays in the country for months. Eventually, he becomes the subject of a Voice of America radio broadcast entitled "Fong and the Indians: The Odyssey of a Communist."

Theroux returns to the main plot before closing the book, offering two different visions of postcolonial Africa: Fakhru's standard Africanist assessment and Fong's more hopeful outlook. Fakhru remains aloof from Africans, holds Naipaulian beliefs about the true state of contemporary Africa, and regards the opportunities for exploitation as the only positive attribute of the continent. Rather than a haven for freedom, Fakhru's Africa, like Fong's, is characterized by complicated dependencies. Africans will keep threatening people like himself but will only be hurting themselves if they deport the Asians. Fakhru reflects: "There were certainties, few, but important ones. The Asians were lost. The Africans did not matter. The British belched lies. The disorder and inconvenience of Africa killed charity and made profit possible. Fong lived down the street. He owed. He had been used, but he was unworn, unsold. The Americans would stay; Africa was a green worm which, in all the childish innocence that their earnest stupidity was made up of, they valued more than treasure. . . . He smiled. Fong was still his" (195).

Unlike previous works in the expatriate tradition, in *Fong and the Indians* the main character's surrender to the African environment does not result in disaster. Whereas Fakhru remains insulated from the African way of life, Fong eventually adopts African habits, accepts the flux of postcolonial life, and develops an optimistic outlook. The grocer, who earlier dismissed East Africa as "Bananaland," now eats the ubiquitous fruit himself: "The food was an indicator of why nothing had ever happened to millions of East Africans: their country, their lives were dominated by bananas. And now his life as well" (197). According to Theroux, "the immigrant's last compromise is his diet" (197). Thus, Fong's new eating habits indicate that he has accepted Africa as his home, as does his new attitude toward the continent: "Africa did not frighten him: it was all accidental, and accidents could not be foreseen. The disordered slowness he knew existed in Africa was an assurance that the accidents would be small; he would not be harmed" (198). Just at that moment a real accident occurs; the milk train from Nairobi derails, presumably making Fong a rich man and freeing him from his obligation to Fakhru. Fong does not concur with the American sentiment that was bandied about at the party for him but which he never understood, that all men are the same. Nevertheless, his judgment of his fellow men is optimistic: "By nature men were different . . . but however much the differences created upset or alarm, still there could not be deliberate evil, for man was good" (198–99).

To his credit, in *Fong and the Indians* Theroux neither completely overlooks independent Africa's problems nor condemns the continent outright; rather, he provides opposing visions, a Naipaulian assessment and Sam Fong's hopeful one. However, following his own disenchantment with Africa in 1968, Theroux offers only the standard Africanist evaluation in his subsequent African novels.

Girls at Play

Written before Theroux decided to leave Africa, *Fong and the Indians* deviates from the standard Africanist assessment of the continent found in going-native works. In contrast, *Girls at Play* clearly reflects his changed attitude toward the continent; it depicts Africa as a corrupting and murderous environment. Rather than realistically depicting urban life as he does in the first half of the earlier book, Theroux concentrates on a small group of unmarried white expatriate women who teach at a school for girls in the Kenyan bush. Lacking the hope, humor, and playfulness of his first African novel, *Girls at Play* ranks with *In a Free State* and *A Bend in the River* as a prime example of Africanist writing among second-generation postwar authors. The moral, physical, and mental degeneration of the white women is complemented by the violence and depravity of the African characters in the book. Illustrating the Naipauls' assessment of contemporary Africa, the women represent the persistent presence of "outpost civilization" in the continent while the Africans in the book embody the permanence of indigenous primitivism.

Theroux's title is ironic because, although the action takes place at a girl's school and the first scene finds a group of them playing field hockey, "Girls" also refers to the women teachers, two of whom engage in increasingly nasty "games" of one-upmanship that affect everyone at the school and eventually escape their control. Theroux intimates the real meaning of the title in the Author's Note, which also announces the expatriate tradition by introducing the notion of corruption: "White women in Africa appear strikingly girlish—even middle-aged ones; there is also a queer queenly aspect to them (perhaps suggested by the tall servants who wait darkly at their elbows), with the same foolishness and decay that one associates with royalty."[26]

The "games" between the headmistress Miss Poole and recently transferred Heather Monkhouse can be attributed to the combination of expatriate "foolishness and decay" and the remote African setting, which allows the women, like Kayerts and Carlier in "An Outpost of Progress," to carry their dispute to foolish extremes because there is no crowd around to dictate acceptable and unacceptable behavior. The headmistress prides herself on the order she has established at the school, an order modeled on that of her father's farm during the colonial era. Heather, on the other hand, thinks of her new school as a "detention camp": "Everyone down there under those red roofs was an embarrassment or they would not have been sent to the bush, like her. Heather could not disgrace the school; it was already in disgrace, and that had happened in Miss Poole's seven years [as headmistress]" (40). Likewise, Heather readily admits that she and people like her are bad for Africans but asserts, "we're the best they'll ever get. Who wants to live in Africa, what white people? Only cranks, fools, failures" (79–80).

The rivalry between the two women begins at the start of the new term when Miss Poole invites the three other white teachers— Heather; B. J., a peace corps volunteer; and Miss Male, a young Englishwoman who rooms with B. J.—over for dinner. Hoping to discourage her teachers from eating too much of the meat so that she can then provide her cats with the remainder, Miss Poole doesn't sharpen her carving knife. Such behavior on Miss Poole's part irritates Heather and she quickly succeeds in returning the favor by getting on the headmistress's nerves. Although the first meal has been a disaster, Heather invites the same group over to her house and a pattern is established. At subsequent repasts, Miss Poole and Heather engage in a kind of dinner terrorism directed at one another that often redounds on B. J. and Miss Male. They serve bad food, set up broken chairs for their opponent to sit in, and generally try to discomfit and horrify each other.

In response to the nastiness of the older two women, B. J. and Miss Male grow closer. They invent a gecko game reminiscent of the cockroach killing contest between Harris and Wilson in *The Heart of the Matter*. With little else to do in their free time, B. J. and Miss Male draw, letter, and number a grid on their wall in pencil and whenever either of them sees a gecko on a square she yells out its location, such as "G-4." As with the Greene episode it so clearly recalls, the gecko "game" not only illustrates the boredom and vacuousness of expatriate life in Africa, it also parodies something more serious in the novel, that is, the "games" engaged in by Heather and Miss Poole.

In *The Heart of the Matter* and *A Bend in the River* one of the last stages of protagonist's degeneration is his betrayal of his servant, which he ultimately regrets; Scobie kills himself shortly after betraying Ali, and Salim feels ashamed that conditions in Zaire make it impossible for him to help Metty. Miss Poole and Heather exhibit no such strong feelings for the Africans who work for them. Their battle

reaches beyond the meals when the women begin ordering each other's servants to perform often ridiculous tasks. Eventually they set
their servants against one another, which leads to violence and results in both women losing their cooks when the two men run away.
After this episode, the dinner parties come to an end, and each
woman tries unsuccessfully to ignore the other.

In the second half of the novel, events get beyond the women's
control because of the primitivism of Africans (to whom Theroux
assigns only two roles; they are either servants or criminals) and
the physically corrupting effects of Africa. Through her desire to get
to know Africans, the naive Californian B. J. unleashes the corruption of Africa, precipitating the demise of herself, Heather, and the
school. Like Gide in Theroux's epigraph from *Travels in the Congo*,
B. J. has been disappointed with Africa, expecting more mystery and
strangeness. Evincing a nascent consciousness of Africanist discourse, B. J. realizes that the Africa she has sought exists only in
books and movies, and she resolves to go back home to San Diego:
"It was, after all, the best place to go: Hollywood was a shortish
drive up the freeway and that is where most of Africa was" (111).

Before she leaves, however, in true Peace Corps fashion she is determined to get to know some Africans. She convinces Wangi, a vet-
eran of the Mau Mau uprising, to show her his village and introduce
her to his family. Along the way B. J. becomes distressed when
Wangi makes what appears to be a rather violent pass at her, but she
thinks nothing more of it when he obeys her command to let go of
her. Still set on getting to know Africans, B. J. later talks a reluctant
Heather into joining her, Wangi, and Wangi's cousin Wilbur, who is
the district education officer, on a kind of double date. At a bar,
Wilbur recalls the scandal that resulted in Heather's transfer and
threatens to blackmail her. Meanwhile, B. J. impulsively announces
her intention to return to the United States, which visibly upsets
Wangi. Wangi presumably rapes B. J. who is heard crying in her
room the next day and is later found drowned in a stream, an apparent suicide. To bribe Heather into silence, Wilbur has Miss Poole
manhandled and deported for negligence in B. J.'s death, thereby el-
evating Heather to headmistress.

While the rivalry between the two white women in the first half of
the novel is cruel, it nevertheless adheres to certain rules. However,
in the second half of the novel, African primitivism turns the
"games" chaotic and deadly. Heather's response to Miss Poole's for-
cible removal from the school indicates the way things have gotten
out of control since the days of the "games": "It was all fair until

this, and I didn't do it" (199). To put a stop to the madness, Heather has decided to turn in Wilbur and clear Miss Poole. However, unbeknownst to Heather, the contest between herself and Miss Poole has not ended. At the school Miss Poole has sheltered an albino African girl, Rose, whom she uses to spy on the other teachers. During the "games," Miss Poole made it clear to Rose that Heather was not only her enemy but Rose's as well. At the darkly ironic end of the novel, as Heather sleeps in what she believes to be a completely deserted school, Rose stabs her to death with the dull carving knife from the first dinner party.

Even before the primitivism and corruption of Africans bring about the death of two white women and the school itself, the physically corrupting influence of Africa takes its toll on Heather and Miss Poole. Soon after the suspension of the "games," the two older teachers' healths begin to suffer. Miss Poole often becomes ill and Heather has to take over some of her duties. Meanwhile, B. J. notices Heather's hair changing color and thinks she is going white with madness. Near the end of the term, Miss Poole accuses Heather of wanting her job. Heather denies the charge but afterward recognizes how dangerous the school in the bush has become for her: "if she took no more precautions and let herself be guided by Africa's bestial nudges, it could easily come about: she, Heather, would be the mad Headmistress rotting away in the bush girls' school" (169–70). At the end of the novel Heather has indeed physically degenerated. She not only has Miss Poole's job but she has come to resemble her. In many previous going-native works, sexual licentiousness is one indication of an outsider's decay. In contrast, Theroux stresses physical rather than moral corruption. The bush environment has deprived Heather of her one true joy in life, her sexuality. She confides to Miss Male: "I feel like a hag. As if I've just let go of all my sex. I don't have any now. When I heard B. J. was dead I got scared; then they roughed up Miss Poole. My sex all leaked out. I don't have any instincts left any more. I'm an old woman" (204).

Unlike *Fong and the Indians*, which offers two opposing assessments of contemporary Africa, *Girls at Play* provides only the bleak and disturbing thoughts of Miss Male shortly before her own departure and Heather's death. Theroux rather unsubtly positions Miss Male's lone vision of Africa near the end of the novel so that it assumes the status of the moral of the story: "There were many culprits in Africa; and there could be no justice because B. J. had been among strangers and had no business there. There were risks in coming to Africa; Miss Male had taken them; she knew she could expect nothing better than the dead girl in the morgue, the terrorized old lady [Miss Poole], the chain-smoker in her parlor [Heather]. Exiles, they had elected to live alone as girls, unmarried among bananas. It was cruel to think, but they had asked for it" (205). This profoundly Africanist passage deserves careful scrutiny. Theroux implies that white women who go to Africa should expect to be raped and murdered by Africans. More generally, in a much starker manner than in *Fong and the Indians* he declares that the efforts of outsiders in Africa are doomed to failure. Given the sharp contrast between his first African novel and *Girls at Play*, the attack on his wife and himself appears to have played a pivotal role in Theroux's attitude toward the continent. This is confirmed by the fact that Miss Male's thoughts on B. J. match Theroux's after he had suffered violence at the hands of Africans in 1968: "I remember thinking: *I have no business to be here*."[27]

Two related symbols reinforce the themes of African primitivism and the futility of white efforts. The first is the image of the playing field, a patch of ordered space surrounded by bush. At the start of the novel, a group of schoolgirls are playing field hockey while a mysterious white figure, presumably Rose, watches them from the bush. This area of cleared ground represents an African cage or prison, an island of order hemmed in by primeval chaos. The image applies equally to the school itself, which the African bush also circumscribes. Symmetrically, in the final scene of the novel, Rose stands alone in the middle of the playing field. Still in possession of the set of keys provided by Miss Poole to facilitate her eavesdropping and fresh from stabbing Heather, Rose represents both the jailer and executioner of the African prison, the playing field and the school itself.

The second symbol, a ruined mosque, represents a failed attempt on the part of outsiders to conquer the chaos of Africa. On the first page, Theroux states, "A discernable order in a place where there are no people (the dry mosque in the dunes) is a cause for alarm; it means failure; the decaying deserted order is a grave marker" (2). At the end of the novel, this is precisely what the school has become, a tombstone for an effort to impose order. Furthermore, the image of the ruined mosque has a historical dimension as well: it represents the unsuccessful attempt by Arabs to establish something with permanence in Africa before the age of European colonialism. Likewise, the now-disbanded farm where Miss Poole grew up, which she regards as a symbol of order, stands for the failed colonial effort to impose an enduring structure on the continent. Thus, the closing of the school in the bush during the postcolonial era represents another, perhaps the final, failure of outside order in Africa.

Jungle Lovers

Theroux's third African novel, *Jungle Lovers*, features some of the realism and humor of *Fong and the Indians* but maintains the standard Africanist evaluation of the continent found in *Girls at Play*. In contrast to his first two African novels, which take place in a fictitious country and a remote bush location respectively, Theroux sets his third African novel in Malawi, which allows him to draw liberally on his own experiences in that country and include many realistic details. The novel divides its attention between representatives of the West's two most important exports: insurance man Calvin Mullet (capitalism) and the revolutionary Marais (Marxism). In Africa, both men lose faith in their ideologies and go native. As with Theroux's two earlier African novels, the title "Jungle Lovers" has more than one meaning. At one point in the book the phrase is used to describe Calvin and his African wife, Mira, but it also refers to expatriates like Calvin and Marais who are attracted to the tropics. These outsiders come to help Africans but become disillusioned because of their flawed civilization, their own insignificance, and the insolubility of Africa's problems. In addition, physical and moral corruption characterize Theroux's Malawi, while his Africans consciously and unconsciously imitate the behavior of whites. Corresponding to these Naipaulian perceptions, the dominant image of *Jungle Lovers* is the prison, recalling the playing field in *Girls at Play*.

Although the action of the novel occurs in 1966, Theroux alludes to political events that transpired in the Central African nation through 1970. The author makes numerous references to Malawi's President for Life, Hastings K. Banda, whom he names Hastings K. Osbong. Just as Theroux regards Malawi as "a political accident, an attempt at order foiled by lusty jungle," he describes its president and his bullying supporters, the Young Pioneers, as "a clownish Papa Doc defended by a *Tonton Macoute* of giggling Youth Wingers who, during the day or when it wasn't raining, put up road blocks and searched for spying Chinese."[28] In addition, Theroux sets a substantial part of the action involving Marais in Lilongwe, a city in the central part of needlelike Malawi. Only a village at the time of independence in 1964, Lilongwe was designated as the site for the new capital, replacing Zomba in the South, in an attempt to increase the infrastructure in the middle of the nation and promote greater unity between North and South. Later the first African leader to be received with full state honors in Johannesburg, in 1966 Banda denied rumors that the change in capitals was being financed by the South Africans. Using Malawi as the location for his third African novel enables Theroux to illustrate specific challenges facing African nations, such as effective leadership and political stability, as well as revenge himself on the regime that deported him.

Absent from *Girls at Play*, humor reminiscent of Waugh occasionally appears in *Jungle Lovers*. Theroux portrays as ludicrous the whole notion of selling insurance to Africans, in the process parodying the vice president of the Hartford Accident and Indemnity Company, Wallace Stevens, who often refers to exotic locations in his poetry. Not only does a fictitious excerpt from *Time* magazine in *Jungle Lovers* use the phrase "black mischief" to describe the political unrest threatening Malawi, but other instances of humor in the book recall Waugh's sharp wit and bitter mockery. According to Theroux, for the African, whose offspring function as a kind of insurance, "the child was the mortician of the man" (232). In another wry twisting of a famous phrase, this one meant to deride the education of Africans, Calvin's black coworker tells him in despair: "We are hopeless. Hobbies—have you read Thomas Hobbies? He was right, life in Africa is nasty, British and short" (265).

In a 1984 introduction to the novel, Theroux ties the political dimension of postcolonial Africanist discourse to his own psyche, "I suppose the insurance man and the revolutionary were the two opposing sides of my personality."[29] Young North Americans drawn by the desire to assist Africans, Calvin and Marais select different methods for doing so. The former regards his decision to sell Homemakers' Mutual insurance to Africans as a "mission" because he "was going there to help" (45), believing that insurance will enable the people to save for the future and protect them in case of disaster. The latter, too, "had come a long way by a painful route to set these people free" (16). His goal is to train, lead, and raise the consciousness of a band of African soldiers who will ignite the spark of popular unrest throughout the region. However, each crusader encounters resistance to his plans. Calvin discovers that Africans have little interest in insurance, are particularly baffled by the concept of fire damage coverage, and neglect to pay their premiums if they do sign up. Likewise, while Marais succeeds in quickly overrunning the north of Malawi, he has trouble restraining his men from wanton violence and destruction, cannot get them to treat him as an equal, and fails to win the local population's support for his

uprising. The prospect of personal failure combined with the corruption of the African environment causes the two outsiders to go
native when they abandon their belief in the Western creeds of capitalism and Marxism. Calvin and Marais realize that their "missions" are false as well as neocolonial, yet, like Theroux, they
cannot shed their Africanist perceptions of the continent.

Lack of work promotes Calvin's thirst for beer and the prospects of
easy sex result in both a divorce from his first wife and his permanent residence at a brothel in Blantyre. A retired British soldier who
also lives at the cathouse, Major Beaglehole, feels affection for
Calvin but worries about "the makings of dementia" in Calvin's
preference for the ugliest prostitutes, which like his mission to sell
insurance derives from his desire to help the less fortunate. Calvin
finds another way to express his empathy for Africans when, returning to his office drunk late one night, he begins writing a book called
The Uninsured. Narrated by a poor African who laments his lot in
life, the book blames the West for Africa's woes and looks forward to
a popular uprising that will end the oppression. Pity, lust, and loneliness cause Calvin to marry Mira Ogilvie, a young African girl
whom he meets along with her brother Nirenda while trying to sell
insurance in the North of the country. After agreeing to take out a
policy, the Ogilvies kidnap Calvin, extorting presents from him for a
few days. Rather than being bitter about the experience, Calvin feels
shame for fleeing from them, paying Nirenda's premiums himself
upon returning to Blantyre. Depressed by the emptiness of his days
there, Calvin returns to the North to propose to Mira only to find that
she has been raped and Nirenda killed by Marais's men. He brings
the girl back to Blantyre where she quickly spends most of the insurance money, becomes Mrs. Mullet, and lives with her husband at
the bordello.

The death of Mira's brother causes Calvin to lose his faith in not
only insurance but the whole Western way of life. Rejecting the mission that brought him to Africa, he now regards insurance as an evil:
"—it was cruel to make them think that they could be saved by insurance. The Africans sat; they were clumsy and perishable; they
had a very old but very narrow culture. . . . Nothing changed, not
even a death in the family altered them, insurance never could.
Some giant would have to snatch up the country like a clogged
ketchup bottle and smack it violently on the bottom for it to change;
but that would never happen either. And besides, the bottle might
turn out to be empty" (161).[30] His assessment of the continent contains the basic gestures of Africanist discourse, that is, evolutionary

language, binary oppositions, and blankness. Now, however, Calvin clearly believes that outsiders cannot help Africans; he sees insurance as one of many unsuccessful Western attempts to aid Africa, equating these outside efforts with corruption: "He had spent more than a year trying to sell insurance. It was, like any stranger's, a charitable but deluded eagerness to help, like crop spraying or reporting on literacy or asking solemnly, 'What's going to happen to those children?' Worse than simply pointless, it was in a word, corruption. Industry polluted, crop spraying made people hungry, tin roofs were hotter than thatch. And literacy simply frustrated and crazed" (163). To escape this Western "corruption," Calvin adopts what he considers to be African habits. He stops going to the office, sleeps with his African wife, refuses to wash, and drinks all day long. Later, after his agency has been nationalized and he has become a civil servant, Calvin spends his days drinking and reading *Boom* comics with Mwase, whom he is supposed to be training. By becoming, as he sees it, "practically an African," Calvin ironically also becomes the outsider who has succumbed to the decay of Africa, the typical Westerner gone native.

As with Calvin, when Marais's mission becomes bogged down, he becomes depressed and susceptible to the effects of the African environment. One by one he betrays his ideals, losing the trust of and trust in his men, becoming introspective and self-pitying, and finally abandoning the revolution and going native. Marais implements extreme forms of punishment for his disobedient soldiers, breeding fear and resentment among his troops and sacrificing his goal of an egalitarian army. After his men have taken Lilongwe, Marais lies to his men and realizes he no longer trusts them. As the revolt stagnates, Marais feels more and more isolated, less and less in control, hating his men as they hate him.

Marais's French Canadian origins are significant because, along with his decision to come to Africa to be where the action is, they link him with Rimbaud, whom Miller regards as a central Africanist figure.[31] Theroux devotes his two epigraphs to the French poet. The first from *Les Illuminations* illustrates Rimbaud's fascination with primitivism before he went to Africa; the second from W. H. Auden's "Rimbaud" concerns Rimbaud the African adventurer and introduces the Conradian theme of lying. Like Calvin, Marais writes a book that corresponds with his mission. Entitled *Principles of Revolt*, it is meant to be a practical handbook on popular revolution written in a simple, factual style. Earlier Marais rejected the romantic, lyrical writing of his youth because it smacked of poetry and corruption: "It was not a poem, but it was trying to be. The aim was all wrong. Poetry was a clever reply, an illness of the ear, a lying substitute for a coarse truth. . . . The little pimpled man wrote of love, the coward of battle. But not even a soldier's image could represent a broken man crying and pleading for his life, the shock of the bullet, the stink of a jungle camp. It was no wonder Rimbaud chucked his poems to come gunrunning in Somalia. Only the unloveliest of textbooks could describe how to win a war" (175–76). As he becomes alienated from his men and disenchanted with the revolution, however, Marais turns his political tract into a diary, growing increasingly self-absorbed and romantic.

At this point Marais abandons the mission that brought him to Malawi, thereby going completely native. He regards the attempt to start a popular revolution as a "mistake." Instead of liberating the country, Marais believes his meddling has done much more harm than good:

The town, like the exploitation was imaginary. This is just jungle, with a few buildings and some voices, all dispensable to Osbong. The image of order was mine. What I didn't see before was that the order is tribal, chiefs and headmen, ancestor worship and bride prices. And no one is angry about that. Politics never got to this level, I don't think there was any exploitation here. No one mentions Osbong: he was my demon. It's still a tribal village, and all we've done is to uproot it and scatter it temporarily. When we leave, as we must, it will go back to being a village, slightly scarred with the memory of deaths. It was always cows and children. (249)

Like Calvin, Marais now believes that outsiders cannot help Africans; in effect he accuses himself of Africanist thinking, of imposing his fantasy on the continent. At the same time, however, this passage recalls Nazruddin's assessment of the land outside of Kisangani in *A Bend in the River*; both assert the blankness of Africa. Just as abandoning his Western ideals is a sign that Calvin has gone native, Marais begins to take on the characteristics of the typical outsider maddened by the tropics. He recalls the story of an old Portuguese, "who, marooned by a failed love affair [which the revolution has become for Marais], went about naked in a pair of rugged sandals. He brandished an ancient shotgun at strangers. He had lost the gift of speech; he was dirty, and his hair was wild" (268). Increasingly, Marais comes to resemble this man, hiding from other people, feeling naked and hunted, and no longer able to write anything in his notebooks.

By the end of the novel Calvin and Marais are two of a kind, outsiders who have lost faith in their missions. Like Marais, Calvin has started a political movement that he no longer believes in and does not have the power to stop. *The Uninsured* has been stolen from his office, printed up as a revolutionary pamphlet, distributed all over Blantyre, and used to fan unrest among the people. Early in the book when the two men meet briefly, Calvin tries to sell insurance to an incredulous Marais. When they meet again near the end of *Jungle Lovers*, Marais comes to take out a policy. At first Calvin refuses, but he sees that Marais has changed greatly. Together they diagnose their common ailment, after which Calvin states that he does not think Malawi is a country and Marais asks what it is: " 'It's a little parish, sort of,' said Calvin. He thought a moment. 'If you got the faith it's okay. If not, not.' 'The only thing worse than having it,' said Marais, with fatigue, 'is losing it' " (292). After paying Calvin one thousand dollars for an insurance policy with Calvin's unborn child named as the beneficiary, Marais returns to Lilongwe apparently to try to stop the revolution. He manages to kill the new leader, who happens to be the waiter at the brothel where Calvin lives, before dying in a fire in his old hotel room. That Calvin winds up receiving the insurance money, thus representing Marais's next of kin, further underscores the similarity between the two outsiders. But while Marais, like Rimbaud, dies young as a result of his adventures in Africa, Calvin returns to the United States with Mira and his black baby boy.

Three Africanist elements characterize the Malawian environment causing both men to give up their Western ideals and go native: corruption, imprisonment, and imitation. Theroux conveys the corruption of Malawi by dwelling on bodily functions (much of the description of Calvin's day to day life concerns his bowel movements and micturition), emphasizing the availability of illicit sex (according to Theroux, if it were located anywhere else, the brothel where Calvin lives would be closed down, but in Malawi it is frequented by expatriates and high government officials), and detailing various instances of death and violence. Before returning to the North to find that Nirenda Ogilvie has been beheaded and Mira sexually abused by Marais's men—who later terrorize Lilongwe by looting stores, burning homes, and killing people—Calvin encounters the first corpse he has ever seen on the street in Blantyre. It is actually the body of a cabinet minister murdered in the brothel by the revolutionary waiter. In addition, late in the novel Calvin overhears a scuffle in the barroom of the whorehouse, which ends with a fatal stabbing by the same waiter.

Not merely corrupt, Theroux's Malawi is a prison for both expatriates and Africans. Early in the novel Nirenda and Mira Ogilvie kidnap Calvin who escapes only to be detained briefly by Marais. Major Beaglehole tells Calvin about being held against his will by a tribe during colonial times and also relates the story of the governor of a prison island in what was then Lake Nyasa who was hacked to death by his prisoners. Late in the novel, when Africans in Blantyre have begun mistreating whites, Calvin dreams of being the governor of the prison island. Marais also finds himself imprisoned in Malawi. When he imprisons one of his soldiers, the man refers to Marais as General Bang-Bang, the African nickname for the governor of the prison island. Lilongwe becomes a prison for Marais even before he realizes that his own men have put him under arrest. Moreover, Calvin's now abandoned book, *The Uninsured*, is all about imprisonment. Written by "A. Jigololo," which means prisoner, the manuscript actually begins to take possession of Calvin and imprison him while he is writing it. Later, when the book is printed and distributed under the title UNITE, BROTHERS, the outsider's sense of confinement expressed within it is transferred to Africans. Unbeknownst to Calvin, his coworker Mwase constantly reads the book, thereby coming to regard himself as a prisoner in Osbong's jail.

The final Africanist characteristic of Theroux's Malawi is African mimicry of Western practices. Instead of rejecting Western ways of living, Africans not only long for them and try to duplicate them but they carry on the projects that the outsiders, Calvin and Marais, have abandoned. When Calvin meets Nirenda and Mira at the start of the novel, the first of many instances of African imitation occurs. After Ogilvie has signed his name to an insurance policy, he hesitates because he cannot fill out his address, claiming that he cannot write. Puzzled, Calvin asks about the autograph on the page. At this point Mira steps in to explain: "That not name. . . . It look like name. But . . . that not name. That *signature*" (10). Mira becomes one of the major imitators in the novel. Following her brother's death, she spends most of the insurance money on Western consumer goods and knickknacks. Likewise, she baffles Calvin by emulating the poses of pinup pictures she hangs all over their room even though he finds her much more erotic than any of the white women in the pictures.

African imitation of the West likewise pervades the Miss Malawi beauty contest sponsored by a Rhodesian skin lightening company, which Mira enters. The whole proceeding amazes Calvin: "One perception held him. It dawned on him that he was watching a minstrel show in reverse, a negative rather than a photograph. Instead of Al Jolson in blackface—popping his eyes and crooning 'Mandy, is there a mister handy?'—black people wearing skin lightener were cavorting around dressed as *bwanas*, *memsahibs* and white showgirls"

(186). At first he believes that the contest is a conscious lampooning of the mockery of blacks by whites; however, as the show goes on, it comes to resemble, right down to the very songs that are sung, a blackface performance put on in 1951 by the Baptist Men's Club in Calvin's hometown. By the end of the pageant, Calvin to his horror realizes that the Africans are not mocking whites but instead imitating white behavior designed to demean blacks.

The theme of imitation, apparent in V. S. Naipaul's discussion of African art in "A New King for the Congo," is one that, according to Theroux, his mentor constantly asserted during the time that the two men knew each other in Africa: "He claimed that there were very few African writers who were not in some ways plagiarists; and several were exposed, though not by Naipaul."[32] Through the events surrounding *The Uninsured*, Theroux incorporates an instance of plagiarism as well as other forms of African imitation into *Jungle Lovers*. Itself a white person's imitation of the thoughts of an African, *The Uninsured* is plagiarized wholesale by an African and distributed to the people in Blantyre who start to believe in and act on its sentiments. Calvin stops writing *The Uninsured*, embarrassed by it because he realizes "no honest African could have written it. Only a fearfully unhappy white person could be the author" (164). However, he discovers that Jarvis Moore, the revolutionary waiter at the brothel, bears a striking resemblance to A. Jigololo. Like Calvin's narrator, Moore has a white liberal pose unauthentic for an African; he is "a caricature of A Jigololo, who was himself a caricature of one wasp's unhappiness" (172). Later, after Moore steals *The Uninsured* from Calvin's offices, has copies printed and distributed, and passes it off as his own, he ironically asserts the veracity of the book: "No white man could have written that" (283).

At the end of the novel, Calvin and Marais learn that, like the "games" in *Girls at Play*, which get out of control, African imitation of Western ways of living cannot be stopped. Although Marais has disavowed the revolution and Calvin has turned his back on *The Uninsured*, the projects the two men started continue to thrive without them. Before his death Marais determines that there never was a time when it would have been possible to stop his men from the destruction they had brought to Lilongwe. Likewise, Calvin recognizes that things would be the same if he had never begun his book: "Calvin's only consolation about *The Uninsured* was that if he had not written it, someone else would have; but he was still annoyed by the thought that the someone would have had to be a stranger to the parish, like himself or Marais" (305). The experiences of these two outsiders gone native do not augur well for contemporary Africa. On the one hand, efforts to help on the part of non-Africans prove counterproductive because of the continent's corruption. On the other hand, lacking originality, Africans are doomed to mimic the West and demean themselves in the process. Even more disturbing, despite Theroux's assertion that the next Evelyn Waugh will be from Africa, this passage indicates that Africanists like himself will continue to represent and influence Africans. *The Uninsured* demonstrates Theroux's consciousness of the ability of language to subjugate Africans. There is no indication, however, that he recognizes that his own novels participate in that process.

While neither as narrowly focused nor as consistently bleak as *Girls at Play*, *Jungle Lovers* nevertheless asserts the futility of outside endeavor in Africa and offers the standard Africanist assessment of contemporary Africa. Like Naipaul, Theroux depicts outsiders as powerless, regards colonialism as a failure, and associates Africa with corruption. As with his mentor, at times he demonstrates an awareness of Africanist thinking and the power of discourse to objectify Africans, but he does not make the connection between them and his own writing. Taken as a whole, Theroux's five years in Africa and three novels about the continent chronicle in miniature the West's initial attitude of hope for postcolonial Africa that quickly turned to disillusionment, and ultimately reverted to Africanist thinking.

Martha Gellhorn

The Weather in Africa

Male authors have always dominated writing about Africa and Africans, despite such notable exceptions as Aphra Behn in the 1600s, Mary Kingsley at the end of the nineteenth century, and the triumvirate of colonial settlers whose works have recently enjoyed great popularity and been adapted to television and film: Isak Dinesen, Beryl Markham, and Elspeth Huxley. The reasons for this are primarily extraliterary. Men went to Africa as explorers, adventurers, and colonial administrators, thereby accumulating experiences to be used in works about the continent. Given this male preeminence in outside literature about Africa, Martha Gellhorn's *The Weather in Africa* (1978) breaks some new ground. A relatively early work about Africa by a woman outsider during the postcolonial era,

Gellhorn's collection of three novellas paves the way for books about Africa in the 1980s by white women such as Maria Thomas, Helen Winternitz, Rachal Ingalls, and Joanne Leedom-Ackerman.

With the exception of Theroux's heavy-handed *Girls at Play*, which sacrifices realism to drive home the going-native theme, the literature about Africa by male outsiders before 1980 tends either to ignore women or assign them flat characters and secondary roles. Books such as *Heart of Darkness*, *The Heart of the Matter*, and *A Bend in the River* focus on one man, either paying little attention to family relationships or depicting the protagonist's estrangement from his family as a stage in the going-native process. In contrast, *The Weather in Africa* contains a number of well-developed female characters from different backgrounds and of various ages, and concerns itself with parents, children, and marriage. Just as in *Girls at Play*, most of the white women in *The Weather in Africa* are alone, either unmarried or divorced, which makes their status in Africa additionally perilous. Although Gellhorn's treatment of women is innovative, she remains firmly Africanist.

Gellhorn first visited Africa south of the Sahara in 1962, when she made a three-month trip across the continent from West to East by a combination of air and land transportation. Greatly preferring Kenya and what was then Tanganyika to Cameroun and Chad, Gellhorn returned to the east coast the following year and rented a home in Mombasa. This began what she has called a thirteen-year "love affair with Africa" during which she visited the continent frequently and established two residences there.[33] By the middle 1970s, however, the "affair" was clearly over as this passage from Gellhorn's long chapter on Africa in *Travels with Myself and Another* reveals: "But Africa has changed, politics and the tourist boom spoiled much of what I loved, and perhaps I have only grown wise enough to know when to give up" (234). Like Churchill, Laurence, and Theroux before her, Gellhorn returns to Africanist thinking as if rediscovering a truth she never should have doubted.

After deciding to "give up" on Africa, Gellhorn wrote "On the Mountain," "In the Highlands," and "By the Sea"—the three novellas that compose *The Weather in Africa*. While her assessment of contemporary Africa is not as consistently condemnatory as that of the Naipauls or Theroux's *Girls at Play*, the continent she depicts is corrupt, leading white characters into isolation, debauchery, mental collapse, and death. In keeping with the second-generation portrayal of whites, Gellhorn's characters are insignificant, often described as "misfits." The Naipaulian theme of isolation receives full treatment in *The Weather in Africa* as does Theroux's image of Africa as a prison. Although Gellhorn implies that independence eradicated the colonialist mentality, she undermines this notion by limiting Africans to the role of servants in all cases but one.

Clearly part of the expatriate tradition, the first short novel, "On the Mountain," focuses on the Jenkins family who have run a hotel seven thousand feet up on Mount Kilimanjaro for thirty-five years. Bob and Dorothy have begun to think about turning over the hotel to their daughters, Jane and Mary Ann, who grew up in Africa and have both returned to newly independent Tanzania after spending some years abroad. It appears that the children have come home to take care of their parents; however, as the African environment preys on the daughters, causing them to go native, the parents wind up retaining their roles as providers for and protectors of their children.

Both over thirty, Jane and Mary Ann come back to Africa to escape imbroglios abroad. In twelve years of pursuing a singing career in Europe, Jane has found neither the success she craves nor a satisfying relationship with a man. Similarly, after a few years in America, Mary Ann has broken off an unpromising engagement and returns home. Strained since they were very young, the relationship between the sisters does not improve when they meet again in Africa. Mary Ann resents shouldering the burden of keeping the hotel's books and managing the staff while Jane contents herself with occasionally interacting socially with the guests. The two women also have divergent attitudes towards Africans. More liberal than her sister but still in the position of commanding Africans, Mary Ann knows well the need to please the Africans who come to the hotel because it exists only at their sufferance. Out of Africa for a dozen years, Jane, on the other hand, retains colonialist views about blacks and their ability to govern themselves, sneering at them until Mary Ann and her parents reprimand her for it.

Despite their differences, the two sisters go native when they become involved in sexual relationships in Africa. Jane attempts to show up her family by fawning over the next African who comes to the hotel. Her subsequent affair with this man, a government employee named Paul Nbaigu, robs Jane not only of her haughty demeanor but also of her looks, self-esteem, and, temporarily, her sanity. On the same night that Jane and Paul begin their torturous affair, Mary Ann meets Jim Withers, an English botanist, who has come to study the rain forest nearby. Soon Mary Ann and the unhappily married Withers fall in love. Their affair causes Mary Ann to neglect her duties at the hotel and nearly ends as ruinously for her as the affair with Paul Nbaigu does for her sister. Unsuccessful in love abroad, in Africa the sisters become involved in relationships that are more dangerous than anything they have experienced previously. The sexual attraction between Jane and Paul is based on the blankness common to much Africanist discourse. Unable to think of anything else, Jane finds herself compulsively drawn to Paul's room: "She felt now like a sleeper at the edge of the whirlpool, dreaming her helplessness and the force that pulled her. She had stopped thinking of her parents, Mary Ann or any inquisitive guests; she was not thinking at all; she was moving slowly towards the powerful drowning centre."[34] Jane soon becomes virtually addicted to sex with Paul, turning to alcohol to overcome her "withdrawal symptoms" when she is not with him.

Like Theroux and Naipaul, Gellhorn depicts racial intolerance as a legacy of colonialism with the potential to destroy people in the New Africa through the relationship between Paul and Jane. As racially biased as his lover, Paul hates whites, blaming them for all the failures and indignities he has endured. At the same time, he detests himself for craving Jane and everything she represents. When he tells her that he will not let their affair jeopardize his future, Jane scoffs at the notion of a career in a "stupid little tinpot African country," thus betraying her colonialist mentality (36). Paul's response turns their affair from sexually obsessive to sadomasochistic and mutually destructive, accelerating Jane's (and his own) decay:

He did not desire her less but saw her now as the enemy, like all whites, in her heart despising his country and his people and thus himself and his hopes. To Jane, they were servants, people without faces, meant to take orders. She would obey him, Paul decided, and she would eat dirt and like it, and then finally she would beg forgiveness for insulting his nation. (36)

Paul hits on a means of totally humiliating Jane, thereby vindicating himself and his country, that ultimately destroys her mental balance and completes her decline. Suggesting for the first time that Jane accompany him during the day, Paul has Jane wait in his car while he finds a local girl whom he sodomizes before Jane's eyes. Despite calling him a "filthy pig," Jane allows herself to be sodomized soon afterward. Feeling he has nearly achieved complete revenge on Jane and all whites, Paul demands that she apologize for her calling his a "tinpot African country." Suddenly recognizing Paul's motivation for enslaving her, Jane has a nervous breakdown. While Mary Ann quickly has her sister sent to a clinic in Nairobi, Paul's final act of vengeance backfires, for he loses his job when his superior learns of his assault on the young girl.

Perhaps because it is not with an African, Mary Ann's affair does not involve the debauchery and cruelty of her sister's; nevertheless, her relationship with Withers proves to be nearly as destructive. Ignorant about birth control, Mary Ann becomes pregnant, suffering in silence rather than telling anyone. At first, Mary Ann considers trying to consult local women for a potion that will induce an abortion. Later she decides to have the child, planning to go away to bear it. However, Withers gets a divorce, learns about the pregnancy, and convinces Mary Ann to inform her parents of her condition.

Gellhorn depicts the departure of the sisters from the hotel shortly after their return as the end of an era; however, the colonial situation wherein whites hold positions of authority and Africans work for them does not change. Deprived of her looks but still bankrolled by her parents, Jane goes to England. Likewise, still pregnant and unmarried, Mary Ann leaves her parents to live with Withers, presumably returning to England with him when his grant expires. The white community interprets the return and subsequent departure of the Jenkins sisters as an indication that "You can't count on children for anything anymore" and that they themselves have become "the last of the settlers" (72). Despite Gellhorn's assertions of change, there is a great continuity to "On the Mountain." At the end, Bob and Dorothy once more take complete charge of the hotel. Moreover, the one African character given a role other than that of a servant has lost his position of power.

Like "On the Mountain," "In the Highlands" contains elements of the expatriate tradition, emphasizes the themes of isolation and enslavement, and criticizes the colonial mentality. The second novella focuses its attention on isolated misfits and, like Theroux's *Jungle Lovers*, relies heavily on the image of the prison. As with its predecessor, "In the Highlands" ends shortly after independence, describing this event as the end of an era for whites in Kenya yet depicting Africans as servants and laborers only. This white predominance also vitiates the major difference between the second novella and "On the Mountain": the suggestion that the races may be able to live together harmoniously in the New Africa.

The main character, Ian Paynter, attempts to surrender to the forces of Africa, thereby going native, but a restrictive colonial society does not allow him to do so. Ian comes to Kenya in 1947 after spending five years as a prisoner of war in Germany and returning home to England to find his family dead. A social misfit, he comes to Africa to enjoy the expansive vistas that contrast with the dark walls he endured during his confinement. At first Ian works on a large estate where he feels uncomfortable around the other whites and is treated like an outcast. When Ian reads a notice about a farm for sale that has been nearly ruined through neglect, he goes to see it immediately. Soon after acquiring Fairview, Ian says to himself *"I'm free"* (103). As part of their decline, the protagonists of going-native works from the colonial period, such as Kurtz and Scobie, betray the colonial mission. Similarly, Ian refuses to participate in the social life of the white settler community and rejects the European doctrine that Africans are "lazy and filthy and ungrateful." He implicitly connects colonialism with military detention but stops short of asserting equality between the races: "He had been treated like an inferior; flea-ridden, half starved, dirty, ragged and helpless while his jailers were clean, well-fed and powerful. All men were not equal, of course, but all men had a right to respect. He meant to trust his watu, assure their needs, and explain the purpose of their work" (106). Unlike the other settlers, he pays his African workers well, gives them new houses, and even works side by side with them. In return for his fair treatment, Ian expects hard work from his men. However, by purchasing a farm and trying to restore it, Ian has already become part of the colonial society, adopting Africanist notions about bringing order to the chaos of the continent. To his chagrin, Ian has to put down a mutiny after only six months, dismissing a few malingerers as an example to the others. The experience ends his days of working with his men and makes Ian feel akin to the Germans who used the same method to maintain control. Depressed and alone, Ian confesses his failure with the Africans on the farm: "They've made me see I can't get on with anyone. I'm a misfit wherever I am" (108).

Ian becomes even more firmly entrenched in the colonial society when he marries Grace Davis, another maladjusted person who comes to Kenya to escape England. She painstakingly embarks on a course of visiting, assisting, and flattering Ian in a desperate but eventually successful play to get the naive farmer to marry her. After the wedding, Grace becomes a totally different person, evincing a contempt for Africans that she never displayed before. In time, Grace turns their life together into a new kind of concentration camp for her husband: "After eight months of marriage, Ian knew he had made a fatal mistake and was imprisoned in it. Of his own accord, like a man doomed, he had destroyed his freedom and built his own private Oflag. He thought of himself with despair. He was a misfit and a failure. But Fairview was not a failure. He had a purpose in life, quite apart from the catastrophe of his marriage" (139).

Ian and Grace separately adopt children who become misfits like their new parents. Glossing over an essential stage in Kenya's history, Gellhorn portrays the Mau Mau emergency as a boon to the Paynters because it gives Grace an excuse to be away from the farm. Near the official end of the Mau Mau uprising, Ian takes a keen interest in an illegitimate and sickly infant girl of mixed Asian and African blood who has appeared at the farm. Kept ignorant of Zena, Grace continues to go to Nairobi regularly after the emergency and learns of a baby white girl that is up for adoption. Needing someone on whom to shower her affections as much as Ian does, Grace obtains custody of Joy. For different reasons, the two girls, like the adults who have adopted them, suffer isolation and are on their way to becoming misfits. Raised in loneliness and being of mixed race, Zena does not understand the games of the African children and is ostracized by them. Ian realizes that he has imprisoned Zena, who can only leave the compound he has built for her when Grace and Joy are not around: "With love and the best intentions, he had put his child into a sort of prison. He seemed to have a special talent for prisons" (170). Similarly, in her desire to make Joy totally dependent on her, Grace has isolated her daughter from other children.

Gellhorn's depiction of the inevitable encounter between Joy and Zena symbolically serves as a microcosm of the colonial situation. When she sees all the toys that Zena has, Joy accuses her of stealing them and then absconds with the toys herself. She plays with Zena everyday, but being the white girl and physically stronger, Joy always takes the dominant role: "If Zena did not do what she ordered, quickly, she pinched Zena who cried and obeyed. Joy was specially fond of games in which she was the Queen, meting out punishment to Zena, the villain or slave. Zena did a lot of kneeling and begging for mercy as the Queen commanded, though her head was often cut off anyway" (179).

Like "On the Mountain," "In the Highlands" depicts independence as the end of an era. When Grace finds out about Zena, she and Joy go to England, living off the profits from the farm. Gellhorn suggests not only that their departure—along with that of a number of white settlers at the time of independence—signals the end of the colonialist mentality but also that many of those who stay compose a new breed, like Ian and Zena, whom the farmer brings into his house, thereby formalizing her adoption. Ian has never feared independence, thinking it only just; Zena fits in at school, where she has made both black and white friends; and together Ian and Zena have apparently formed a bond that cuts across racial barriers. Both the relationship between the white man and the mixed-race girl and the harmony that exists at Zena's school appear to offer a non-Africanist picture of the New Africa. Likewise, Ian's thoughts at the close of the novella echo Fong's hopeful outlook on life at the end of Theroux's *Fong and the Indians:* "What's the matter with you, Ian Paynter? Use your greying head. Think of the accidents. Who could ever have foreseen . . . that you'd be here . . . with this particular child as the centre of your life? . . . Bad accidents too like going to the Karula Sports Club for the second and last time in nearly twenty years and meeting Grace. How does it cancel out? . . . You won't know until you're dead, will you? And what's the point in worrying about the future? Let the future take care of itself, since you certainly can't" (199).

Although Gellhorn's assessment of postcolonial Africa in "In the Highlands" seems to contrast with that of its predecessor, her depiction of black-white relations once again belies her assertion that independence represents the end of an era. Ian continues to run his farm, supervising African laborers and making enough money to support himself and the expensive tastes of his estranged wife. Throughout "In the Highlands," Africans appear only as servants and farmhands, and Gellhorn gives no indication that this will change with the end of colonial rule. Independence has eliminated the presence of whites with colonialist mentalities like Grace, but more liberal expatriates such as Ian remain to impose order on the African landscape and export the continent's raw materials. Reminiscent of first-generation writers, Gellhorn suppresses the political realities of Africa during the 1950s. Treating the Mau Mau rebellion in any depth would have required her to create more rounded African characters. She not only avoids but misrepresents the uprising, mentioning it only briefly and depicting it as a godsend for the Paynters. Even Ian's adoption of Zena is problematic. Rather than taking in and showering his affection on a black child, Ian becomes infatuated with the exotic Zena whose mixed blood differentiates her from the Africans who work on the farm.

"By the Sea," the last short novel in Gellhorn's collection, provides a harshly Africanist assessment of the continent, boiling down the

expatriate tradition to its simplest form. Because of Africa's corruption, the product of its inherent primitivism and the failed civilization of the Western-run tourist industry Gellhorn decries in
Travels with Myself and Another, death results from the two instances when the black and white worlds intersect.

"By the Sea" tells the story of yet another lonely white person
who comes to Africa to escape her troubles. Diana Jamieson is a
middle-aged divorced American whose life was shattered by the
death of her only son at the age of eight from leukemia. However, in
contrast to settlers like the Jenkins and the Paynters who make Africa
their home, Mrs. Jamieson has just come to a hotel on the Kenyan
coast for two and a half weeks as a tourist. Although she considers
herself daring, almost an explorer, for coming to such an exotic
place, she soon discovers that she is merely part of the herd: "I was
quite wrong to believe that flying off to Africa was extraordinary and
a dashing thing to do. Every nationality is here, treating Africa as
just another tourist resort, French people, Germans, Italians, some
cruise ship Americans, all kinds of British Commonwealth, and
three pairs of giggly Japanese" (204). For the first two weeks of her
vacation, Mrs. Jamieson talks to no one and does not leave the hotel.
Looking for something exciting to do, she decides to take a day trip
to a local sightseeing attraction, venturing into the African landscape for the first time. As Mrs. Jamieson drives her rented car down
the road at fifty miles an hour, fantasizing that she is a Livingstone or
Stanley, a small African boy darts out into the street, colliding with
the white woman's car and breaking his neck instantly.

Back in Mrs. Jamieson's hotel room, the second fatal encounter
between Africa and the West takes place. After finding her in the
ditch, the police take the incoherent Mrs. Jamieson back to her room,
where, medicated for a slight head injury, she oscillates between
consciousness and unconsciousness. During her lucid moments,
Mrs. Jamieson tries to reconstruct the important events of her life,
continually returning to the death of her son; at other times she has
nightmares about the accident. While Gellhorn may be suggesting
that the callousness of the tourist industry is responsible for the
death of the black boy, she leaves no doubt that Mrs. Jamieson's second deadly confrontation with an African derives from the continent's primitivism. Juma, the waiter assigned to bring food and
drinks to Mrs. Jamieson's room, roughly wakes her from her sleep
and tries to extort money from her in the name of the dead boy's father, but he cannot recall exactly what his friend who put him up to
this told him to say. Pinned down by Juma, addled by drugs and

sleep, Mrs. Jamieson fuses the accusation that she killed the African boy with the accusation that she killed her own son. She breaks free, runs frantically out on the balcony, and plunges to her death.

Through Mrs. Jamieson's white physician, Dr. Burke, and Miss Grant, a white manager of the hotel, Gellhorn provides the final, harshly Africanist assessment of the continent in *The Weather in Africa*, which recalls not only her disdain for the tourism in contemporary Africa and her decision to "give up" on the continent but also Miss Male's statement at the end of *Girls at Play* about the fate of white women in postcolonial Africa. When Miss Grant comments that it is fortunate that none of the guests were up early to see the body, Dr. Burke sarcastically replies, "Bad for tourism. . . . Mustn't upset the tourists. Our great national industry" (236). A moment later the novella ends with Miss Grant's reflection on Mrs. Jamieson, "Poor woman. She should never have come to Africa" (236).

William Boyd

A Good Man in Africa

William Boyd's *A Good Man in Africa* (1981) is a fitting culmination to the novels in the expatriate tradition by second-generation postwar writers. As in the fictions by V. S. Naipaul, Paul Theroux, and Martha Gellhorn, the non-Africans in Boyd's book are insignificant and unheroic. However, rather than merely emphasizing the helplessness of these outsiders as one more symptom of the tragedy of contemporary Africa, Boyd depicts whites in Africa as bumbling incompetents and milks the conventions of the expatriate tradition for all the humor they are worth. Although firmly Africanist, Boyd's comic rendition of the tradition entails a recognition that its basic elements are not grounded in fact but rather literary conventions ripe for parody.

While its setting and comic intent link *A Good Man in Africa* with Waugh's *Black Mischief*, Boyd's humor comes at the expense of white characters rather than Africans. Most of it is generated by the misfortunes of the protagonist, Morgan Leafy, an Englishman who has spent three years as the first secretary of the British Commission in Nkongsamba, a city in Kinjanja, West Africa, a former English colony celebrating its tenth year of independence. Overweight, balding, alcoholic and libidinous, Morgan is one of Theroux's expatriate Tarzans: a white man starting to wilt, sweating profusely, with nothing particularly objectionable about him, who has let the body take over.[35]

The insignificance and incompetence of the whole British community—from Arthur Fanshawe, the deputy high commissioner, on down—serve as a comic version of the powerless outsiders, such as Salim, Calvin, and Marais, found in other second-generation works. Given their mediocrity, it comes as no surprise that when the British officials in Nkongsamba receive an order to implement a delicate diplomatic operation, the undertaking results in embarrassment for the United Kingdom and precipitates a political debacle for Kinjanja.

Like Naipaul's Zaire and Theroux's Malawi, Boyd's Kinjanja is both physically and politically corrupt. Using Morgan as his mouthpiece, early in the novel Boyd launches into a three-page diatribe on the ugliness, poverty, and disease of Africa. Nkongsamba resembles both "a giant pool of crapulous vomit on somebody's expansive unmown lawn" and "some immense yeast culture, left in a damp cupboard by an absent-minded lab technician, festering uncontrolled, running rampant in the ideal growing conditions."[36] In an echo of Kurtz's "Exterminate all the brutes," a depressed Morgan dreams of dropping a nuclear bomb on the town but reflects that the effort would probably be futile, like his recent attempt to kill a cockroach in his home. Using an insect as an image for Africa makes perfect Africanist sense: like the continent, the insect epitomizes corruption and menaces white men who have failed in their efforts to wipe out or control it.

Outside writers often emphasize death as a means of illustrating the corruption of Africa. Just as Calvin in Theroux's *Jungle Lovers* sees his first corpse on the streets of Blantyre, so Morgan comes face to face with a dead body for the first time when the Fanshawes's servant, Innocence, is struck dead by lightning. The Kinjanjans attribute the death of Innocence to the god Shango, who must be appeased by a large funeral service before the corpse can be buried, but no one will pay for it so she quickly decomposes. Boyd also thematizes the Africanist projection of decay onto Africa when Morgan contracts gonorrhea from his African mistress. In a scene recalling Scobie's consultation of the bank manager's medical encyclopedia to learn the symptoms of angina in *The Heart of the Matter*, the news sends Morgan to a bookstore where he pores over a book called *Sexually Transmitted Diseases* and lets his imagination run wild with infections that might be corrupting his body.

As in many earlier Africanist works during the postcolonial era, political corruption and violence go hand in hand with the physical decay in Boyd's Africa. Kinjanjan politicians regularly engage in "weekend shopping sprees in Paris and London, village-sized parties with guests shuttled in by helicopter, [and the] forced requisition of Kinjanjan Airlines planes for private use" (180). This kind of graft has stirred the ire of the people and more importantly the military, resulting in political turmoil and violence. Students take over the university by force, the police set up roadblocks and shoot anything that moves, and the army mobilizes for a coup d'etat.

In addition to depicting a thoroughly corrupt environment, Boyd creates a protagonist ripe for succumbing to its influence. In *A Good Man in Africa* he brilliantly exploits the conventions of the expatriate tradition for his comic ends. The epigraph from "A Voyage," by W. H. Auden, announces the tradition and lists three possible outcomes for outsiders who journey to exotic locations: "Somewhere a strange and shrewd tomorrow goes to bed, / Planning a test for men from Europe; no one guesses / Who will be most ashamed, who richer, and who dead" (8). In contrast to such tragic going-native works as *Heart of Darkness, The Heart of the Matter, A Burnt-Out Case,* and *Girls at Play,* where the punishment for succumbing to the corruption of Africa is death, in *A Good Man in Africa* Morgan Leafy pays for his primarily sexual indiscretions by enduring one humiliation after another. One of the funniest incidents occurs when he experiences a pain in his groin, cannot find a fresh pair of underpants, and to his extreme embarrassment finds himself with his trousers down at the university hospital trying to explain to Dr. Murray that his underwear does not normally look so shabby: " 'I think I should say these are not my normal . . . ' he began in a rush. 'My steward refused to wash . . . So I had to . . . I do have some perfectly good ones . . . ' This was *appalling,* he screamed to himself. . . . It was useless, he let his underpants fall and looked anguishedly at the ceiling. The average human body, such as the one he possessed, couldn't tolerate, he felt sure, the extremes of shame and humiliation that his had been subjected to recently" (149–50). An even more humbling episode transpires when Fanshawe's daughter asks Morgan to take her to a dance at the club and then makes it clear that tonight is the night. On his way to take Priscilla back to his place, Morgan encounters Murray in the men's room. He informs Leafy that he does indeed have gonorrhea. The scene that ensues at Morgan's apartment proves humiliating for both Priscilla, who keeps taking her clothes off, and Morgan, who, zombielike over the news he has just received, attempts to put them back on her. When she realizes that he is not joking, Priscilla hotly demands that Morgan drive her home, believing him to be impotent, and within a matter of months she is engaged to Morgan's subordinate, Dalmire.

Boyd's corrupt Africa not only allows Morgan's sexual desire to go unchecked, it also causes him to engage in unsavory acts, commit crimes, decay physically, and participate in non-Western customs. Ordered to dispose of Innocence's corpse any way he can before the Christmas party at the Commission, Morgan turns body snatcher, sneaking the decaying body into the trunk of his car in the middle of the night. However, when the servants refuse to work the next day, Morgan receives a frantic command to put Innocence back. That night he becomes an arsonist, setting an abandoned car ablaze to create a diversion so that he can restore the body to its original location. In the process, Morgan scorches his face, loses an eyebrow, and singes his hair. After all he and Innocence have been through, Morgan elects to pay for the funeral to appease Shango. This act alone does not prove that Morgan has adopted African beliefs, but his misfortunes in the continent have made him fatalistic, which to Boyd links him with the Africans. Morgan sees himself as someone at the mercy of forces he can neither control nor understand, and this, according to Boyd, is what Shango represents for the Kinjanjans.

By exploiting its conventions for humorous ends, *A Good Man in Africa* serves as a fitting culmination to the second-generation works in the expatriate tradition. Helpless and often foolish, characters like Naipaul's Salim, Theroux's Calvin, and Gellhorn's Jenkins sisters are already parodies of such intellectually and spiritually monumental figures as Kurtz, Scobie, and Querry. Boyd recognizes the comic possibilities of the insignificant outsider in Africa and sees how ripe the clichés of the expatriate tradition are for generating humor. Parodying a literary tradition demands a level of metaconsciousness that identifies conventions and stereotypes for what they are and then pushes them a step or more too far. Boyd's Kinjanja is anything but realistic, yet, in contrast to the fictional Africas of other authors in the expatriate tradition, it does not claim to be authentic. While he remains firmly within the expatriate tradition, exploiting Africanist conventions remorselessly, Boyd targets the shortcomings of expatriates rather than Africans and refuses to write a tragic novel about contemporary Africa. Building on Boyd's metaconsciousness, third-generation postwar writers openly acknowledge and actively subvert the conventions of the established ways of writing about Africa in attempts to avoid automatically perpetuating the subjugating effects of Africanist discourse.

Walter Abish

Alphabetical Africa

Africa, explored and excavated and neo-capitalized as it now is, remains—
for Mr. Abish as for Moravia, as it was for Leakey and Livingstone, for Gide
and Hemingway, for Rider Haggard and Edgar Rice Burroughs, for Burton
and Speke and Mungo Park and Prince Henry the Navigator—an invitation
to the imagination.

—John Updike, "Through a Continent, Darkly"

In *Alphabetical Africa* (1974) Walter Abish has constructed an elaborate word game spread across fifty-two chapters ranging in length from one to nine pages. Abish uses only words beginning with the letter a in the first and last chapters, only words beginning with the letters a and b in the second and penultimate chapters, and so on until the twenty-sixth and twenty-seventh chapters, where he allows himself words beginning with all the letters in the alphabet. Although Abish's admittedly excessive work perpetuates Africanist myths, like Boyd's *A Good Man in Africa* it eschews the tragic depiction of the continent common to other second-generation works. More important, the whole conception of the book involves a recognition of how much Western writing about Africa is a language game. Just as Burroughs and Bellow did not need to go to Africa to produce their fantasies about it, Abish requires nothing more than a dictionary and an acquaintance with a handful of Africanist texts to create his own.

Abish makes clear that his concern in the book is language: "Feeling a distrust of the understanding that is intrinsic to any communication, I decided to write a book in which my distrust became a determining factor upon which the flow of the narrative was largely predicated."[37] Abish chooses Africa as the setting for his book because of its linguistic variety and its associations with the fantastic. The diversity of the continent enables Abish to roam from Angola to Zambia, encounter giant ants and Zanzibar's dogs, and mention Ashanti architecture and Swahili words such as Zaa, Zaba, and Zabadi. Moreover, because of the long tradition of fantasy works written about the continent, setting the book in Africa enables Abish to concoct a fantastic, nonsensical plot comprising invasions, murders, nymphomaniacs, stolen diamonds, and bilingual ants.[38]

Although Abish repeats a number of Africanist clichés—"all history is hearsay in Africa" (21), "killing is easier in Africa" (27)—the book is often metafictional, self-effacing, and parodic. In this paragraph from the first chapter, for example, Abish pokes fun at himself and his whole endeavor: "Africa again: Angolans applaud author, after author allegedly approached an American amateur aviator, and angrily argued against America's anachronistic assault. Afterward all applaud as author awarded avocado and appointed acting alphabet authority" (2). Moreover, in addition to repeatedly describing the other characters in the book as creations from the author's earlier works, he calls himself "an unreliable reporter" (56). Abish also declares himself to be "on a paper chase. A lovely English paper chase, only it's in darkest Africa" (39) and recognizes that "Africa is a favorite topic in literature, it gives license to so much excess" (58). Likewise, through his use of exaggeration, irony, puns, and allusions, such as his description of Quat, the transvestite ruler of Tanzania, as an African Queen, Abish occasionally parodies Africanist discourse. Thus, the serious purpose behind *Alphabetical Africa*'s facetiousness is to cause the reader to reassess the stereotypes of outside writing about Africa.

John Updike

The Coup

In his review of *Alphabetical Africa*, John Updike asserts the appropriateness of the African setting for Abish's lexical gymnastics, but he overlooks the metafictional nature of the book and the way this and the author's alphabetical gimmickry reflects not on Africa but on those who write about the continent. Relying on Africanist oppositions, asserting the continent's blankness, and equating the continent with a fantasy world, Updike links the capriciousness of Abish's approach to the putative randomness of Africa: "there is a nice rightness to setting such a work in Africa, where incantations are still potent and national boundaries slice across tribal realities as arbitrarily as the alphabet schematizes language. Teeming yet vacant, mysterious yet monotonous, Africa permits this literary experiment. *Alphabetical Asia* would not have been so funny, *Alphabetical America* would have been cluttered with reality, *Alphabetical Antarctica* would have been blank."[39] This unashamedly Africanist attitude has particular relevance to Updike's own fantasy work about the continent. Although *The Coup* (1978) resembles Nabokov's *Pale Fire* more than *Alphabetical Africa*, it nevertheless fits squarely in the tradition of Burroughs's *Tarzan of the Apes* and Bellow's *Henderson the Rain King*. All three works use the continent as a backdrop on which to project a white Western male fantasy that says more about America than Africa. Updike's innovation, if it can be called that, is to put his Africanist attitudes in the mouth of a black African protagonist, Colonel Hakim Félix Ellelloû, erstwhile president of the arid, impoverished, landlocked country of Kush.

Updike touches on a number of themes that occupy other second-generation writers. Ellelloû's name, which means freedom, and his position recall the theme of independence treated previously by V. S. Naipaul and Theroux. Because the protagonist rules a sovereign African nation, the Naipaulian theme of leadership likewise comes into play. Moreover, as in Theroux's novels, Updike's Africa becomes a battleground for capitalism and communism, as the Soviet-backed Ellelloû tries to uphold the purity of his Islamic-Marxist revolution against the forces of American-inspired consumerism. However, while Updike recognizes the importance of these political issues, in contrast to Naipaul and Theroux he examines them only superficially.

Like the scenes set in New England in *Henderson the Rain King*, the most vivid writing in *The Coup* concerns Ellelloû's four years at McCarthy College in Franchise, Wisconsin. More important, as with Bellow, many of Updike's African scenes can be read as an allegory of American life. Responding to Ellelloû's pronouncement that "Africa held up a black mirror to Pharaonic Egypt, and the image was Kush,"[40] Deborah McGill has written, "One might say of *The Coup*: it holds a white mirror to postcolonial Africa, and the image is Connecticut."[41] George W. Hunt, SJ, provides more evidence that Ellelloû's African experiences are merely a camouflage for distinctly American phenomema. Citing a 15 December 1978 interview of Updike by Dick Cavett on PBS, Hunt reports, "Updike has described *The Coup* as an allegory of America's Watergate Crisis, and Ellelloû's drift into exile from 1973 on parallels Nixon's similar drift. His subsequent efforts to compose a memoir also recall Nixon, as do the results."[42]

The United States has formed Ellelloû's unbalanced character and therefore bears responsibility for the contradictions of Kush under his rule. At McCarthy, Ellelloû falls in love with a girl named Candy who embodies white middle-class America while at the same time he fraternizes with the small coterie of African-American students who introduce him to Islam and Communism. Although Ellelloû wants to believe that only the separatist and revolutionary aspects of his American education have influenced his policies as president of Kush, the materialistic values of middle America have also had an effect on him, as indicated by the fact that Ellelloû brings back to Africa both intellectual radicalism and Candy as his wife.

Like Ellelloû, upon returning to Africa *The Coup* cannot escape the United States. After serving in the military of Kush during its early years as an independent nation, Ellelloû leads a coup in 1968 that overthrows the king and takes power himself. He adopts a staunchly anti-American stance, turning Kush into a Soviet client state, endeavoring to keep the country free from the effects of consumerism, and rejecting any aid from the United States. Holding himself personally responsible for the drought that strikes Kush when he assumes power, Ellelloû embarks on a series of trips to various parts of his country in what he regards as a graillike quest to bring water to his parched nation and make the Sahara green. While on these absurd journeys, the president finds evidence that American materialism has penetrated Kush. Driving through an isolated part of the country, Ellelloû and his bodyguards inexplicably see a flatbed truck carrying crushed American automobiles. Earlier Ellelloû glimpses two golden parabolas in the desert, which subsequently prove to be the arches of a McDonald's. Ultimately, Ellelloû loses his political power in what he thought was the most remote corner of Kush, a previously unknown city that resembles Franchise in the 1950s and bears his own name.

Unlike Burroughs and Bellow, Updike did go to Africa in 1973 as a Fulbright Lecturer. At first glance *The Coup* seems much more realistic than either *Tarzan of the Apes* or *Henderson the Rain King*. References to the drought in the Sahel in the early 1970s, quotations from the Koran, and a hostility toward America lend Updike's book an air of authenticity. All of this, however, like Burroughs's use of the theory of evolution and Bellow's borrowings from Burton and others, disguises the white Western fantasy that lies below the surface. A closer analysis reveals Kush to be an amalgam of Africanist imagery, as Arnewiland and Waririland are in *Henderson*. In her essay on *The Coup*, Joyce Markle treats some of the geographical impossibilities of the novel, relying on an unpublished manuscript by Barry Amis, an African-American with extensive African experience. Amis makes it clear that Updike constructs Kush out of elements from very different parts of the continent: "The area [Updike] describes is one which might include parts of present-day Mali, Niger, and [Burkina Faso]. In this area one does not find Indian shops (which are a feature of East Africa) nor does one find *souks* (which are a feature of North Africa). Juju is not a feature of the lives of the overwhelmingly Moslem population and Tuaregs do not have slaves. Young women do not walk around "utterly naked" in front of their parents and others, driving a Mercedes through the Bad Quarter is an automotive impossibility."[43]

The source list at the start of the book, the apparent third-world sensibility, and the superficial acknowledgement of weighty issues, mask the presence of Updike, the Africanist who reviewed Abish's *Alphabetical Africa* and firmly believes in the continent's blankness and innate corruption. Just as no coup actually occurs to topple Ellelloû, so the novel *The Coup* does not represent a whole new direction for white writing about Africa. A careful analysis reveals that the novel is merely Updike's fantasy. Again drawing on Amis, Markle asserts that the book's true voice is neither African nor black. According to Amis, "There is nothing in the novel that is authentically African. The customs are not African, the language is not African, and the characters are not African" (298). Moreover, Ellelloû's narrative contains statements that betray a white bias. The protagonist's claim that "In Kush we never cease dreaming of intercourse between dark and fair skin, between thick lips and thin lips" (57) elicits the following response from Amis: "whether or not such a fantasy has any basis in American society, it certainly has none in the African region Updike purports to depict" (299).

After discerning Updike's fingers controlling the strings of Ellelloû's narrative, the task of enumerating the Africanist elements of *The Coup* becomes much easier. Ellelloû consistently refers to the blankness of the continent while his imagery and conduct illustrate the corruption of Africa. In reference to *The Coup*, Updike has claimed to have "always been attracted to hidden corners" and chosen Africa because it was "the emptiest part of the world I could think of."[44] The book's epigraph from the Koran, "Does there not pass over man a space of time when his life is blank," introduces the concept of the void and the quotation from Melville at the start of the fourth chapter, "Beneath the stars the roofy desert spreads / Vacant as Libya," reinforces it. Moreover, an anecdote from Ellelloû's school days in Wisconsin drives the notion of blankness home. While discussing his final exam in an African history course with Professor Craven, Ellelloû answers Craven's complaint that there seemed to be "something missing" in the response by suggesting, "Perhaps that is the very African ingredient" (215). Echoing the prevalent Africanist association of the continent with mortality, Ellelloû uses a death's-head as an image for Kush: "But even memory thins in this land, which suggests, on a map, an angular skull whose cranium is the empty desert" (16). Ellelloû's behavior throughout the novel demonstrates the corrupting effects of Africa. He not only orders that a pile of American relief goods be ignited, thus killing a State Department official who is perched on top, he personally beheads the former king in a ceremony designed to blame the deposed ruler for the continuing drought.

Ellelloû eventually comes to resemble the insignificant white characters in works by other second-generation writers—alienated, corrupt, irrelevant, and powerless. Eschewing a personality cult, Ellelloû is largely unknown in his nation and on his various trips often travels in disguise. He begins to feel like a guest in his own country and the population comes to regard him as crazy. In addition to murdering his adversaries, Ellelloû grows increasingly insane, in the process putting personal whims before the good of the country. He would rather have Kush starve to death than become contaminated by the forces of materialism. As a result of his madness, Ellelloû loses touch with political realities. While he is off like a medieval knight on a personal quest to save his country from disaster, his underlings take charge, negotiate deals with the United States, and start to develop Kush's economy. After being abandoned in the town with his own name, Ellelloû reads of his own disappearance and death. The final indication of his insignificance comes when he bargains for a pension for himself and his family and moves to the South of France to write his memoirs.

Thus, what at first appears to be a realistic novel from the perspective of an African, proves to be a white Western male fantasy that relies on Africanist images to allegorize America. Just as Naipaul uses the African Ferdinand to condemn his own continent at the end of *A Bend in the River*, Updike disparages Africa through his native protagonist.

NOTES

1. For an example of the controversy Naipaul's writing has engendered, see the exchange of letters between Michael Thelwell and Irving Howe over Howe's review of *A Bend in the River* in the *New York Times Review of Books* 13 May 1979, which has been reprinted as "Contra Naipaul" in Thelwell's *Duties, Pleasures, and Conflicts: Essays in Struggle*, Amherst: University of Massachusetts Press, 1987, 200–207. See also Adewale Maja-Pearce, "The Naipauls on Africa: An African View," *Journal of Commonwealth Literature* 20 (1985): 111–17.

2. See V. S. Naipaul, "Conrad's Darkness," *The Return of Eva Perón*, New York: Vintage, 1981, 221–45.

3. Paul Theroux, "V. S. Naipaul," *Sunrise with Seamonsters*, Boston: Houghton, 1985, 100. See also V. S. Naipaul, "Prologue to an Autobiography," *Finding the Center*, New York: Vintage, 1986.

4. Richard Wright's *Black Power* (New York: Harper, 1954) describes his sojourn in what was then the Gold Coast.

5. Shiva Naipaul, *North of South: An African Journey*, New York: Penguin, 1980, 14–15. Subsequent references are to this edition.

6. Here, Naipaul not only echoes the rhetoric of the expatriate tradition but adds a twist to it: just as prolonged exposure to Africans corrupts whites, extended contact with the flawed civilization imported from Europe denigrates Africans.

7. V. S. Naipaul, "A New King for the Congo: Mobutu and the Nihilism of Africa," *The Return of Eva Perón*, New York: Vintage, 1981, 205. Subsequent references are to this edition.

8. Throughout the essay, Naipaul makes little or no mention of the repression and torture characterizing the Mobutu regime, nor does he discuss the Western economic and military support that the president receives. For these reasons, Naipaul's travel account of Zaire differs markedly from that of Helen Winternitz, which will be examined in chapter four. See pp. 113–17.

9. V. S. Naipaul, "The Crocodiles of Yamoussoukro," *Finding the Center*, New York: Vintage, 1986, 90. Subsequent references are to this edition.

10. Miller, *Blank Darkness*, 172.

11. V. S. Naipaul, *In a Free State*, New York: Vintage, 1984, 8. Subsequent references are to this edition.

12. For an even more revealing source for *A Bend in the River*, see Naipaul's *A Congo Diary*, Los Angeles: Sylvester, 1980.

13. V. S. Naipaul, *A Bend in the River*, New York: Vintage, 1980, 15–16. Subsequent references are to this edition.

14. Lynda Prescott, "Past and Present Darkness: Sources for V. S. Naipaul's *A Bend in the River*," *Modern Fiction Studies* 30 (Autumn 1984): 547–59.

15. In contrast to Kurtz, whose presence dominates all of *Heart of Darkness*, Huismans only appears in the first third of *A Bend in the River* and receives little consideration thereafter. This is not to imply that the amount of time characters appear in a work alone determines their importance. Kurtz isn't actually encountered until near the end of *Heart of Darkness*; nevertheless, he is an important presence throughout, becoming an obsession for Marlow. Similarly, the Reverend Torvald Neilson in Lorraine Hansberry's *Les Blancs*, who like Huismans is killed on a journey into the bush, never actually appears on stage; nevertheless, events take place in and around Neilson's mission, the reporter Charlie Morris comes to Africa to do a story on him, his wife and colleagues discuss the Reverend at length, and the falsehood at the heart of his character and his years in Africa is one of the significant themes of the play. Thus, Neilson's presence in *Les Blancs*, more substantial than that of Huismans in Naipaul's novel, links him more closely to Kurtz and Salim.

16. Such an assessment of postcolonial Africa, and Zaire in particular, is by no means peculiar to Naipaul, as a recent newspaper article on a city in the Bandundu province of the central African nation reveals: "The wheel of history, it almost seems, has come full circle here. Nearly a century ago, when the first Europeans ventured into Zaire's vast interior, Kikwit was a small village whose people and institutions existed in a quiet, self-contained world wholly uninterrupted by the frenetic rhythms of modernity. The village gradually disappeared as a social and cultural force as Belgium . . . exploited the region's mineral and agricultural wealth, transforming Kikwit into a provincial trading center. . . . Today, the legacy of Kikwit's colonial past is swiftly disappearing. 'Civilization is coming to an end here,' said René Kinsweke, manager of Siefac, a chain of food stores, as he spoke of how Kikwit has become a dispiriting tableau of chaos and catastrophe. 'We're back to where we started. We're going back into the bush.' " Kenneth Noble, "Once a Colonial Jewel, a City Hurtles Backward," *New York Times* 15 November 1991, A4. Five days later a *Times* editorial not only quoted from Noble's article but also took its Naipaulian title, "Back to the Bush in Zaire," from it.

17. The Tarzan Theroux describes in his essay does not correspond exactly with the Tarzan of Burroughs's novels. Theroux claims that Tarzan out of the jungle would be meaningless; however, as noted in the first chapter, in *Tarzan of the Apes* the foundling Lord Greystoke remains a heroic figure in both Europe and the United States and is able to express himself quite eloquently. Apparently Theroux is using the caricatured Tarzan of the comics and movies to better make his point about the insignificance of white expatriates in Africa.

18. Paul Theroux, "Tarzan Is an Expatriate," *Sunrise with Seamonsters*, Boston: Houghton, 1985, 33. Subsequent references are to this edition.

19. Paul Theroux, "When the Peace Corps Was Young," *New York Times* 25 February 1986, nat'l ed.: 31.

20. See Paul Theroux, "The Killing of Hastings Banda," *Sunrise with Seamonsters*, Boston: Houghton, 1985, 63–75.

21. Paul Theroux, "V. S. Naipaul," 95.

22. Paul Theroux, "The Killing of Hastings Banda," 71.

23. Margaret Laurence experienced a similar disillusionment. See p. 42 above.

24. This statement corresponds to an equally startling one to be found in Theroux's review of John Updike's *The Coup* (which will be discussed in the final section of this chapter): "More important than the Americans who will read this book are the Africans who will at least understand what it is they have been trying to say," "Updike in Africa," *Bookviews* 2 (December 1978): 36. Apparently Africa did not produce an Evelyn Waugh between 1971 and 1978, so Africans had to listen to Africanists such as Theroux and Updike to comprehend themselves and their continent.

25. Paul Theroux, *Fong and the Indians*, Boston: Houghton, 1968, 10. Subsequent references are to this edition.

26. Paul Theroux, *Girls at Play*, Boston: Houghton, 1969. Subsequent references are to this addition.

27. "Introducing *Jungle Lovers*," *Sunrise with Seamonsters*, Boston: Houghton, 1985, 328.

28. Paul Theroux, *Jungle Lovers*, Boston: Houghton, 1971, 122. Subsequent references are to this edition.

29. Theroux, "Introducing *Jungle Lovers*," 329.

30. This phrasing recalls a profoundly Africanist passage in Gertrude Stein's *The Autobiography of Alice B. Toklas* (1933): "Gertrude Stein concluded that negroes were not suffering from persecution, they were suffering from nothingness. She always contends that the african is not primitive, he has a very ancient but a very narrow culture and there it remains. Consequently nothing does or can happen." *The Autobiography of Alice B. Toklas*, New York: Vintage, 1961, 238.

31. Miller, *Blank Darkness*, 139–65.

32. "V. S. Naipaul," 93. Theroux is probably alluding in part to the famous case of alleged plagiarism involving Yambo Ouologuem's 1968 novel *Le Devoir de violence*. Although garnering great critical acclaim and receiving the Prix Renaudot for the book, Ouologuem was accused of using passages from Graham Greene's *It's a Battlefield* and other works in his novel. For a discussion of the subject see chapter seven of Miller's *Blank Darkness*.

33. Martha Gellhorn, "Into Africa," *Travels with Myself and Another*, New York: Dodd, 1979, 109–234. Subsequent references are to this edition. See also "Monkeys on the Roof," *The View from the Ground*, New York: Atlantic Monthly, 1988, 260–68.

34. Martha Gellhorn, *The Weather in Africa*, New York: Avon, 1981, 30–31. Subsequent references are to this edition.

35. Leafy also appears in two earlier stories by Boyd, "Next Boat from Doula" and "The Coup," *On the Yankee Station*, New York: Penguin, 1982, 61–68, 157–79.

36. William Boyd, *A Good Man in Africa*, New York: Penguin, 1982, 17. Subsequent references are to this edition.

37. Walter Abish, *Alphabetical Africa*, New York: New Directions, 1974, back cover. Subsequent references are to this edition.

38. The fantasy that Abish's book most resembles is Raymond Roussel's *Impressions of Africa* (1910).

39. John Updike, "Through a Continent, Darkly," *Picked-Up Pieces*, New York: Knopf, 1975, 350–51.

40. John Updike, *The Coup*, New York: Fawcett, 1978, 14. Subsequent references are to this edition.

41. Deborah McGill, "Boy's Life," *John Updike: A Collection of Critical Essays*, ed. David Thorburn and Howard Eiland, Englewood Cliffs, N.J.: Prentice, 1979, 165.

42. George W. Hunt, SJ, *John Updike and the Three Great Secret Things: Sex, Religion, and Art*, Grand Rapids, Mich.: Eerdmans, 1980, 198.

43. Joyce Markle, "*The Coup:* Illusions and Insubstantial Impressions," *Critical Essays on John Updike,* ed. William R. Macnaughton, Boston: G. K. Hall, 1982, 283–84. Subsequent references are to this edition.

44. Donald J. Greiner, "*The Coup,*" *John Updike: Modern Critical Views,* ed. Harold Bloom, N.Y.: Chelsea, 1987, 141.

4

Third-Generation Postwar Writers: Political Engagement within the Traditions

Most humanistic scholars are, I think, perfectly happy with the notion that texts exist in contexts, that there is such a thing as intertextuality, that the pressures of conventions, predecessors, and rhetorical styles limit what Walter Benjamin once called the "overtaxing of the productive person in the name of . . . the principle of 'creativity,' " in which the poet is believed on his own, and out of pure mind, to have brought forth his work. Yet there is a reluctance to allow that political, institutional, and ideological constraints act in the same manner on the individual author.

—Edward Said, *Orientalism*

In books published in the middle to late 1980s, the third generation of outsiders who have written about Africa since 1945 recognize the Africanist baggage that the political assessment, expatriate, and fantasy traditions carry with them, and they understand that any portrayal of Africa necessarily has political ramifications. Helen Winternitz, Jonathan Raban, Maria Thomas, and J. G. Ballard actively acknowledge or subvert the conventions informing earlier depictions of the continent. These authors carefully choose and often draw attention to the language they use. Instead of attempting to be objective, third-generation writers make clear their biases, which are no longer so definitively tied to Western interests. Despite this recognition that the established ways of writing about Africa have perpetuated Africanist myths, these authors do not completely abandon the dominant traditions. As a result, they revert at times to Africanist stereotypes.

Winternitz explicitly announces her political agenda in *East along the Equator*, attributing the terror present in Zaire to American support for the Mobutu regime rather than Africa's innate "primitivism." Raban and Thomas choose different methods to subvert the expatriate tradition. While *Foreign Land* depicts England, instead of Africa, as the environment that causes the protagonist to go native,

Antonia Saw the Oryx First devotes equal attention to a black and a white protagonist, favorably depicting the latter's movement toward and momentary adoption of the former's Weltanschauung. Frequently acknowledging that his book is a fantasy, Ballard explores the obsessive nature of the Africanist mentality in *The Day of Creation*. Despite their attempts to eliminate Africanist discourse's subjugating effects, however, in varying degrees each of these third-generation postwar authors relies on Africanist clichés as a result of writing in one of the established traditions.

Helen Winternitz

East along the Equator

Like Churchill's *My African Journey*, Helen Winternitz's *East along the Equator* (1987) clearly and unapologetically states its political agenda. Churchill uses his book to recruit young Englishmen for service in East Africa and to drum up public support for the empire's policies. First- and second-generation postwar travel writers rarely exhibit such honesty. Waugh tries, unsuccessfully, to ignore politics in *A Tourist in Africa*; the Naipauls hide their political motives behind a facade of neutrality. Winternitz, in contrast, acknowledges the political nature of travel writing. In her introduction, she explains her reasons for journeying to Zaire in 1983 to write *East along the Equator*. She aims to trace the impact of outsiders on the Central African nation, in particular the effect that the United States' economic and political support for the Mobutu regime has had on the citizenry. Rather than simply regarding the continent as the corrupt combination of failed colonialism and indigenous "primitivism," as second-generation postwar writers commonly do, Winternitz argues that Western interests play a central role in contemporary Africa.

Winternitz's methods for gathering information differ significantly from those of her predecessors. Unlike the Naipauls, who treat their travel works as nonfiction novels, Winternitz is a journalist and approaches her subject accordingly. Thus, she refuses to indulge in the Africanist shaping of experiences the Naipauls acknowledge in *North of South* and "The Crocodiles of Yamoussoukro." Winternitz sets out to meet, travel with, and interview Zairians, including members of the opposition. Her knowledge of Swahili and some Lingala enables her to talk to the people directly. All this entails certain risks, which at the end of her journey become quite real. But Winternitz's tactics make her a participant, gathering information firsthand rather than relying on rumors filtered through the expatriate and embassy communities. In addition, she has re-searched her topic thoroughly; her list of suggested reading includes such recent studies as Nzongola-Ntalaja's *The Crisis in Zaire* and Crawford Young and Thomas Turner's *The Rise and Decline of the Zairian State.* Despite her anti-imperialist objectives, Winternitz's book belongs to the political assessment tradition, which histori-cally has been dominated by Africanist discourse. Early in the book, she presents binary oppositions and at times imposes images on the African landscape. However, after seeing the interior of Zaire for her-self, becoming acquainted with the people, and suffering detention and interrogation at the hands of the secret police, Winternitz rejects the Africanist clichés that equate Africans with savagery and reas-signs blame for the cruelty and terror that persists in the Central Af-rican nation.

Winternitz outlines her political agenda at the start of the book. Accompanied by fellow *Baltimore Sun* reporter Timothy Phelps, Winternitz travels to Central Africa to assess Zaire in the light of American investment in the Mobutu regime. In her introduction she informs the reader that the African nation has been a client and ally of the United States for over twenty years, ever since Patrice Lu-mumba, the country's democratically elected Prime Minister, was assassinated with the blessings of the CIA; that cobalt, uranium, and geopolitical considerations have replaced slaves and ivory as the reasons for outside interest in the former Belgian Congo; and that the Reagan Administration has steadfastly supported Mobutu despite his becoming one of the world's richest men while Zaire has become one of the world's poorest nations.[1] Winternitz then succinctly states the purpose of her trip: "We were going to see firsthand, as few Westerners have, what has happened in the interior of Zaire as the result of America's sponsorship of Mobutu."[2]

She later broadens the scope of her investigation to include Arab and European influences on the Congo and takes pains to dissociate herself from the imperialists who came to the region: "we did not remotely resemble the grand expeditionary forces that had preceded us into Africa's interior in search of slaves, ivory, or glory. We car-ried no trading beads or rifles, and nothing like the portable boat [Stanley's] expedition had lugged across Africa. We were not out to claim anything in the name of civilization, nation, or ideology" (11). Even the title of the book is political. Winternitz travels "east along the equator," up the Zaire from Kinshasa to Kisangani and then over-land to Goma. This is a reversal of the route of Henry Morgan Stan-ley; her purpose for coming to Central Africa is also diametrically opposed to his. Originally departing from Zanzibar in 1875, Stanley fought his way down the Congo and eventually reached the Atlantic in 1877, opening up Central Africa for exploitation by Leopold II of Belgium.

She punctuates her description of the boat ride she makes from Kinshasa to Kisangani with references to the history of Western involvement in the region in an attempt to dispel Africanist clichés. Before describing how the greed of the slave trade replaced the good will and cooperation between Central Africans and the Portuguese in the fifteenth century, Winternitz asserts: "The story of the first meeting between Europe and the Kongo Kingdom . . . is almost too sad to tell. But to ignore it is to assume that savagery is native to the African continent and that Westerners had nothing to do with the brutality that has marked Africa's history" (39).

This careful attention to history enables Winternitz to avoid the blanket indictments of whites and blacks that characterize the Naipauls' travel works on Africa. Because she has studied the history and politics of Zaire, she can pinpoint responsibility for past brutality and current oppression. Throughout the book Winternitz blames American support of Mobutu for the bleak conditions in Zaire. She wants American policy toward Zaire to change for not only humanitarian but also practical reasons. One resident of Kinshasa warns that when Mobutu finally goes, the people will recall that the United States supported him. "The Americans," he claims, "are inheriting Mobutu's unpopularity" (24).

At the end of the book, Winternitz looks with hope to the departure of American-supported dictators such as Marcos and Duvalier. She condemns Ronald Reagan's 1986 pledge of continued military and economic support for Zaire and his description of Mobutu as "a voice of good sense and good will," countering it with her own assessment: "Mobutu has continued to serve as a prostitute to American interests in Angola and elsewhere on the African continent" (270).

Although Winternitz openly declares her political intentions and strives to distance herself from previous outsiders, she occasionally relies on typical Africanist gestures such as projecting images on the putative blankness of Africa. Although she claims that her reasons distance her from previous travel writers, Winternitz journeys to Zaire not only to achieve political goals but also to fulfill a long-standing dream of finding the source of the Congo. Her desire to pursue the starting point of this great waterway links her more closely than she realizes to imperialist explorers like Stanley and Livingstone. Moreover, her description of the river's source as "the essence of Africa" connects her with Africanist authors like Conrad and

Greene, who use phrases such as "heart of darkness" and "the heart of the matter."

Just as Conrad projected onto Africa the blank space found on nineteenth-century European atlases and Greene equated the shape of the continent with that of the human heart, Winternitz engages in Africanist map reading, too: "On a map, the [Zaire] river looks like a snake and its tributaries like a profusion of tails, curving through the middle of Africa, its head at the Atlantic and its longest tail far miles inland. Malebo Pool resembles the lump a freshly swallowed monkey, or other luckless jungle creature, might make in the gullet of the ophidian river" (34). Although Winternitz intends to show that savagery is "not native to Africa," her imagery undermines her argument. Perhaps in an attempt to heighten the adventure of her undertaking, Winternitz slips into an Africanist technique reminiscent of Churchill's image of the rhino standing in front of Mount Kilimanjaro. However, whereas Churchill consciously uses Africa's fauna and landscape as an emblem for the evolutionary gap he perceives between the continent and the West, Winternitz seems unaware that her description of the river attributes death, savagery, and even evil to Africa.

An even more telling example of how Africanist discourse informs the author's writing even when it contradicts her stated purpose occurs in Winternitz's description of the last night on the steamship before reaching Kisangani. Spending her days trying to improve her Lingala with the merchants and her nights drinking and dancing in the makeshift bars on the barges attached to the steamboat, Winternitz interacts with Africans in a way rarely paralleled by previous travel writers. At their invitation, she shares a bottle of Zaire whiskey with the captain and his officers. Clearly she regards this as a moment of rare communion; however, in her attempt to describe its significance, she alludes to the fabled blankness and darkness of Africa: "I finished the glass and drank another. Outside the big windows of the pilothouse, dry lightning licked along the horizon in untamed counterpoint to the beams from the ship's spotlights. The whole world, the seen and the unseeable, was intoxicated. We needed to shout, to sing, to dance, to procreate, to fill the vast, lush vacancies with illuminating purpose" (118). Reinforcing Africanist stereotypes, the Conradian phrasing at the end of this passage counteracts Winternitz's efforts to create a new discourse on Africa.

Near the end of *East along the Equator* Winternitz succeeds in meshing her language with her political purpose. Returning to Kinshasa, she interviews the resilient Tshisekedi wa Mulumba, a former ally of Mobutu who split with the president, becoming a member of the Group of Thirteen, the only vocal opposition in Zaire. After the interview, an agent of the Centre National pour Recherche et Investigations (CNRI), the Zairian security police, hijacks Winternitz and Phelps's cab. They are taken to CNRI headquarters, held for questioning, and for more than a week forced to return daily for interrogation, often in Cell 3, a room notorious for the tortures that have been performed there. Describing this frightening experience, Winternitz redirects the negative connotations of Africanist discourse so that it applies to those people and institutions responsible for the brutality that exists in Zaire: "This cell was indeed the heart of darkness, the corruption at Africa's essence, the place where human reason failed" (263). Winternitz proceeds to summarize her journey: "We had traveled into the center of Zaire, looking for a legendary darkness, but found rivers and forests that were home to millions of people who had not forgotten how to laugh or dance even as they fought every day to survive" (263). She then provides an overview of the country's history that consciously reverses the Africanist association of the West with light and Africa with darkness:

Zaire's darkness was not geographic. It was not a fruit of the entangling forest, but a creation of man. The dark legacy of the Portuguese slavers . . . has carried through the years of the tyrant Leopold, to Mobutu and his system grounded in torture, repression, and corruption. Those who put Mobutu in place and have kept him there have been foreigners, first among them the American policymakers, who can pretend, as the Belgians and other Europeans did, that they have been bringing light to the darkness. They can pretend, but perhaps not forever, that shoring up one of Africa's premier dictators is going to make the world more democratic. (263)

East along the Equator illustrates how Africanist discourse, operating through one of the established traditions of writing about Africa, can undermine an author's attempt to distance herself from the language used by previous writers who have depicted Africa. At the same time, however, Winternitz's book also evinces an author eventually mastering Africanist discourse and consciously reversing it in accordance with her political intentions.

Jonathan Raban
Foreign Land

Helen Winternitz attempts to get beyond the Africanist clichés that characterize the political assessment tradition. Not until she pays careful attention to her language, however, does she succeed in matching her execution with her intention. In an analagous manner, Jonathan Raban consciously subverts the expatriate tradition in his novel *Foreign Land* (1985). Unlike the first- and second-generation postwar writers, he depicts England as the "foreign land" that causes his protagonist, a Briton returning home after many years in Africa, to go native morally, physically, and mentally. He also inverts standard Africanist oppositions, privileging Africa over Great Britain. Similar to Winternitz, however, Raban's relationship to an established tradition causes him to repeat certain Africanist clichés. He, too, addresses this problem by making language an explicit issue, demonstrating in a scene of reading involving the protagonist and a newspaper account depicting turmoil in Africa, how Africanist discourse can affect the attitudes of even a knowledgeable and sympathetic Westerner.

In contrast to *Heart of Darkness, The Heart of the Matter,* and *A Bend in the River,* in which outsiders fall morally as a result of exposure to African corruption, Raban portrays an Englishman who returns to Great Britain from Africa, finds it a foreign and corrupt land, and goes native. The only Englishman in Bom Porto, George Grey enjoys his life in the largest city of the now-independent country of Montedor. All the people know him, greet him, and try out what English they know on him, for "[i]n this Portuguese cake slice of Africa, English was the language not of colonialism but of romance."[3] However, after twenty years of running one of West Africa's most important bunkering stations, George at sixty learns that his services are no longer required. Although he could stay on as a consultant, George returns to England, moving into his deceased parents' retirement cottage in St. Cadix on the coast of Cornwall.

Instead of depicting a corrupt Africa, Raban attributes licentiousness and decay to England. Once a quiet seaside village, St. Cadix has degenerated into a seedy and morbid port of call. The significantly named Mr. Jellaby tries to interest George in adult videotapes when he comes to the cottage to install a television and later contemplates filming a pornographic movie on George's boat. George grows increasingly impatient to "step off the edge of England and float free" because St. Cadix also literally becomes a place of death for him. Sleeping in his boat one night, he awakens to the noise of an object striking the hull, which turns out to be the corpse of a woman who committed suicide, leaving a note accusing her neighbors of being "the living dead."

When George goes to London to visit his daughter Sheila, Raban intensifies the reversal of the expatriate tradition, using standard Africanist oppositions but privileging Africa over England. What George sees traveling by cab through some of the toughest sections of London shocks him and makes him nostalgic for Africa: "It looked a lawless country. The blocks of workers' flats were dirtier, more sprawled and raggedy, than those of Accra and Dar Es Salaam; there was more trash blowing in the streets than there was in Lagos. Everywhere there were slogans, spraygunned on the walls, signboards, standing sheets of corrugated iron. KILL THE PIGS HEROIN EAT SHIT FUCK THE GLC. George thought sadly of the innocent VIVAs of Montedor; no one wanted anything to live long here" (95). Corresponding to the filth outside the cab, the driver keeps up a steady stream of obscenities.

Raban pushes the reversal a step further, turning the United Kingdom into the subject for a *National Geographic*–type exposé of bizarre native rites. George recalls his incredulity at reading about the Dirty Protest by IRA prisoners at Maze prison: "These men had expressed their indignation against the government by turning themselves into giant babies. They didn't wash. They threw their food on the floor and ate with their hands. They practised incontinence and daubed the walls of their cells with their own excrement. Sitting, out of the sun, in the Rua Kwame Nkruma, George had followed this story as if he was reading up on the customs of some remote and terrifying tribe. In Britain? Surely not" (97). Nonetheless, what George sees confirms the newspaper account: "Yet this new London looked like a dirty protest. It was wrecked and smeared." (97).

Approaching old age, lacking a sense of purpose, and confronting this corrupt environment, George begins to go native, deteriorating morally, physically, and mentally. Retirement forces George to contemplate his own physical decay and the prospect of death. Refusing to give up, as many of those in St. Cadix have, he prepares to take drastic measures to assert his existence and freedom. However, without friends or responsibilities, George has nothing regulating his life. He begins to do things he would not consider doing when he was in Africa, such as using tainted money to buy himself a boat and taking dangerous risks.

During the struggle for independence in Montedor, a Portuguese fishing patrol vessel was sabotaged at George's bunkering station while he was away. George held himself partially responsible for the nine men who died and felt manipulated by his friends in the revolutionary movement, especially after the president of the new republic had presented him with a Swiss bank account worth over forty thousand dollars. Because of its origins, George has always refused to touch the money. Now, however, he decides to use it to buy a ketch in which to sail about England. With a copy of *Heart of Darkness* in his bag, George flies to Geneva to withdraw the money in cash. While there he accepts a proposition from a prostitute, rationalizing that this is "exactly what an Englishman was supposed to do On The Continent that to say yes was to do no more than bow politely to the force of custom" (120); however, the interlude proves unsettling and unsatisfying. George demonstrates his sense of guilt and criminality after he succeeds in getting back to England with the money: "He couldn't work it out at all, but somehow he had got away scot free" (127).

Both George and his boat have succumbed to the forces of corruption. Built the year he was born and retired to pleasure cruising after years of commercial service, George's ketch becomes an image for him. The *Calliope* provides George with a purpose for the first time since his return, and he finds working on her therapeutic: "Cleaning out the boat, he found he swabbed and scoured a lot of the grimier recesses of himself" (132). However, in overhauling the boat and himself, George overlooks one thing. Having used what he once considered blood money to purchase the *Calliope*, George, like his boat, has some "rot in the stempost."

In addition to compromising his moral principles, George goes native physically and mentally. Calling Sheila to inform her that he plans to sail up the Thames to see her in London, he confides, "I'm making a pretty thoroughgoing job of going to seed" (227). He lets his hair become long, grows a beard, and begins to drink too much. His judgment also becomes questionable. Despite a major storm system approaching southern England, George sets out for London, relying on dead reckoning. On the journey he hears and converses with all the important voices of his past and present, becoming so wrapped up in his memories that the *Calliope* nearly runs into a tanker in the fog.

When the corruption of England becomes too much for George, he abruptly and desperately severs his ties with the place where he was born. At Rye, George is stopped by a customs man who becomes quite suspicious upon hearing that George has been pleasure boating in a fierce storm and has large sums of cash with him, bringing a dog on board to sniff out drugs and warning George he will be watched. For George this is the final straw; England has become too corrupt and suspicious a place for him to stay. Without returning to St. Cadix or calling anyone, George buys ample provisions and sets off for the flux and freedom of the open sea.

Although *Foreign Land* subverts the expatriate tradition by depicting England as the place where an outsider abandons his normal pattern of behavior, Raban relies at times on Africanist clichés that link Africa with corruption. George returns to a licentious, squalid, and death-filled England that shocks him after the peaceful life he has enjoyed in Africa. Nevertheless, Raban presents Africa as the source of George's decay. It is not the physical decay of the continent, however, that ultimately affects George; rather, it is the official corruption of the New Africa. George's bank account is just one symptom of a much broader phenomenon. Upon ascending to power, the once honorable Aristide Varbosa becomes a vain and greedy leader. His need to be flattered plunges Montedor into a political crisis after George leaves the country, cutting George off from the place he considers home.

Raban's awareness of language somewhat mitigates his clichéd portrayal of Africa. He makes ineffectual communication and the deterioration of language two of his major motifs and thematizes the effect of Africanist discourse. Not only does George find himself unable to get in touch with Montedor after he learns of the crisis, but he and his daughter continue to talk at cross purposes after his return to England. Moreover, throughout the book George sports a baseball cap that gradually loses all of the letters of its logo. Graffiti and verbal abuse bombard him in London, and in St. Cadix he cannot understand the language of contemporary England: the jargon of television. More important, Raban depicts Africanist discourse's influence on an informed and sympathetic Westerner. At the Royal St. Cadix Yacht Club someone points out to George a badly jumbled two-paragraph newspaper account of the trouble in Montedor. At first George responds with skepticism, weighing the article against his firsthand knowledge of Montedor: "George's anxiety gave way to petulance: what did they mean—'a *small* West African state'? It was twice as big as England" (135). Later, however, the story begins to influence George's attitude toward Montedor. Doubts about his former home cause George to compose a letter to his Montedoran lover as if it were "an anonymous ransom note":

No one tampered with anybody's letters in the Montedor that George knew. But the country of the Sunday Telegraph report was not the one he knew: the scary thing about those two scrambled paragraphs was the way they made Montedor sound just like any other flimsy, tarpaper Third World state—a cockleshell nation that would capsize at a puff of wind from the wrong quarter. He'd been to places like that and knew how appallingly quickly they tipped over: one morning you woke to shooting in the streets; in a week you'd got used to the sight of men you'd once met being blind-folded for their public executions in the sandy town square. But not—surely—in Montedor? Please not in Montedor. (137)

The last two sentences of this passage recall George's earlier response to the account of the Irish prisoners in H-block—"In Britain? Surely not." In both cases language objectifies people, treats them like exotic species, distances and dehumanizes them. Significantly, the West and not Africa bears responsibility for this corrupt use of language. Although Raban cannot completely divorce himself from Africanist discourse, he actively reverses its binary oppositions and thematizes its effects. In the end, Montedor may be just another corrupt African country on the brink of civil war. Raban illustrates that England can be viewed the same way. It is all a matter of perspective and the language one chooses.

Maria Thomas

Antonia Saw the Oryx First

Maria Thomas first went to Africa in 1971. She spent twelve years there, and learned to speak several African languages. In 1989, she died tragically in the plane crash that also killed Congressman Mickey Leland. The structure of her novel *Antonia Saw the Oryx First* (1987) makes it unique among books by non-blacks about Africa. Instead of focusing on an outsider's encounter with the continent, Thomas divides her attention equally between a white and a black protagonist. Moreover, her book subverts the expatriate tradition, not by depicting the decline of an outsider who comes in contact with a corrupt first-world environment, as Raban does in *Foreign Land*, but rather by portraying a Westerner going native in Africa in a positive way. In addition, Thomas's metaconsciousness exceeds that of Raban. She openly decries Africanist attitudes and blames them for isolating whites and blacks from each other. However, in thematizing the separation between the races, she reinforces Africanist oppositions. Paradoxically, *Antonia Saw the Oryx First* attacks Africanist thinking profoundly yet frequently echoes such Africanist writers as Elspeth Huxley and Beryl Markham.

Second-generation postwar writers such as Paul Theroux, V. S. Naipaul, Martha Gellhorn, and John Updike shifted the focus of fictional works about Africa away from tragic white male heroes like

Kurtz and Scobie. Maria Thomas goes a step further in *Antonia Saw the Oryx First*, which concerns a white American woman (Antonia Redmond) and a black African woman (Esther Moro). The novel's rather arcane title actually holds the key to its organization and to an important link between the dual protagonists. Like the bull oryx Antonia saw as a child with "horns so straight and balanced it seemed he had only one, a unicorn,"[4] the novel's structure is an optical illusion. The first six chapters alternate between Antonia and Esther; soon, however, their lives become so intertwined that each of the remaining chapters involves both women. Moreover, seeing the oryx first represents saving life, a purpose to which both Antonia, who is a doctor, and Esther, who becomes a faith healer, devote themselves. By spotting the oryx before her father and the other male hunters on a trip to Ethiopia, Antonia spared the animal's life because of Bill Redmond's personal code dictating that he not kill the first animal he sees.

After meeting one another in Dar es Salaam as a result of searching for their lost fathers, Antonia and Esther assist one another in their quests for wholeness. Bill Redmond was a coffee farmer who loved Africa. Despite bureaucratic difficulties, Antonia remains in the continent partially out of fealty to her father's memory. Esther's father, Mumsumbi, at one time an assistant to a German doctor, had grown to despise what he saw as African ignorance, preferring Western methods and technology. After Mumsumbi's death, a male relative arranges for Esther to become the youngest wife of a rich man who lives far away from her native people. Recalling her father's lectures against African customs, Esther hides her menstruation and then flees from her husband's village to escape circumcision. Ironically, while she works as a prostitute in Dar es Salaam, a Greek sailor brutally performs the same operation on Esther with a broken Ouzo bottle. Antonia is the doctor who treats her when she is brought to the hospital. After they meet, the women play a major role in each other's search for a sense of completeness. Antonia feels dispossessed of her past and hopes that by staying on in Africa she can somehow recover it. Similarly, as a result of her mutilation, Esther longs to be whole again. Her mistreatment at the hands of African institutions and Western rapacity enables her to empathize with others who suffer and work for their recovery as well as her own.

Previous works in the expatriate tradition depicted a corrupt environment undermining the morals or the sanity of an outsider; in contrast, *Antonia Saw the Oryx First* portrays going native in a positive way. Antonia's submission to Africa takes place in four stages:

she strives for a resolution to the alienation she feels in the continent; she enters into a relationship with Esther based on mutual respect and need; she learns the truth about Africanist thinking and her profession; and she briefly regains the ability to experience emotion.

Like other expatriates in fiction about postcolonial Africa, Antonia experiences powerlessness, flux, and alienation. Most whites have left the country, but Antonia remains, believing that she has something to work out between herself and the continent where she was born. Antonia regards her life as "a contract she had made before the real costs were known. She was developing a capacity to drift on events as they came, as though her sense of right and place were all in a state of flux and her surrender to the flow a form of victory in itself, the character of expatriate life now that there were no solid empires holding things up. Nothing but a chaos of international politics that had no root in what was real. She believed there was still a bargain to be made, a deal, a way to catch up with what had been taken from her own history" (7–8). In previous works in the expatriate tradition, succumbing to the unregulated forces of Africa foreshadows disaster. Here, however, it is a positive step, enabling Antonia to become friendly with Esther and eventually understand her own feelings of isolation.

Rather than Esther becoming just one more patient Antonia has treated, a relationship develops between them. At first it appears that Antonia is counseling Esther so she can mentally recover from her wounds. In time, however, it becomes clear that Antonia needs Esther as much or more than she needs Antonia. Esther associates Antonia with her medically trained father. In a semiconscious state after Antonia has tried to save her, Esther longs to reach out to Antonia: "She wanted to know the white doctor and the things the white doctor knew, a kind of sharing, moving arm in arm, so close that secrets passed outside of language through the rubbing of the skin and the contact of the hair" (33). Significantly, Esther seeks communion with Antonia beyond language.

Antonia finds herself increasingly involved in Esther's life. After she is released, Esther starts coming to visit Antonia at the hospital, at first claiming that Antonia has put frogs in her blood through a transfusion but later coming just to talk. In turn, upon learning that Esther is sick, Antonia takes a taxi to Mikrosheni, gets custody of Esther when the police arrest her for prostitution, and becomes the object of gossip at the hospital because of their relationship. During their discussions the link between the two women becomes clearer:

"They were both attracted to something in the raveling themes of sickness and healing and the nature of men, like wobbling reflections in a sideshow mirror—this black village girl and the white doctor" (120–21). Esther tells Antonia she is drawn to people who suffer and has tried to heal them; she expresses her desire to be a doctor or a nurse, vowing to learn to read and write so she can become educated about medicine. In addition, Esther starts giving a crippled boy a kind of water therapy that leaves him more flexible and eventually enables him to walk again. She informs Antonia of this success at the same time that the doctor's frustrations with the hospital's poor standards have reached their peak. Instead of discouraging Esther, Antonia congratulates her, becomes closer to her than ever before, and symbolically blesses Esther's inchoate career as a faith healer: "Perhaps it was wrong, but there was less reason to urge her into a nurse's uniform, even if she did manage to read and write, so she could blunder around the wards in a place like this killing old men. No, it was better somehow for Esther to be where she was, doing what she was doing. It was the reason, because Antonia had caught her euphoria, that she had reached for her hand, out on the port road, two women with a secret, daring the world. To the very last touch of fingers at arms' length. An African good-bye" (160).

In addition to developing a meaningful relationship with an African, Antonia begins to question the methods and efficacy of her Western medical training. Her approach to healing differs greatly from Esther's and increasingly the white doctor regards her own methods as inadequate. Rather than touching people as Esther does, Antonia is cut off from her patients, her hands encased in rubber gloves. Like Naipaul's Salim, with Africans she has always felt "a part of them apart: a ghost who was immune, not only physically to whatever was being suffered out there, but in her heart" (37). Antonia has the intellect to be a doctor but she wonders whether she has the emotion: "She couldn't remember having the compulsion to heal the sick the way Esther did, never had been moved that way by the sound of the world coughing, or the sight of its blood. Technician, even in life" (165). Whereas Esther wants to learn more about the mystery of disease, why some people suffer while others do not, everything is black and white to Antonia, explainable through science. As she tries to establish the validity of Esther's healing, Antonia cannot break out of her scientific way of looking at things; she is "someone who had to see to believe, someone spiritually hemmed in by the burdens of proof" (181).

Although Esther drops out of Antonia's life when she travels around the country healing people, Antonia follows her exploits in the paper and, before leaving Africa, sets out to find her former patient "as if Esther were unfinished business, the only thing she had to tidy up before she broke away" (255). After talking with people who have witnessed Esther's healing, Antonia meets her at a former colonial hotel, called the Lawns. Here Esther's recovery becomes complete and Antonia realizes the truth about her sense of separation from the continent where she was born. Previously, despite the joy that healing people gives Esther, she has felt incomplete because she has never become pregnant. She has regarded herself as less than a woman, barren because the sailor slashed her. Looking at herself in the full length mirror of the hotel, Esther imagines herself pregnant and notices for the first time that she has in fact become whole again: "Something strong informed her, beyond memory; she could see her own healing now that her friend had come, what she had been promised that morning when she woke receiving the stranger's blood. Parts had come together, easy to see in the glass, her whole nakedness. She would not have dared to look before, but here the long mirror would not be refused" (286).

Unlike Esther, Antonia does not gain a sense of completeness as a result of their final encounter; nevertheless, she learns the truth about herself and experiences emotion for the first time in years. The explanation for Antonia's alienation lies in her Africanist attitudes, which, despite her attempts to dissociate herself from the outlook of other outsiders, were instilled in her early and cannot be overcome. Antonia is aware of Africanist thinking in others, particularly writers, and condemns them for it. During her moment of deep despair over the inefficiency at the hospital, she reflects bitterly on those who come to Africa for brief periods and then depict it as hopeless: "she could see the smug faces of those who observed Africa out of hotel windows, from behind their cameras, in their reports. Telling the world how it was sad, but true: things had been better in the colonial days" (159). Later, when government harassment of outsiders intensifies, Antonia adopts a "placid paranoia" but strives to avoid the Africanist pronouncements of those who write about the continent: "It was all you could do, save making excuses for yourself or your kind, or even for Africa. Other misanthropic types—travel writers, researchers, reporters, advisers, developers—found it entertaining to watch their dire predictions of ruin come true. Offering the evidence. There was that king, Bokassa. . . . After the coup, his enemies found human babies in deep freeze, trussed up as roasts. There were massacres in Burundi, in Guinea-Bissau. Dead children in the streets of Addis Ababa. There was Idi Amin" (248).

More than just attempting to avoid Africanist ways of thinking, Antonia begins to see that her methods of healing people are just as ritualistic as those of the *waganga*, the witch doctors. As she loses faith in her ability to help people, she recalls an anthropologist's description of native medicine, written in "a detached documentary tone reserved by those determined not to patronize or prejudice" (251). In the book the nonsensical methods of the healers speak for themselves. Antonia laughs when she thinks how the anthropologist would depict her methods of treating people, "using his uninflected prose to describe the rituals of technology, the intrusive tests, the painful medications, the diagnostic stabs in the dark, the death at last, at her hands, mired in another kind of myth, another kind of blindness" (252). By portraying England as a "foreign land" in his reversal of the expatriate tradition, Raban illustrates the effect that language and perspective can have. Here Antonia realizes that with the proper approach and method of description both Western and native medicine can be made to appear ridiculous.

Antonia discovers that her profession is at base Africanist when she finds Esther at the Lawns. Coming back to the colonial hotel, Antonia unwittingly returns to the place where her desire to be a doctor originated. Still unconvinced of Esther's gift, Antonia thinks of all the operations she has performed. She has never doubted that her own methods were the ones best suited to help the patient. These thoughts lead her to remember an amputation she witnessed at the hotel when she was a child: "Nothing had ever made her think that this was not all there was to it. Or that stunned, staring at a child's rotting hand, she had watched an English woman cut it off and believed that somehow, in that violent act, she had taken charge against the chaos. An act Antonia had performed so many times herself since then" (270). Antonia realizes that her career and Western medicine in general are based on an Africanist mentality. According to Thomas, the intention of both is not to reach out and soothe Africans in pain but rather to stop the infection of Africa from spreading to the West. Confronted with a seriously ill patient a short time later, Antonia feels inadequate without the gadgets and technology of her trade; neither she nor Western medicine can offer anything human to this man: "Without her tools, her medications, her knives, she was helpless as a doctor, stripped bare like the emperor in the children's story who had been tricked to nakedness" (285). Thomas implies that Antonia feels doubly exposed because she can no longer hide behind her Africanist illusions.

The final stage of Antonia's going-native process occurs when she succeeds momentarily in experiencing emotion and perceiving a reality beyond that explicable by Western science. Neither Esther nor Antonia has been able to help Nkosi, Esther's companion who lies dying at the Lawns. With no faith in her own ability to save him, Antonia starts to believe in Esther's powers. At the same instant that Nkosi dies, Antonia has a vision of him walking outside of the hotel. She is uncertain about how to regard what she has seen, wondering "what emotions had called it up, in time to join her with his death?" (290). Although as a result of this vision Antonia understands Esther better than she had before, she nevertheless regards the barriers between them as insurmountable. While Esther stays to aid the "sick ones," Antonia returns to the United States.

Despite subverting the expatriate tradition, attacking Africanist attitudes, and indicting Western medicine as Africanist, *Antonia Saw the Oryx First* reinforces binary oppositions that isolate Africans and non-Africans. Thomas's dual focus represents an innovation within the expatriate tradition, but she nonetheless relies on a standard Africanist opposition in making Esther's search for wholeness physical and Antonia's spiritual. Moreover, the novel frequently echoes earlier Africanist works, particularly on the subject of separation between the races. In addition to alluding to Churchill, Conrad, Gide, and Hemingway, Thomas depicts Esther reiterating Elspeth Huxley's assertion about separate worlds for blacks and whites and patterns Antonia's childhood on Beryl Markham's. Esther's sense of two worlds, "side by side" (20), recalls Huxley's assessment of the colonial situation in Kenya as "two worlds [that] revolved side by side," which she compares to the two arms of an egg beater whirling independently but never touching.[5]

Likewise, the choice of Markham as a model for Antonia reinforces the notion of separation. Like Markham, Antonia used to play with African children, meet their families, and eat their food. She also had a close relationship with her father's servant Sayid "Until she was too big. Until he called her 'memsaab' " (131). Here, Thomas paraphrases one of the most significant passages of *West with the Night*. In it Markham equates the end of her childhood with the realization of the economic and racial hierarchy in colonial Kenya. Kibii, her childhood playmate, returns to her to ask for work, addressing her not as "Beru" (Beryl) but "Memsahib."[6] Through these echoes of earlier Africanist texts, Thomas makes the final separation between her protagonists seem inevitable.[7] As with Winternitz and Raban, relying on the established traditions of writing about Africa causes Thomas to repeat certain Africanist clichés.

Even though Thomas reverts to Africanist oppositions in *Antonia Saw the Oryx First,* her novel makes a profound statement about the barrier Africanist discourse presents to communion between Africans and non-Africans. Antonia has learned that her Africanist attitudes have cut her off from Africa but sees no way to remedy the situation. Despite all the progress she has made toward reducing the alienation she feels in Africa, Antonia gives up short of true communion with the continent and its people. While Esther seeks to reach people beyond language, Antonia is too bound by language to imagine an existence outside of it.

J. G. Ballard

The Day of Creation

Like the other members of the third generation, J. G. Ballard in *The Day of Creation* (1987) consciously acknowledges the tradition in which he writes. He thematizes Africanist discourse, yet relies on many of the basic gestures of writing about Africa found in earlier writers. In this fantasy, Ballard examines the obsessional nature of Africanist discourse and argues that its impact in television and films outstrips that of printed sources. Despite this metaconsciousness, however, Africanist oppositions, the notion of blankness, and the imposition of images and fictions upon the continent pervade the novel. Winternitz, Raban, and Thomas strive to dismantle Africanist discourse by actively subverting the traditions in which they write but occasionally revert to Africanist clichés as a result of writing in the established traditions. In contrast, because of his fascination with obsessions, Ballard chooses to explore the Africanist mentality in *The Day of Creation,* using many of the basic gestures of Africanist discourse to do so.

The protagonist and narrator, Dr. Mallory, is a World Health Organization employee stationed at Port-la-Nouvelle, a small town in the northern province of an arid Central African republic. After dreaming one night of a great river inundating the Sahara, he devotes himself to an irrigation project that he hopes will make his vision a reality. Later, an African working under his command dislodges an old oak tree and a pool of water appears. The pool grows into a stream, connecting up with a major waterway, created as a result of an earthquake that occurred two hundred miles away. Mallory nevertheless claims that he created the river, names it after himself, and regards it as a part of his own body.

Both the river and a twelve-year-old girl called Noon become obsessions for Mallory. Absurdly claiming that the river has destroyed his irrigation plans, Mallory wants to strangle it. He steals an old car ferry and sets off for the source, accompanied by Noon and Professor Sanger, a myopic documentary filmmaker. Chased by the police, malnourished, and diseased, Mallory and his crew travel through a changed environment until they reach a polluted town that serves as the headquarters of the guerrilla movement. Bent on destroying his namesake, Mallory convinces the movement's leader to dam the river, an act that coincides with the river's decline. As the river dies, Mallory has a change of heart, sailing to the river's source in an attempt to save it only to witness the final spring run dry.

The Day of Creation—unlike *Tarzan of the Apes, Henderson the Rain King,* and *The Coup*—clearly and frequently announces itself a fantasy. From the beginning Mallory's talk about his dreams, his readiness to admit that his obsession colors his interpretation of reality, and other characters' doubts about his ability to distinguish what is actually happening from what is going on inside his head make it clear that the work belongs to the realm of the fantastic. This impression becomes reinforced at the end of the novel when Mallory suggests that what he has just narrated may not have taken place. Moreover, while Ballard's book echoes the work of a number of Africanist authors, notably Conrad and Flaubert, it specifically acknowledges its predecessors in the fantasy tradition. Not only does Mallory share Elleloû's "dream of a green Sahara" and refer to himself as a "rain-king," but an entranced Noon watches videotapes supplied by Sanger of 1940s Hollywood melodramas depicting "a female Tarzan, played by a statuesque Texas blonde, . . . leading the cowed villagers against a gang of slave-traders."[8]

As in so many of his earlier fantasy works, in *The Day of Creation* Ballard investigates an obsessive personality. Mallory's Africanist mentality is a perfect subject for such an analysis. Much of the protagonist's manic journey can be read as an allegory of European colonialism in Africa. Like many of the Victorian explorers who preceded him, Mallory dreams of leaving his mark on Africa. By "creating" the river, Mallory compares himself with God, often evoking the Bible to describe his exploits: "I sensed around me the atmosphere of a new world. I breathed the fresh, Edenic air, almost believing that I had planted and watered a forgotten corner of the original Creation garden" (55). In addition, Mallory imagines himself and Noon as Adam and Eve and sets about "the naming of new things." Not content with taking credit for creating the river, Mallory wants it named after himself and even leases it for one thousand dollars from the local police captain so he can officially own it.[9]

Mimicking the European colonialists, Mallory believes his exploits also make him a great philanthropist. His river has cured the people "of their malaise, and irrigated their arid lives" (82). Once the river has flooded the Sahara, the doctor sees himself becoming "the third world's greatest benefactor" (101). Moreover, Mallory claims he has created prepubescent Noon, the erstwhile guerrilla who has a special affinity with the river: "Seeing her, I was almost certain that I had thrown my spit on to the ground and created the river, which in turn had given life to this child" (108).

Despite his avowed desire to be the creator of a new world, Mallory sets out almost immediately to destroy the river. He regards it as an enemy with whom he is dueling. The contradiction between the doctor's intentions and his actions is aptly conveyed in the oxymoronic title Noon gives Mallory: "Doc Mal," the physician of disease. Like so many Westerners who came to Africa supposedly to help the people only to harm them, Mallory brings garbage and sickness to the people via the river. Mallory readily admits the irrationality of his behavior, blaming it on his obsession: "I had become so obsessed with myself that I had seen the Mallory as a rival, and measured its currents against my ambition. Like a child, I had wanted to destroy the river, afraid that I could not keep all of it to myself" (231).

In one section of the novel, Ballard stresses the textual nature of the fantasy environment that results from the new waterway. The doctor terms a flock of birds "cryptic letters of a stylised alphabet," which he interprets as a warning from the river's source (150). A fisherman punting his outrigger resembles "a painted stroke on a Chinese scroll" (151), while the wriggling form of a snake in the beak of an egret covers the air "with a calligraphy of pain" (152). However, Ballard regards Africanist discourse found in film rather than in print sources as the most powerful.

Along with medicine and garbage, celluloid is the major Western export to Ballard's Africa. As boundless as Mallory's Africanist obsessions and egotism are, video proves itself even more formidable by stripping Mallory of his "creations": the river and Noon. As oxymoronic as "Doc Mal," the blind filmmaker Professor Sanger espouses the disturbing philosophy that eventually "everything turns into television" (57). Telling Mallory "you may already be the subject of a new documentary about a man who invents a river," Sanger mentally films the doctor's journey up river. Because of Mallory's "physical and moral decline," the professor regards this as a classic going-native story and interprets the physician's wish to destroy the river as "an attempt to destroy television's image of the world" (157). In addition, once Noon sees Sanger's videotapes of Hollywood films, Mallory must relinquish to the filmmaker the "education" of the child he believes he created. Video also vitiates Mallory's sole sexual encounter with Noon, a surreal, fever-colored scene that occurs in stuttering light resembling "the silver flicker of old arcade peep shows" (222).

At the end of the novel, Sanger's usurpation of Mallory's dreams becomes complete. After the river dies, Mallory is carried downstream by its final wave accompanied by Sanger, who provides a documentary voiceover. The doctor uses the language of film to describe what he witnesses on the trip back to Port-la-Nouvelle: "As we lay in the metal shell we saw the whole process of creation winding down to its starting point like a reversed playback of Sanger's imaginary documentary about my quest for the Mallory's source" (253). Confirming video's powerful influence, Mallory can only recall his adventure through Sanger's documentary rendition of it: "I remember our journey to the Mallory's source in terms of Sanger's imaginary travelogue. That alone seems to give meaning to all that took place" (253). By implicitly arguing that television and film represent the most subtle and effective forms of Africanist discourse, Ballard echoes Kwame Nkrumah's assertion that Hollywood and the mass media help the West dominate Africa.[10]

In his exploration of the Africanist mentality, Ballard relies on many of the basic gestures of Africanist discourse. The entire novel follows an emptiness-fullness, dream-nightmare, life-death pattern. Mallory regards Port-la-Nouvelle as a blank location, "the dead heart of the African continent, a land as close to nowhere as the planet could provide" (16), upon which he is fated to impose his fictions. From the beginning, however, the doctor's vision of a river bringing life to the dying Sahel seems destined to become a disaster: "The *dream* of a green Sahara, perhaps named after myself, that would feed the poor of Chad and the Sudan, kept me company in the ramshackle trailer where I spent my evenings after the long drives across the lake, hunting the underground contour lines on the survey charts that sometimes seemed to map the profiles of a *nightmare* slumbering inside my head [emphasis added]" (15–16). Although the Mallory changes the environment and brings large amounts of water to people who have had to struggle for it, because of the disease and pollution the river brings, it quickly becomes a "bad dream" and a "poisoned paradise." Moreover, by the time Mallory approaches the river's source, the once life-giving waterway resembles a "leaking cadaver" flowing through the "gutter of a vast natural abattoir."

Although Ballard's purpose in *The Day of Creation* differs from that of the other members of the third generation, like them he acknowledges the tradition in which he writes and offers a critique of the Africanist mentality. More than any previous author he stresses the powerful effect Africanist discourse has on outsiders and Africans through television and films. However, by choosing to write in the fantasy tradition, Ballard often relies on the basic conventions of Africanist discourse.

Despite their metaconsciousness, all of the third-generation postwar writers make use of Africanist clichés to a certain extent. Even though they acknowledge or subvert the traditions in which they write, these codified ways of depicting Africa are so steeped in Africanist discourse that the authors occasionally must use its basic gestures. The authors of the fourth category realize that to eliminate Africanist clichés from their writings, they must completely abandon the established traditions. Therefore, they go a step beyond the third generation, recognizing that to render Africa accurately the story of the West's development of the continent must be reconceptualized and rewritten.

NOTES

1. In the late 1980s, as a solution to the Angolan civil war began to look increasingly probable, the United States's support for the Zairian leader waned. The recent unrest in Zaire and Mobutu's inability to quell it stem in part from the refusal of Western governments to continue to bolster the president's notoriously corrupt regime.

2. Helen Winternitz, *East along the Equator*, New York: Atlantic Monthly, 1987, 7. Subsequent references are to this edition.

3. Jonathan Raban, *Foreign Land*, New York: Penguin, 1986, 23. Subsequent references are to this edition.

4. Maria Thomas, *Antonia Saw the Oryx First*, New York: Soho, 1987, 262. Subsequent references are to this edition.

5. Elspeth Huxley, *The Flame Trees of Thika*, New York: Penguin, 1986, 154.

6. Beryl Markham, *West with the Night*, San Francisco: North Point, 1983, 149.

7. In this respect, the end of the novel resembles the parting of Aziz and Fielding at the conclusion of Forster's *A Passage to India*. For a discussion

of the significance of that final scene within colonial literature, see Abdul JanMohammed, "The Economy of Manichean Allegory: The Function of Racial Difference in Colonialist Literature," *Critical Inquiry* 12 (Autumn 1985): 59–87.

8. J. G. Ballard, *The Day of Creation*, New York: Farrar, 1988, 15, 208, 158. Subsequent references are to this edition.

9. There may also be a New Testament reference in the names of Mallory's two companions: "Noon" suggests the Arabic for bread; "Sanger" derives from the French word for blood.

10. Kwame Nkrumah, *Neo-Colonialism: The Last Stage of Imperialism*, London: Nelson, 246. See also p. 78 above.

5

Genealogical Rewriting of Suppressed History and Silenced Voices

Nobody, up to now, has doubted that the "good" man represents a higher value than the "evil," in terms of promoting and benefiting mankind generally, even taking the long view. But suppose the exact opposite were true. What if the "good" man represents not merely a retrogression but even a danger, a temptation, a narcotic drug enabling the present to live at the expense of the future? More comfortable, less hazardous, perhaps, but also baser, more petty—so that morality itself would be responsible for man, as a species, failing to reach the peak of magnificence of which he is capable? What if morality should turn out to be the danger of dangers?

—Friedrich Nietzsche, *The Genealogy of Morals*

Third-generation postwar writers recognized the distorting effects of the established traditions of writing about Africa and sought to mitigate them by acknowledging or subverting the traditions. Despite such efforts, however, the Africanist clichés deeply embedded in the political assessment, expatriate, and fantasy traditions often emerged at some point in these works. The writers of the fourth category, also comprised of works written in the 1980s, adopt more radical means of responding to Africanist discourse. Abandoning the established traditions, William Boyd, T. Coraghessan Boyle, Peter Dickinson, and William Duggan engage in what can be seen as a genealogical rewriting of the history of the West's relationship with Africa. Rather than attempting to depict contemporary Africa, as the third generation of postwar writers do, the authors of the fourth category reexamine and reconceive the West's relationship with Africa, either focusing on a specific historical era or incident, such as exploration, colonial administration, and the European importation of war to the continent, or utilizing a longer perspective by depicting the impact of Western influences on a specific group of Africans over a three-hundred-year period.

In varying degrees, the works of the fourth category amount to exercises in Nietzschean *wirkliche Historie* rather than traditional history. In "Nietzsche, Genealogy, History," Michel Foucault describes the difference between the two: "The former transposes the relationship ordinarily established between the eruption of an event and necessary continuity. An entire historical tradition (theological or rationalistic) aims at dissolving the singular event into an ideal continuity—as a teleological movement or a natural process. 'Effective history,' however, deals with events in terms of their most unique characteristics, their most acute manifestations."[1] The novels of the fourth category search for *Herkunft* or descent, a strategy, according to Foucault, that "is not the erecting of foundations"; instead, "it disturbs what was previously considered immobile; it fragments what was thought unified; it shows the hetereogeneity of what was imagined consistent with itself" (147). Rather than accepting and building upon the Africanist image of Africa and Africans embedded in the established traditions of writing about Africa, as was done by first-, second-, and third-generation postwar writers, authors of the fourth category abandon these traditions, seize upon incidents overlooked by Africanist writers, and even rewrite quintessential Africanist texts. While all the works by writers of the fourth category go back into history for their subject matter, far from being historical novels, they possess a non-Africanist perspective and/or methodology specific to and unavailable before the 1980s.

A transitional work bridging the gap between second-generation postwar writing and that of the fourth category, William Boyd's *An Ice-Cream War* (1982) lampoons whites in Africa in a manner similar to *A Good Man in Africa*. Instead of focusing on postcolonial Africa, however, Boyd's second African novel concerns the First World War in Africa. Britain, and to a lesser extent Belgium and Portugal, did battle against the Germans in an arduous, senseless, and at times farcical struggle across what are now Kenya, Tanzania, Mozambique, and Zambia that actually outlasted the fighting in Europe. In a reversal of the expatriate tradition, Boyd depicts the war as a madness imposed upon Africa by Europe.

T. Coraghessan Boyle employs more radical techniques in *Water Music* (1981), rewriting the experiences of Mungo Park. Because of his position in the history of European exploration of Africa and the uncertainty surrounding various aspects of his *Travels*, the choice of Park is significant. One of the earliest and most renowned African explorers, the first white man to see the fabled Niger, Park generated great interest in Africa among Europeans, prompting further exploration that tipped the balance of power in the region in favor of Europe and eventually lead to the establishment of England's first colony in West Africa. In addition, Park's life and particularly his death at Boussa have been a continual source of controversy. From the beginning there were rumors that Park did very little of the writing to be found in the account of his first trip in 1795. Moreover, the description of the last stage of his second journey was at best third-hand and has never been completely substantiated. The "writerly" aspects of Park's *Travels* and his life, to use Roland Barthes's term, clearly appealed to Boyle, who feels completely justified in being "deliberately anachronistic" in the novel.[2]

Peter Dickinson uses a double focus in *Tefuga* (1986). He devotes alternating chapters to the diary of the young wife of a British district commissioner in Northern Nigeria in 1924 and the filming of a movie about her life on location sixty years later under the direction of her son. Incomplete in themselves, the two narratives must be read together to get a true sense of what actually occurred in 1924 as well as since that time. Dickinson deftly equates Betty Jackland's struggle against male oppression with the struggle of the Africans against their British rulers; language and art become political acts serving the goals of both feminism and national liberation.

Whereas Boyd, Boyle, and Dickinson devote their attention to a single era or event and focus primarily on Europeans, William Duggan chooses to tell the story of a group of Africans from their first encounter with white men in the early 1700s until the present. The first two volumes of a projected trilogy, *The Great Thirst* (1985) and *Lovers of the African Night* (1987), depict the history of the BaNare people of Kalihariland. Duggan goes beyond any previous outside author writing about Africa by attempting to use African methods to tell an African story. Complete with family trees, his novels aspire to be written transcriptions of the oral history of the BaNare. Instead of writing a strictly linear, Western-style history of southern Africa, Duggan organizes *The Great Thirst* around the important members of BaNare society from the early eighteenth century through World War I and *Lovers of the African Night* around locations where significant events involving the BaNare occurred from the period between the world wars through the mid-1970s.

William Boyd

An Ice-Cream War

Like *A Good Man in Africa*, *An Ice-Cream War* depicts the efforts of whites in Africa as foolish and futile. However, whereas Boyd's first novel, faithful to the expatriate tradition, attributed the impossibility of positive, moral action to the corruption of contemporary Africa, his second portrays war as a madness and corruption that the Europeans import to Africa during the colonial era. The phrase "an ice-cream war" sums up the senselessness of an endeavor characterized by incompetence, lack of communication, mutilation, and death, in which even personal vendettas fail. There are neither heroes in Boyd's novel nor are there any significant African characters, even though Africans made up the majority of soldiers and suffered the highest numbers of casualties. Boyd presents the war as a predominantly white undertaking, with whites revealing themselves at their worst.

The main characters of Boyd's novel are the Cobb brothers, Gabriel and Felix. The former, a lieutenant in an Indian regiment, has to cut his honeymoon short when the war becomes imminent. After many delays he leads a platoon of ill-trained Indian soldiers with whom he cannot communicate into battle against the Germans at Tanga. Severely wounded and captured, Gabriel spends the war in a prisoner of war camp in the south of German East Africa. There he works as a hospital orderly, deliberately aggravating his wounds so he can stay on to gather information.

After unsuccessfully trying to enlist when the war starts, Felix goes to Oxford only to find it largely deserted except for men training to become officers. He enters into an affair with Gabriel's wife, Charis, who, wracked by guilt writes to her husband about her infidelity and then commits suicide. Tortured by guilt himself, Felix embarks on a mad plan: he joins the British forces in Africa in order to find Gabriel and prevent him from receiving Charis's letter. Shortly before Felix finally reaches Gabriel's camp, the latter flees, only to be pursued by Captain von Bishop, whose men misunderstand his orders and kill Cobb. After finding his brother's body, Felix vows revenge. At the conclusion of the fighting, he goes to von Bishop's house in Dar es Salaam to kill him, only to find that after surviving over four years of fighting the German has died of influenza.

After indicating the folly and futility of the war in Africa in his prologue, Boyd illustrates its horror and insanity through Gabriel's experiences at Tanga and Felix's participation in the British effort to drive their enemies out of German East Africa. The prologue consists of a genuine letter from a British soldier to his sister at the outbreak of the war. In it he repeats his lieutenant's prediction that "the war here will only last two months. It is far too hot for sustained fighting, he says, we will all melt like ice-cream in the sun."[3]

An important port near British East Africa, Tanga seemed a logical and easy target for England's first major attack on the Germans.

Instead, the invasion turned out to be an unqualified disaster. Because the Royal Navy had negotiated a truce with the Germans that the army was about to break, the British decided to inform their enemies of the plan to attack Tanga, giving the Germans an opportunity to reinforce the port that they had already written off. Even without the element of surprise the much larger British forces should have had little trouble taking Tanga. Poor intelligence, inadequate training, botched orders, mass desertions, friendly fire, and swarming bees, however, transformed a sure victory for the British into a rout by the Germans. Gabriel finds himself abandoned by his men, rashly shoots at a German patrol whose return fire kills his exposed corporal, and stumbles into enemy controlled territory, where he is repeatedly bayoneted and taken prisoner.

Felix's quest to find Gabriel parallels the quixotic British effort to encircle the much smaller and more mobile German forces whose goal was to hold out as long as possible. Fantasizing that he is Stanley gone in search of Livingstone, Felix tries to intercept Charis's letter, which has long been lost, and did not in fact mention him, as he feared. Having forded numerous swollen rivers, suffered through fevers, and barely survived on greatly reduced rations, Felix eventually catches up with Gabriel only to discover his decapitation at the hands of von Bishop's uncomprehending native soldiers. Through Felix's reflection on his experiences as a soldier, Boyd drives home the insanity of the war: "He realized that he'd been a soldier now for nearly two and a half years—since July 1916—and he had never fired a shot in anger. What kind of a war was it where this sort of absurdity could occur? . . . He knew that he was not responsible for the way events had turned out, that it was futile to expect that life could in some way be controlled" (368). Nevertheless, by plotting to kill von Bishop, Felix tries and fails one last time to settle a personal score in "this mad, absurd war."

Although the depiction of native soldiers mutilating Gabriel on two separate occasions might be seen as a perpetuation of the Africanist association of blacks with primitivism, Boyd shows that European incompetence and insanity ultimately bear responsibility for these acts as well as all of the other instances of mutilation, suffering, and death resulting from the war. British ineptitude brought about the wholesale slaughter at Tanga while von Bishop's inability to communicate with his scouts caused them to kill Gabriel. Moreover, Felix suffers a form of mutilation near the end of the war as a result of purely European stupidity. Assigned as an intelligence officer in Portuguese East Africa even though he cannot speak the

language, Felix nearly dies when his incompetent superior acci-
dently fires a shell in his direction.

To further emphasize the folly of the war the Europeans imposed
on Africa, Boyd eliminates heroism from his novel; survival becomes the highest ideal to which his characters can aspire. For this
reason, he largely ignores the German Commander, Colonel Paul von
Lettow-Vorbeck, whom historians have recognized as a brilliant tac-
tician for successfully thwarting and eluding a much larger and better equipped Allied fighting force for over four years. Boyd goes
even further, however, rewriting certain historical details to show
the Europeans in the worst possible light. In *On to Kilimanjaro*—an
account of the Great War in Africa based on the memoirs of participants and the British *Official History of the War*—Brian Gardner
portrays intelligence officer Captain R. Meinertzhagen as the only
British military man with the tactical expertise to rival Von Lettow-
Vorbeck.[4] To underscore the war's farcical aspects, Boyd not only incorporates some of the most bizarre details from Meinertzhagen's
account of the failed invasion at Tanga into his novel but he also
turns Meinertzhagen into Major R. Bilderbeck. Like Meinertzhagen,
Bilderbeck is an intelligence officer shocked by the British bungling
at Tanga; however, Boyd portrays him as a cruel and eccentric fa-
natic, who, rather than being invalided home like Meinertzhagen,
goes insane and is later found dead. According to the officer who replaces him, Bilderbeck "used to stand on the parapets of the
trenches at night yelling insults at the jerries. Then one night he
cracked. He was last seen sprinting off in the direction of the enemy,
waving his gun, screaming something about 'his girl' and how the
huns were preventing him from finding her" (311). Boyd emphasizes
that the war rather than Africa causes Bilderbeck to become "de-
ranged." In contrast to works in the expatriate tradition, such as
Boyd's first novel, which confirm Richard Burton's assertion that
"madness comes from Africa," Boyd's second novel depicts Europeans bringing the insanity of war to Africa.

In *An Ice-Cream War*, William Boyd eschews the second-postwar
generation's association of corruption and primitivism with Africa
and Africans. Similar to works of the third-postwar generation, he
reverses the expatriate tradition by depicting the First World War as
a madness Europeans imposed upon the African continent and its
people. Going beyond this approach by reexamining the history of
the West's relationship with Africa and thereby undermining certain
Africanist assumptions, Boyd engages in a new, genealogical kind of

outside writing about Africa, one which other authors will explore in even more radical ways.

T. Coraghessan Boyle

Water Music

Postmodern and antiheroic like *An Ice-Cream War*, T. Coraghessan Boyle's *Water Music* is far more innovative in its techniques and extreme in its political engagement. In his "Apologia" Boyle announces that the impetus behind his novel "is principally aesthetic rather than scholarly," allowing him to be "deliberately anachronistic," invent "language and terminology," and stray from his orginal sources: "Where historical fact proved a barrier to the exigencies of invention I have, with full knowledge and clear conscience, reshaped it to fit my purpose."[5] Depicting Mungo Park as a boor, adding perspectives that the explorer omitted, and reversing Africanist discourse, Boyle rewrites a germinal text that had a profound effect on European exploration, colonization, and objectification of Africa. Unlike Park's *Travels in the Interior Districts of Africa* (and most other Africanist texts), *Water Music* contains a fully realized African character and devotes much of its attention to lower-class English life, focusing principally on Ned Rise, the real hero of the novel.[6] In the process, Boyle demythologizes European "civilization," exposes Africanist writing as a fiction, and portrays Europe and Africa as equally corrupt.

The Scotsman's position in the history of the West's penetration of Africa and the writerly aspects of his life and work make Boyle's choice of Park significant. The timing of Park's expeditions, "at the end of the Age of Enlightenment and the beginning of the Age of Imbursement" (4), was pivotal. According to Peter Brent, "if it had not been for Europe's new wealth, for its increasing population and its exacerbated nationalism, it is unlikely that Mungo Park would have been on the Niger at all."[7] Park's two journeys into West Africa in 1795 and 1805 foreshadowed the power shift in the Sudan away from African rulers and toward Europeans that occurred during the nineteenth century. On his first expedition, privately bankrolled by the African Association, Park, along with two native guide/interpreters, traveled at the sufferance of African rulers, who occasionally harassed and imprisoned him. He succeeded in reaching the Niger but had to turn back soon afterward, returning to Gambia via a slave coffle. For his second trip, Park received financial support from the government, instructions from the colonial secretary, a military rank, and forty men from the garrison at Goree. Beset by bad weather, disease, bees, fires, and crocodiles, the explorer's party had dwindled to four men by the time they reached the Niger, down which they sailed until they were apparently killed at Boussa. Park's expeditions generated tremendous interest in Africa among Europeans. In "The Colonial Consequence," the final chapter of his book on the explorer, Brent asserts that British and French colonialism in West Africa and the continent as a whole "was the real conclusion" of Park's efforts (191).

The veracity of Park's *Travels* has always been open to dispute: the explorer may not have written the description of the first journey attributed to him, while that concerning the second is an incomplete, multivalent, and suspect document, comprising entries from Park's notebooks, the journal of one of his guides, and a hearsay account of the explorer's death at Boussa. J. Wishaw, who wrote a memoir of Park for the 1815 edition of the *Travels*, concludes that Bryan Edwards, a slaveholding friend of the explorer and the secretary of the African Association, "probably had a large share in composing" the account of Park's first expedition. Moreover, Wishaw disputes Park's glowing description, in a letter to Mrs. Park, of the men he recruited from Goree—who were mostly transported convicts—and concedes that "the circumstance of Park and Lieutenant Martyn leaping hand in hand with the soldiers into the river [at Boussa], is much too *theatrical* to be literally true."[8]

The facts relating to Park's demise have never been satisfactorily established. When Park had been missing for four years, Isaaco, the guide who had taken him to the Niger, investigated the explorer's fate, obtaining the journal of Amadi Fatouma, which eventually became the final section of *Travels*. According to Fatouma, the guide hired to lead Park down the river who departed from the explorer shortly before Boussa, eyewitnesses claimed that Park was ambushed and drowned. Certain aspects of Fatouma's story have been questioned. How were men from Yauri, who were at least a day behind Park's party, able to get ahead of them? Also, if the boat capsized at Boussa as Fatouma reports, how does one account for a book of Park's showing no signs of water damage being given to the Lander brothers when they visited there in 1830? Rumors of a white man living in the jungle reached England, intensifying speculation about Park that persisted even after the *Times* announced his death on 3 May 1819. Hugh Clapperton visited Boussa in 1825, finding the natives "uneasy" and "strangely evasive" when questioned about

Park. Compounding the mystery surrounding the explorer, in 1827 Park's oldest son Thomas set out from Accra in search of his father, never to be heard from again.[9]

Like a number of postcolonial novels set in Africa, *Water Music* features a powerless, incompetent, comical, white protagonist; Boyle's innovation is to go back in history and portray a heroic European explorer this way.[10] The novel begins with a moment of complete embarrassment for Park. During his month's captivity by the Moors at Benown, the ruler Ali treats Park like a freak, forcing him to appear naked before all the members of the court so they can appraise him. In this way Boyle subtly reverses Africanist discourse: rather than Park objectifying the Africans as in the *Travels*, the explorer becomes the foreign entity whom the Africans study. Park himself reflects on the difference between his expectations and the realities of exploration: "the explorer never dreamed it would be like this—so confused, so demeaning. And so hot. He had pictured himself astride a handsome mount, his coat pressed and linen snowy, leading a group of local wogs and half-wits and kings to the verdant banks of the river of legend. Yet here he is, not at the head, but somewhere toward the rear of the serpentine queue wending its way through all this parch, a prisoner for all intents and purposes, his horse wheezing and farting, his underwear binding at the crotch. Is there no sense of proportion in the world?" (64)

Instead of confirming the images of saintliness and superiority typically found in explorers' accounts of their experiences in Africa, Boyle's Park is a klutz. In a slapstick scene during his first journey, after falling from his horse, the explorer appears before Queen Fatima as an emissary of the British Crown covered with offal; then, entangling himself with some animals, he brings down half the tent and falls across Fatima. Similarly, in an episode that adumbrates future disasters, at the beginning of his second expedition Park loses his sea trunk ten minutes after landing at Goree.

In addition to turning Park into a bumbler, in a scene that partially explains the title of the novel, Boyle depicts the civilization of Europe as a thin veneer masking its corruption. After Park returns from his first trip, he attends a performance of Handel's *Messiah* and feels the words and music "washing him in the sweetness and light of civilization, whispering of precision and control, of the Enlightenment, of St. Paul's and Pall Mall, of the comfortable operation of cause and effect, statement and resolution." Park then contrasts these attributes of Europe with the "darkness," "chaos," and "barbarity" he endured in Africa. However, just at that moment the mad king,

George III, bursts Park's Africanist reverie, shouting down the singers and calling for "Water Music!" (99).

Boyle further illustrates Park's jejune civilization by depicting him as a savage and a crude racist during his second expedition. When an African is caught stealing from the explorer's coffle, Park momentarily thinks of the ideals associated with English civilization, asks himself "What in God's name am I doing?" and then shoots the unarmed man (355). Having led Park to the Niger for the second time, Johnson/Isaaco counsels Park as a friend not to travel down the river and warns him against Amadi Fatouma. The explorer responds by angrily shouting, "Get out, nigger!" (386).

In rewriting Park's *Travels*, Boyle includes voices omitted by the explorer. The author fuses the principal guides from Park's two journeys, adding copious biographical details, to produce a fully realized African character who not only knows both Europe and Africa but belongs as much to the late twentieth century as the early nineteenth. Boyle's character is a composite of Johnson, who accompanied Park for much of his first expedition, and Isaaco, the guide who led Park and his men to the Niger on the second.[11] Johnson has seen all sides of eighteenth-century black-white relations. A Mandingo born Katunga Oyo, he worked twelve years on a plantation in the Carolinas after being sold into slavery, served as his master's valet in England, where he acquired a classical education, a taste for literature, and in 1772 his freedom. In 1790 he was transported back to Africa for killing a racist in a duel. His varied experiences make him wiser, more tolerant, and more learned than the middle-class Park, whom he regards as a "half-witted, glory-hungry son of a crofter" (102).

Johnson's perspective is not only comprehensive but also contemporary, enabling him to see what Park cannot and providing the reader with ironic comments on Park's adventures. He recognizes the absurdity of Park's claim to be the first to solve the mystery of the Niger with an ancient African town all around him, equates the virgin birth and Jacob's Ladder with African superstitions, and translates the people's reactions to Park—for example, their belief that whites eat rather than enslave blacks because the latter never return. In addition, Johnson's language is filled with anachronisms, being a mixture of jive talk, Black English, and vocabulary beyond Park's comprehension. He calls Park "brother," uses the word *hon-kee* to describe the "harmless white man" to African rulers, and refers to the continent as the "heart of darkness" in an attempt to impress on Park the seriousness of native religious practices.

More important, Johnson plays a vital role in the relationship between history and fiction that is a recurrent theme in the novel. When it begins to appear to the members of the African Association that Park has failed in his quest to find the fabled river, they debate the authority of classical writers such as Herodotus and Pliny on the subject of the Niger. Sir Reginald Durfeys, Johnson's former master, cites the testimony of his erstwhile servant to support his belief that the Niger flows eastward, but is shouted down by the other members who will only accept white men as authorities. During the discussion, Lord Twit adopts a Nietzschean outlook, declaring "all our cherished histories . . . are at best a concoction of hearsay, thirdhand reports, purposeful distortions and outright fictions invented by self-aggrandizing participants and sympathizers" (98–99). Boyle portrays Park confirming Twit's assessment of history and perpetuating Africanist discourse. When Johnson reads a page from the explorer's notebook, he is shocked to find it "a distortion and a lie," telling Park, "you're suppose to be an explorer. The first white man to come in here and tell it like it is. A myth-breaker, iconoclast, recorder of reality. If you ain't absolutely rigorous, down to the tiniest detail, you're a sham" (121). Park replies that people do not want the truth: "When they read about Africa they want adventure, they want amaze. They want stories. . . . And that's what *I* intend to give them. Stories" (121–22).

Peter Brent notes that explorers were middle-class heroes, representatives of "a million armchair explorers" at a time when "much nearer at hand than in the tree shadowed interior of Africa lay another colonised and unconsidered nation, the nation of the labouring poor" (171). Through the character of Ned Rise, Boyle incorporates a lower-class perspective into *Water Music* and depicts Europe as ridden with disease, filth, poverty, perversion, and drug abuse. Rise also serves as an ironic double for Park and a parody of Christ, to whom many "saintly" explorers implicitly compare themselves. Because of his ability to survive, Rise eventually becomes the hero of the book, regarding Africa as a place to begin a new life instead of a place of death.

Boyle portrays Rise's existence as an unbroken chain of misery, cruelty, fraud, and drunkenness, more corrupt than anything to be found in Africa: "Not Twist, not Copperfield, not Fagin himself had a childhood to compare with Ned Rise's. He was unwashed, untutored, unloved, battered, abused, harassed, deprived, starved, mutilated and orphaned, a victim of poverty, ignorance, ill-luck, class prejudice, lack of opportunity, malicious fate and gin. His was a childhood so totally depraved even a Zola would shudder to think of it" (34). The hardships of growing up "like an aborigine" have taught Ned how to be cunning and how to survive. Early in the book he mounts a live sex show for London gentlemen featuring two English prostitutes and a male Congolese owned by Lord Twit. When the police raid the performance, Ned slips away, jumps into the icy Thames to elude the constables, survives being frozen solid, and is presumed dead by his enemies.

Ned's birth and his second "resurrection" link him ironically with Park and Christ. His mock nativity, complete with straw in a place nicknamed "The Holy Land," takes place the same year that Park is born. Similarly, Christmas 1797, the very day that Park returns to England from Africa after being thought long dead, Ned is hanged at Newgate flanked by two thieves for the murder of Lord Twit, only to miraculously come to life when surgeons try to dissect him. Other coincidences connect Park and Rise long before they meet in Goree, where Ned, a transported convict, becomes part of the explorer's second expedition. At the start of the novel, for example, a hungover Rise feels "a bit like an explorer setting foot on a new continent" after a night of debauchery (6), while Park feels "almost as if he'd drunk too much claret or gill-ale" as a result of being starved by the Moors (8).

During Park's second journey, Ned's ability to survive propels him to the forefront of the novel. In addition, his experiences with the corruption of Europe enable him to regard Africa in a non-Africanist way. Recognizing Park's incompetence after his friend Billy Boyles is killed, Ned realizes that everyone will die unless he takes charge. Ned is now "a man with a purpose, a man who would fight and scratch, manipulate and maneuver—a man who would survive" (334). As Park grows increasingly passive, Ned acts to save the lives of the small party, becoming de facto second in command and the explorer's confidant. Reflecting that Park would not have anything to do with him in London, Ned reconsiders his attitude towards Africa: "Homeless, fatherless, with neither prospects nor hope, Ned has begun to see this bleak, stinking, oppressive continent in a new light, as a place of beginnings as well as endings" (420).

In Boyle's reconception of Park's *Travels*, all of the explorer's enemies from both his journeys lie in wait for him and his party at Boussa. But rather than Park and his lieutenant going overboard hand in hand, Ned Rise and the explorer plunge into the river fighting over a pistol. Moreover, true to his name, Ned once again survives certain death, being taken in by pygmies with whom he shares a love for music. Responsible for the rumors about a white man alive in the jungle, Ned has escaped from the European "civilization" that produced and then hounded him, having found in Africa his kingdom on earth: "He was no outcast, no criminal, no orphan—he was a messiah" (435).

The postmodern era has produced many outside antiheroes in Africa but always in an Africanist context. Boyle breaks out of the trap, rewriting history and creating, despite his humor, exaggeration, irreverence, and scatology, a more authentic picture of Africa and African-European relations.

Peter Dickinson

Tefuga

Peter Dickinson calls *Tefuga* a "novel of suspense," but to characterize the book simply as a mystery would be to do it an injustice. Written from a feminist perspective and celebrating the power of language and imagination, this politically conscious novel not only rewrites the history of colonial administration and its consequences but explodes clichés about the corruption and violence of Africa commonly found in Africanist works. Structurally, *Tefuga* employs a dual focus. The eight even-numbered chapters come from a diary written between December 1923 and December 1924 by Betty Jackland, the young wife of a British district officer overseeing the Kiti region of northern Nigeria. The nine odd-numbered chapters describe the filming of Betty and her husband Ted's story on location sixty years later by their son, Nigel, for British television. In a statement that provides the key to Dickinson's novel, Elongo Sisefonge, Betty and Ted's former houseboy who now rules as Sarkin (emir of) Kiti, warns Jackland about judging Africans' motivations too quickly: "you may perceive certain facts about Nigeria, but unless you can also feel certain other facts you do not know the truth and have no right to pronounce. This is as true now as it was in your parents' day, for all your modern open-mindedness."[12] Jackland can "perceive" certain facts, but the capacity to "feel" certain other facts, which his mother possessed, is also needed to understand colonial and contemporary Nigeria. In its alternating chapters, *Tefuga* provides both ways of looking at things.

Through his feminist and political themes, Dickinson breaks down the barriers Africanist discourse erects between outsiders and Africans. The combination of Betty's description of the communion she feels with African women and the assertion of women's vast imaginative capacity by Mary Tressider (Nigel's current lover who plays his mother in the film) suggests the extent to which, in a white man's world, Betty is linked to the Africans. In addition, Betty's fresh-eyed, largely unbiased observations illuminate the ignorance and indecision informing British Indirect Rule while six decades later Nigel's efforts to make his film force him to come to grips with colonialism's enduring effects on Nigeria; seen together these two perspectives allow the reader to realize the political motivations behind the actions taken by the Kitawa while under British rule.

Having just recently married a much older man, partly to escape a difficult family situation, Betty comes to Kiti without clearly formed ideas about Africans or British colonialism. Recording information about Indirect Rule in Northern Nigeria in her diary as she learns it, she points out, often unconsciously, the system's flaws and contradictions. In contrast to the French, who tried imposing their culture on and took a more active military and administrative role in their African possessions, the British were undecided about attempting to change African culture and ruled through local political leaders, such as the hereditary emirs in Nigeria. Betty reports that British colonial officers, solely responsible for huge areas and subject to frequent relocations, rarely knew the languages of their subjects and often failed to understand the complicated system of alliances and rivalries existing among the people they ruled. Unaware of the special relationship between the emir in Kiti Town, a Hausa, and the numerically dominant Kitawa tribe, the British precipitate a number of crises over taxes in Kiti. Likewise, ignorant of the Kiti language, the colonialists are cheated out of revenue by the emir. Moreover, by projecting their own male-dominated system on the Kitawa, they underestimate the power that women have within the tribe.

Seen from Betty Jackland's perspective, the Elongo who works as her houseboy is an honest, caring African. Seen from Nigel Jackland's perspective sixty years later, the Elongo who served his parents was a spy planted by the Kitawa to gather information and thwart British efforts to rule the tribe. Similarly, viewed through Nigel's eyes, the Elongo who reigns as Sarkin Kiti is corrupt; however, if Betty were alive to observe her former servant, she would presumably find him a man who has selflessly devoted his life to his people. The truth about young and old Elongo, like that about colonial and contemporary Nigeria, lies somewhere between the two assessments or, more accurately, requires that a person adopt both perspectives at once.

The result of this dual focus—and of Dickinson's novel—is the reversal of Africanist discourse. On the one hand, subversive, politically motivated actions, such as Elongo's spying, demythologize the clichéd image of Africans as radically other, possessed by mysterious motivations. The Kitawa act out of a desire for freedom, something the British should be able to understand but which the conflict between their ideals and their imperialist aspirations does not allow them to acknowledge. In particular, by revealing the political reasons for the ritualistic murder of the new emir on Tefuga Hill, Dickinson exposes the Africanist association of Africans with primitivism as simplistic. On the other hand, Betty's ability to "feel" certain facts is also needed to counteract the oppositional tendency to regard Africans as anarchists and criminals. Although Elongo and Femora Fong deceive Betty, she never regards them as dishonest or duplicitous; she senses the genuine fear that prompts their actions and never doubts that their intentions are good.

Dickinson attacks Africanist discourse by breaking down the barriers separating Africans and outsiders during colonialism. Stressing the links between Betty Jackland and the Kitawa, he pinpoints white male oppression rather than African "primitivism" or inferiority as the cause for these barriers. Betty experiences several moments of communion with the Kitawa women, moments she cannot share with her husband, resulting from a special female affinity in the areas of creativity and imagination, which Mary Tressider as a performing artist of the 1980s also understands. However, Betty's links with the Kitawa are not limited to the women of the tribe. As a subjugated people, all of the Kitawa suffer under a form of oppression that resembles the one confronting white women in European society during the 1920s. It is with Elongo, the future leader of his people, and his "aunt" Femora Fong, the most charismatic and ultimately the most-powerful member of the Kitawa tribe, that Betty has the most in common.

With no other white person to talk with than her husband and no specific duties to perform, Betty channels her energies into creative endeavors—learning Kiti, painting, and writing. Each of these seemingly harmless activities, either consciously or unconsciously, becomes a tool in the Kitawa's and Betty's own struggle against oppression.

Because it is a difficult language spoken nowhere else, the British administrators have never bothered to learn Kiti, relying instead on the emir's assistants to translate for them. Desiring to make contact with people, Betty decides to learn it from Elongo, whom she in turn teaches English. Knowing Kiti gives Betty an advantage over Ted; she can speak with the Kitawa directly when the couple goes on tour. She delights in conversing with the local women who have their own female language, which they teach her. However, when one of the emir's men sends a Hausa guard to "protect" Betty, the women refuse to speak with her and Betty suspects the emir's people are trying to hide something. This is confirmed by Betty's clandestine encounter with Femora Fong who talks about the emir's brutality and claims that the Hausa are using the language barrier between the British and the Kitawa to exploit her people. While Ted dismisses these accusations, Betty gathers proof of the emir's monetary abuses. Aware that the Kitawa use a counting system based on twenties, encompassing toes as well as fingers, Betty discovers that the Hausa have used the British ignorance of this system to cheat them out of taxes.

When Ted approves of the armed-guard policy over her protestations, Betty begins to see herself as one of the oppressed, someone whose right to communicate freely has been abridged. Betty realizes that because of Ted's power, she, like the Kitawa, must understand her husband better than he does her: "It's his world, so it's the shape he makes it, and I have to fit into the bits left over, so I've got to understand where that is" (100). Gradually, Betty recognizes a parallel between the emir's domination of the Kitawa and Ted's control over her. The Kitawa themselves recognize the difference between Betty and her husband. When Femora Fong tells her she is "not the White Man," Betty is shocked at first but then reconsiders: "No, I am not a White Man. I am not. How extraordinary. I share more with this black savage who I'll probably never see again than I do with dear Ted, who I'm going to spend the rest of my life with" (151).

As with her communication skills, Betty's talents as an artist bring her closer to the Kitawa. An accomplished watercolorist, Betty initially paints to capture various sights for posterity and sharpen her skills. Soon, however, her art becomes a means of gaining access to forbidden areas, transmitting secret messages, and spurring people to action. After Elongo informs Betty that his sister has been stolen and made a member of the emir's harem, Betty succeeds in making contact with her by doing a painting of Kama Boi's palace. While capturing some of the emir's wives on paper as the others watch, Betty feels a powerful bond with them: "There was something there, working through me—not just me, all of us—a force, a spirit, something to do with us all being women. They gathered it, standing behind and around me, and then it came funnelling through me into the pictures I was painting, making them special. I don't believe, however much practice I have, I'll ever do anything as good as those sketches in my whole life" (51). The way these women are forced to live appalls Betty, who begins to see a connection between their lives and her own, and she resolves to do "something about KB and his wives" (57). To this end, she goes behind her husband's back, sending Bevis de Lancey, Ted's immediate superior and an art lover, a picture of a village not on the tax rolls in an attempt to expose Kama Boi's dishonesty, an act that initiates an investigation eventually leading to the emir's deposition.

More important, Betty's art provokes the Kitawa women to take drastic measures. Although the British now suspect there are villages that have not been paying taxes, their investigation fails to uncover any until Betty uses her painting, her fluency in Kiti, and her affinity with the Kitawa women to convince them to show her one of these "toe" villages. Like Betty, Femora Fong is a woman of great imagination who uses her art for political ends. In her desire to have Kama Boi removed, she fabricates the toe village, which Betty draws for de Lancey. Moreover, it is Femora Fong's dream that foretells the end of Kama Boi's reign and the subsequent ineffectiveness of British rule. Eventually all of the women of the tribe claim to have dreamt this dream and even Betty herself experiences it. Depicting the frightful images from this dream on paper, Betty forces a group of Kitawa women to take her to a nearby toe village.

In contrast to her picture of the dream, the final and most significant political consequence of Betty's artistic and language skills occurs without her willing it to happen. As the Kitawa women paint themselves for the ceremony on Tefuga Hill signifying the bond between the new emir, a twelve-year-old Hausa boy, and the Kitawa—a ceremony that has traditionally been sealed by a human sacrifice—Betty is drawn to them and asks whether she can make some sketches. The women deliberately, at least in Femora Fong's case, misinterpret Betty's explanation of the British-rigged ceremony and her fragmentary drawings of their body parts, which she intends to assemble later on a larger sheet of paper. In what becomes known as the Tefuga Incident, the Kitawa women dissolve their tribe's longstanding relationship with Kama Boi's family by falling upon and literally ripping apart the new emir. To the British, this is another instance of Africans' inscrutability and "primitivism." However, Dickinson depicts the incident as a politically motivated murder.

Writing in her diary grows into an even more powerful political act for Betty than talking with the Kitawa or painting pictures.

Through recording events in her journal, Betty recognizes that both she and the Kitawa are oppressed. In a passage that links her with Elongo, Betty refers to herself as a "spy" in men's country. When she describes her and Femora Fong's victory over Kama Boi, Betty regards herself as writing women's history: "We've won! I've won. Yes. It was really me. If I hadn't been there it wouldn't have been any good. Oh, some day, in five years, or ten, someone would have found out [about the toe villages]. But I did it, this year. It was my own private war, and I won. Now I'm going to write it all down, before the men start telling it their way" (185).

Betty's art not only enables her to bring down the person oppressing the Kitawa, but may also free her from the dominating force in her life, her husband. Like *Oedipus Tyrannus*, which has been compared to a detective story because the protagonist struggles to find the truth of his existence, in Nigel Jackland *Tefuga* contains a character seeking the truth about his origins. Moreover, hindsight reveals the event on Tefuga Hill to be a political assassination. However, it is not until the final pages that Dickinson's novel begins to resemble a mystery in the conventional sense. Only then do we learn that Ted commits suicide soon after Betty's departure for England and that Betty's diary may be the cause. After the debacle of the Tefuga Incident, reading about Betty's betrayal of him is presumably too much for Ted. In this politically motivated "murder," Betty is once again linked with the Kitawa. Femora Fong's dream predicted the ineffectiveness of British rule after Kama Boi's ouster, designating Elongo as the cause for this. Before she leaves Kiti, Betty gives Elongo instructions about disposing of the diary, which she knows he is unlikely to follow. Thus, if Ted's death is a murder, then Betty and Elongo are coconspirators.

Even more radical than what it says about colonial Africa are *Tefuga*'s implications for the continent today. Second-generation postwar Africanist writers frequently attributed official corruption and military coups to African "primitivism." In a similar way, Nigel Jackland regards the dishonesty and violence he encounters in Nigeria as purely African problems. Believing he has no connection with the colonialism that once existed in Nigeria, Jackland fails, at least initially, to see the link between the system his parents were part of and the country's current political situation—one in which the military maintains a high profile and the old emir system still survives. His discussions with Major Kadu and Elongo, however, force Jackland to rethink his position. The army alternately harasses and assists the British film crew, which consequently brings Jackland and the Major together. During a discussion of the respective limitations of democracy and martial rule, the officer asserts that colonialism created the corruption in his country, "These [dishonest] people only do these things because they are operating in system where is nobody to stop them. No sanction of custom, of tolerable dealing. You destroy all that. You leave us only the sanction of the gun" (63).

Events also bring Elongo and Jackland together, providing them with an opportunity to exchange ideas. Without the emir's help, Jackland would not have been able to shoot in Kiti. During the filming of a scene in Old Kiti Town, a disgruntled youth decries "Elongoism," provoking the emir to defend himself to Jackland and explain what has happened in Kiti since 1924. When a military coup takes place shortly before Jackland plans to leave Nigeria, Elongo appeals to him for assistance in fleeing Kiti. The unusual circumstances enable the two men to discuss colonial and contemporary Nigeria. Rather than being symptomatic of African "primitivism," as works in the expatriate tradition frequently assert, Elongo explains that the coups and corruption have longstanding and clearly discernable political causes. On the one hand, eschewing bitterness, the Sarkin soberly, even sympathetically, assesses the military men who are pursuing him. He understands their need for scapegoats and predicts that within a year they will be overwhelmed by the insurmountable problems they have taken on. On the other hand, resenting Jackland's suggestion that his rule has seen its share of corruption, Elongo explains that a model emir under British Indirect Rule would find it difficult to succeed in postcolonial Nigeria because, while laudable, ethics by themselves do not help get politicians elected: "Anyone who is not a fool can perceive the pragmatic benefits of honest government, but that does not necessarily mean he feels them in his heart. Your father and his kind actually felt deep admiration for probity, and determination to show it themselves, but they did not manage to instil that feeling in the peoples they ruled. All they left us with is the rhetoric of probity. The virtues we genuinely feel are different—generosity, spontaneity, boldness, bravura, personal authority. You will tell me you can't run a country on those. I tell you you can't run even a small province in Nigeria without them" (206).

Elongo's statement underscores the purpose of Dickinson's dual focus—to reverse Africanist discourse—by asserting that the violence and corruption of postcolonial Nigeria, like the actions of Betty and the Kitawa during colonialism, have complex political origins. Through his feminist and political themes, Dickinson exposes the falsity of the Africanist concept of "primitivism." In addition, opting for realism rather than parody, he goes beyond Boyd and Boyle by not only rewriting a page in the history of the West's relationship with Africa but providing a historically grounded, non-Africanist approach to contemporary Africa as well.

William Duggan

The Great Thirst *and* Lovers of the African Night

In the first two installments of his projected southern African trilogy, William Duggan rewrites the history of African-European relations in a more profound way than any other non-African. Whereas many earlier postwar authors concentrate on a limited period of time—first-generation writers on colonial, second- and third-generation writers on postcolonial, Boyd on colonial, Boyle on precolonial Africa—Duggan's novels span three centuries, depicting the continent before, during, and after the colonial era. Further, in contrast to most outsiders who have written about Africa, Duggan focuses on Africans, not Europeans, and uses a style that aspires to be a transcription of an oral narrative to tell their story. Finally, *The Great Thirst* and *Lovers of the African Night* are highly politicized novels, linking the hardships the BaNare have to endure as a result of their proximity to South Africa with the struggle of the blacks in that country against the white minority government.

The Great Thirst traces five generations of the BaNare in detail, focusing its attention on Majamaje, "Eater of Rocks." Before the arrival of the Boers, the BaNare migrated from South Africa to Kalahariland, a country similar to but not identical with Botswana, forcing the original occupants, the Bakii, out to the desert village of Loang while they inhabited Naring. Over the years, a series of peoples besiege the BaNare: the Zulu or Imitation Zulu, the Boers, the Wall Makers, and finally the English. Only the latter actually conquer them, and the BaNare are largely oblivious to this, thanks to Mojamaje, but all of these peoples, as well as the Bakii and the Bushman, influence the tribe. A natural disaster, the Great Thirst or drought, proves an even more awesome threat than the invasions, but the BaNare manage to survive this, too.

Mojamaje's story begins with him as a nine-year-old being pinned against a rock while the BaNare battle a group of Boer cattle raiders. His father is killed but Mojamaje survives, and a song, the first of many, is composed about him. He becomes the first BaNare to go to South Africa, learn Boer and English, marry a person with non-

African blood, and serve in the English army. It is Mojamaje, at ninety the oldest member of the tribe and the subject of many songs, who meets with the British district commissioner and fifty soldiers when they march into Naring. With his knowledge of the English and their language, Mojamaje once again saves the BaNare. His death, sometime between World War I and II, certainly signals the end of an era for the BaNare; however, during his lifetime, their world has already been dramatically changed by the waves of Africans, Boers, and Britons who have swept through Kalahariland.

Shorter and more concentrated than its predecessor, *Lovers of the African Night* portrays the BaNare from the end of World War II until approximately the mid-1970s. Whereas Duggan organizes the main sections of *The Great Thirst* around people, he structures his second novel around places. Nevertheless, the book does have a hero(ine): she is Ata Four, one of an outcast family of women who live on the outskirts of Naring, entertain men as a means of survival, and never marry. Similar to Mojamaje, Ata Four breaks new ground, becoming the first Ata to help out in the BaNare's fields, work for English people and learn their language, chase a man who has deserted her, get married, and open her own business.

While Ata and later her son Kanye play significant roles in the South African struggle and strive to reverse the fate of the Atas, Mojamaje's grandson Boko tries to save the BaNare from foreign exploitation and their own complacency. Not until the chief's recklessness is made clear when a fire he sets destroys Naring, however, does the tribe elect Boko their leader, indicating that a form of democracy has replaced monarchy in the tribe, which is now part of a newly independent country. Ata returns to a devastated Naring in triumph, the mother of the BaNare's new hero, Kanye, for whom Mojamaje has been a constant inspiration. Kanye's declaration that the BaNare in South Africa need to know there is a home they can return to inspires the tribe to rebuild Naring.

Unlike Africanist writers who stress or create differences between blacks and whites, Duggan emphasizes the importance of racial integration in the history of the BaNare, depicts Europeans as part of a series of forces that invade Naring, and treats Western technology as yet another innovation to which the tribe must adapt. One of the keys to the BaNare's survival is their assimilation of other peoples. After the BaNare drive the Bakii to Loang, the latter intermarry with Bushmen, but they become part of the BaNare when Mojamaje's mother, Ma-Mojamaje, becomes the first Bakii to marry a member of the dominant tribe. The *Mfecene* not only brings Zulu and Imitation

Zulu to Kalahariland but also large numbers of refugees escaping their raids, many of whom become BaNare. As the whites penetrate deeper into South Africa, Griquas, Boers, and Indians come to Naring as traders. Furthermore, Mojamaje and others after him journey to South Africa, intermarry and often bring relatives back to Kalahariland. Finally, the English post a district officer at Naring, eventually resulting in English blood being mixed with the wide variety of African and Boer blood flowing through BaNare veins. This willingness to incorporate different peoples into their tribe contrasts markedly with the racial intolerance of white South Africans, which Duggan's novels amply document.

As with the racial question, Duggan puts Western technology in the proper perspective. While the Boers with their rifles and the English with their cannons are formidable adversaries, the BaNare succeed in maintaining their autonomy, just as they have previously turned back technologically superior invaders, such as the Zulu and Imitation Zulu, who use short stabbing spears instead of long throwing spears. In fact, the most serious dangers the BaNare face are drought and internal rivalry. The Great Thirst not only kills crops, reduces the BaNare livestock to a few goats, and causes the women to stop menstruating, but it also places tremendous pressure on the tribe's fragile cohesiveness: "So far in the turmoil of South Africa the BaNare's luck had held out. [Mojamaje's brutal grandfather] Tladi, raids, refugees, Boers, English, [the scheming missionary] Stimp, perfidious [Chief] Pia, all these disruptions produced lasting strains and cracks that a drought might multiply, shattering the BaNare after all, to share the same fate in the end that South Africa suffered."[13] Likewise, the fire that destroys Naring in *Lovers of the African Night* results as much from internal dissension among the BaNare that keeps them from heeding Boko's warnings about the chief's improprieties as from carelessness.

As Duggan himself points out, the adaptability of the BaNare figures as prominently in his fiction as their greatest hero: "[the story of the Great Thirst] gives a true picture of Mojamaje's heroism, a thing easily misunderstood but important to know, for he lived in a time when the world changed completely and the BaNare struggled to survive within it" (15). In addition to new people, new languages, new means of warfare, and new forms of government, the tribe must adjust to changes in agricultural methods, the advent of money, the appearance of diamond and gold mines in Kimberley and Johannesburg, and the legalization of racism in South Africa, among other things. Stretching from the eighteenth to the late twentieth century,

The Great Thirst and *Lovers of the African Night* together provide the most comprehensive view of African-European relations to be found in works by outside authors. Duggan goes a step beyond Dickinson, depicting the precolonial as well as colonial events that have helped to shape postcolonial Africa.

Duggan's focus on the BaNare and his attempt to use African methods to tell an African story set his novels apart from anything else written by an outsider. Duggan creates a large number of fully realized African characters, from Mojamaje's fierce grandparent Tladi, who expands the BaNare's influence out to Loang, through Ata Four's son Kanye, who protests the mandatory teaching of Afrikaans in South African schools. Clearly, however, Mojamaje and Ata Four, are his most impressive achievements. Although there are a number of important similarities between these risk takers and protectors of their people, *Lovers of the African Night* is as much a woman-centered novel grounded in the present as *The Great Thirst* is dominated by great men of the past.

Moreover, the results of Duggan's approximation of an oral narrative, complete with genealogies in the case of *The Great Thirst*, are, at least from a non-African prespective, beautiful and satisfying; however, this technique also raises important questions. Duggan's attempt to produce a written imitation of oral narration is unique among outside works about Africa. His novels contain elements from each of the five major categories Jan Vansina lists in his typology of oral traditions: formulae, poetry, lists, tales, and commentaries.[14] Nevertheless, the validity of Duggan's approximation of oral testimony can certainly be questioned. How accurate is this depiction of southern African storytelling and how much has Duggan had to alter or simplify the process of oral transmission so that it will be comprehensible and aesthetically pleasing to his Western audience?

Relying on simple rhymes and adding a liberal dose of humor, Duggan includes many songs about Mojamaje and other BaNare in his narrative that contribute to the oral flavor. For example, the first song about Mojamaje celebrates his surviving a Boer cattle raid despite being pinned helpless against the rocks: "All through the night / Through the terrible fight / Mojamaje kept watch by the door / First he ate a rock / Then he ate a bullet / Then Mojamaje ate a Boer" (14). Not only does Duggan make the BaNare's customs and actions seem reasonable and inevitable but outsiders like the Boers and English appear foreign, illogical, vicious at times, and intrusive. However, his emphasis on racial integration and adaptability shows that Duggan has not merely ridden the Africanist pendulum to the other extreme. Mojamaje is certainly not an eater of rocks, nor does he perform all the exploits the BaNare attribute to him, yet through Duggan's story we realize that he truly is a monumental figure to his people and deserving of commemoration. As a result, the contrast between the BaNare and people who lack an oral tradition is striking. The tribe's ancestors are truly present to them because their stories keep them alive, truly heroic because the BaNare have retold, debated, and reassessed the experiences of their forbears. The oral style also allows Duggan to use repetition effectively; recurrent symbols, coincidences, and leitmotifs serve to remind the reader, as a *griot* would remind his audience, how things fit together.

Although Duggan focuses on Kalahariland rather than South Africa, his novels are highly politicized, boldly incorporating some of the most explosive events in the struggle against apartheid. As with his imitation of oral narration, the honesty of such a practice might be questioned if Duggan had not made the connection between the BaNare and blacks in South Africa clear from the beginning and, through Ata and Kanye, established the need for autonomous ancestral homelands such as Naring as sources of inspiration for those engaged in the racial struggle. The BaNare's names, language, titles, and general geographical location in and around the Great Thirstland of the Kalahari identify them with the Tswana people who inhabit Botswana and the neighboring parts of South Africa.[15] Although Duggan takes some geographical liberties, Kalahariland resembles Botswana in its terrain, its proximity to South Africa, its status as a High Commission Territory administered by the British during the colonial era, the language that its people speak, and its comparatively recent independence. Duggan takes his greatest liberties, however, in his description of South Africa.

When the BaNare migrated from South Africa to Kalahariland before the arrival of the Boers, they left a place called Taung. It is to Taung that Mojamaje and many BaNare after him go when they journey to South Africa. There, Mojamaje meets and marries Maka, who is half Boer, and later brings some of his Boer relations back to Naring with him. Ata also travels to Taung when she chases after the man who abandoned her, a BaNare called the Jackal. Perfectly comfortable with being a successful second class citizen in South Africa, the Jackal looks forward to the construction of Sharpetown, a government built and regulated community, for working blacks only, scheduled to replace Taung village. Now the Jackal's wife, Ata is horrified by the government's bulldozing of Taung village and repulsed by the prospect of Sharpetown. Refusing to live there, Ata is the first to set her pass aflame during a demonstration that prompts the government to shoot dead sixty people and wound another two hundred in an episode clearly based on the massacre at Sharpeville outside of Vereeniging in 1960. An event with important consequences for the struggle against the South African government, in *Lovers of the African Night* the pass protest causes Ata to become the saviour of Kalahariland because the government's brutal response convinces the British not to turn over the territory to South Africa. Approximately sixteen years later, Ata's son is immortalized on front pages across the world when he defiantly hurls stones at troops firing on students protesting the enforced use of Boer as the medium of instruction in black schools. Occurring once again in Sharpetown (rather than Soweto), the event makes Kanye a hero in both South Africa and Kalahariland.

Instead of plundering famous events to sensationalize his story, Duggan makes it clear that the struggle of South African blacks is the BaNare's struggle as well, one that began even before the Battle of the Rocks when the young Mojamaje was pinned against a cliff wall, facing an armed force of Boer cattle raiders. That early scene serves as a metaphor for black and white relations in southern Africa over the last three centuries. Trapped, confronting almost certain doom, black people must not only survive but learn as much as they can from their enemies, so they and their descendants may be better prepared for the next encounter.

By focusing on one group of Africans over a period of time encompassing the precolonial, colonial, and contemporary eras, using African methods to tell an African story, and clearly connecting the BaNare's struggle for survival and autonomy with that of blacks in present-day South Africa, Duggan has made a tremendous breakthrough. *The Great Thirst* and *Lovers of the African Night* rewrite the history of black and white relations in the continent, reverse Africanist discourse, and provide the most authentic portrait of Africa yet produced by an outside author. It will be interesting to see where the final installment of his trilogy will take him, if he in fact completes it. Unless he goes backward or forward in time, he will have to limit himself to just about a decade. In any event, his first two novels stand out as towering achievements, whetting the appetite for more.

NOTES

1. Michel Foucault, "Nietzsche, Genealogy, History," *Language, Counter-Memory, Practice,* ed. Donald F. Bouchard, Ithaca: Cornell University Press, 154. Subsequent references are to this edition.

2. Roland Barthes, *S/Z*, trans. Richard Miller, New York: Hill, 1974, 4.

3. William Boyd, *An Ice-Cream War*, New York: Penguin, 1983, 12. Subsequent references are to this edition.

4. Brian Gardner, *On to Kilimanjaro*, New York: MacFadden, 1964.

5. T. Coraghessan Boyle, *Water Music*, New York: Penguin, 1983, x. Subsequent references are to this edition.

6. Boyle adds another perspective absent from *Travels* by constructing a subplot involving Park's wife, Ailie, about whom historians have been able to uncover little. He also presents a lower-class woman's experiences through the character of Fanny Brunch.

7. Peter Brent, *Black Nile: Mungo Park and the Search for the Niger*, London: Gordon, 1977, 168. Subsequent references are to this edition.

8. J. Wishaw, "Life of Mungo Park," Mungo Park, *Travels in the Interior Districts of Africa Volume II: Last Journey, Life*, New ed. London: Murray, 1817, xcvi–xcviii, cxxvii.

9. See "Life of Mungo Park," cxxlviii; *Black Nile*, 162, 167, 185; Sanche de Gramont, *The Strong Brown God: The Story of the Niger River*, Boston: Houghton, 1976, 100–101; Christopher Lloyd, *The Search for the Niger*, London: Collins, 1973.

10. Boyle is not the first to take liberties with Park, however. John Gray's bizarre novel, *Park, A Fantastic Story* (1934), depicts a fifty-nine-year-old Mungo Park strangely transported to a futuristic England where Catholic Africans hold sway.

11. In *Water Music*, shortly after Park "discovers" the Niger on his first trip, Johnson is attacked by a crocodile (an event that actually befell Isaaco), much to the chagrin of the explorer who thinks him dead. In Johnson's village seeking a guide for his second expedition, Park learns that Johnson, now calling himself Isaaco, is alive and willing to lead him once again.

12. Peter Dickinson, *Tefuga*, New York: Pantheon, 1986, 207. Subsequent references are to this edition.

13. William Duggan, *The Great Thirst*, New York: Dell, 1985, 225. Subsequent references are to this edition.

14. Jan Vansina, *Oral Tradition: A Study in Historical Methodology*, Trans. H. M. Wright, Chicago: Aldine, 1965, 142–164.

15. For a recent account of the *Batswana*, see Marianne Halverson, *Under African Sun*, Chicago: University of Chicago Press, 1987.

Conclusion

In their works about Africa since 1945, non-black outsiders have become increasingly aware of discursive formations, recently seeking methods of circumventing their stultifying and hegemonic influences. By the early twentieth century, three means of depicting the continent, all imbued with the basic gestures of Africanist discourse—binary oppositions, image projection, and evolutionary language—had been firmly established. These were the political assessment or travel book tradition, the expatriate or going-native tradition, and the fantasy tradition. Postwar outside writing about Africa comprises three generations that descend directly from the dominant traditions and a fourth category that deliberately eschews them.

Written during the age of high imperialism, Winston Churchill's *My African Journey*, Joseph Conrad's *Heart of Darkness*, and Edgar Rice Burroughs's *Tarzan of the Apes* stand as quintessential examples of three ways of portraying Africa that continued largely unaltered until the 1960s and only in the 1980s began to be subverted or abandoned. Churchill makes no attempt to disguise the political agenda of his travel book, in essence mapping East and Central Africa for further British exploitation. In Kurtz, Conrad depicts the Westerner "maddened by the tropics," corrupted by the lack of restraint and the condition of unlimited power that Africa offers him. Without firsthand experience in the continent but well versed in Africanist discourse and Darwin's theories, Burroughs concocted a fantastic Africa so popular among the general public that he became one of the most widely read authors in history.

From 1945 to the early 1960s, first-generation postwar writers such as Evelyn Waugh, Graham Greene, and Saul Bellow rely heavily on the established traditions and largely or totally ignore the political realites of Africa during the twilight of the colonial era. Waugh's *A Tourist in Africa* is a half-hearted attempt to write a between-the-wars travel book on the eve of widespread African independence. Inspired if not obsessed by Conrad, Greene sets two going-native novels in Africa, *The Heart of the Matter* and *A Burnt-Out Case*, avoiding contemporary political events to focus on various states of religious belief and disbelief. In *Henderson the Rain King*, the fantasy tradition offers Bellow the opportunity to allegorize America without fettering his imagination to a location grounded in reality. In contrast to previous authors, Greene and Bellow display a consciousness of Africanist discourse; however, they choose to use it for their novelistic purposes rather than attempt to mitigate its underlying violence.

A significant exception to the apolitical nature of the first generation are the largely reactionary novels inspired by the Mau Mau revolt in what is now Kenya. In addition, Margaret Laurence's transitional work, *This Side Jordan*, not only addresses political change in Africa but predicts a bright future for the continent.

Predominately comprised of works from the 1970s, second-generation postwar writing about Africa is much more openly political than its predecessor. An early work, Paul Theroux's *Fong and the Indians* possesses an optimism reminiscent of Laurence's *This Side Jordan*. Both writers, however, became disillusioned with the New Africa by the end of the 1960s, as Africanist attitudes reintrenched themselves. Theroux's later works on the continent echo the political assessments of V. S. and Shiva Naipaul, who regard postcolonial Africa as the hopeless combination of failed colonialism and indigenous primitivism.

Second-generation postwar works in the expatriate tradition by Theroux, V. S. Naipaul, Martha Gellhorn, and William Boyd no longer portray whites in Africa as heroic figures but rather as powerless, often inept individuals at the mercy of forces they cannot control. The elder Naipaul's *A Bend in the River* offers a new wrinkle by making an Indian born in Africa his protagonist; nevertheless, the novel is vigorously Africanist, accentuating the corruption of independent Africa. Similarly, John Updike's *The Coup* features an African as the main character, but below its veneer of authenticity the novel is a firmly Africanist white male fantasy.

Second-generation postwar writers do, however, go beyond the metaconsciousness of Greene and Bellow. At times, Theroux, V. S. Naipaul, Updike, and Walter Abish recognize that language itself can subjugate Africans, but they fail to acknowledge the extent to which their own works perpetuate this process. A parody of postcolonial works in the expatriate tradition, Boyd's *A Good Man in Africa* is a fitting culmination to second-generation writing. Though unashamedly Africanist, his novel treats the basic elements of the expatriate tradition as literary conventions ripe for parody instead of established facts.

Aware that Africanist discourse informs the dominant means of depicting the continent, during the 1980s third-generation postwar authors openly acknowledge or actively subvert the traditions they utilize. Helen Winternitz makes clear her opposition to American support for the Mobutu regime in the introduction and refers to specific historical events throughout *East along the Equator*. Jonathan Raban reverses the expatriate tradition by depicting England instead of Africa as the "foreign land" that corrupts his protagonist. Likewise, Maria Thomas portrays going native positively in *Antonia Saw the Oryx First*, depicting a mutually beneficial relationship between a white American and a black African woman. Repeatedly announcing that his work is a fantasy, J. G. Ballard explores the obsessional nature of the Africanist mentality in *The Day of Creation*.

Third-generation postwar writers frequently make language a subject of their works, illustrating the ways in which words themselves can objectify people. Raban thematizes the effects that Africanist discourse can have on an outsider knowledgeable about and sympathetic to the continent. Thomas criticizes not only researchers and travel writers who condemn Africa but even Western medical personnel for their Africanist attitudes. The power of the established traditions, however, causes the writers of the third generation to occasionally repeat Africanist clichés, despite their metaconsciousness.

By avoiding the dominant traditions completely and reconceiving the history of relations between Africans and Europeans, authors of the fourth category engage in Foucauldian genealogy, seeking to reverse Africanist discourse by focusing on events that belie its continuity. In *An Ice-Cream War* William Boyd retells the story of the First World War in Africa, showing it to be a madness the West imposed upon the continent. T. Coraghessan Boyle rewrites Mungo Park's expeditions to West Africa in *Water Music*, adding an African and a lower-class English perspective absent from Park's influential *Travels*. In these works Boyd and Boyle reject the Africanist myth that opposes Western civilization with African primitivism.

Peter Dickinson and William Duggan go even further, demonstrating the connections between past occurrences and present conditions in the continent and the links between Africans and non-Africans. Dickinson's *Tefuga* compares the oppression of white women in 1920s European society with the situation of Africans under colonialism. In addition, he shows that the violence and official corruption of contemporary Africa have complex political causes, many of them rooted in colonialism. In *The Great Thirst* and *Lovers of the African Night*, Duggan focuses on the interactions between one group of African people and their black and white neighbors over a span of three hundred years, showing how, in contrast to the racially intolerant minority that controls South Africa, the Ba-Nare have survived adversity through assimilation and adaptability. Unique among outsiders who depict the continent, Duggan attempts to use African methods to tell an African story by aspiring to capture the flavor of oral narrative in his novels.

Now that some non-black writers have recognized the distorting effects of Africanist discourse and sought to subvert or totally abandon the established ways of writing about the continent, the opportunity exists for more outsiders to create powerful, sensitive, historically grounded works about Africa. Fourth-category writing should not be regarded as an end in itself, the means of depicting Africa to which all future outsider authors should aspire and conform. Rather, it is likely that the genealogical writing of the fourth category will come to be seen as a necessary, corrective phase separating the Africanist writing of the past from the non-Africanist writing yet to come. Unquestionably, Boyle, Dickinson, and Duggan deserve credit for rewriting the history of African-European relations, but much remains for outsiders writing about Africa to accomplish.

Although vigorously Africanist, second-generation postwar writing focused its attention on postcolonial Africa. Similarly, third-generation authors addressed contemporary conditions in the continent, despite at times reverting to Africanist clichés. Because of the groundbreaking work of fourth-category writers, the stage is set for outsiders to produce works about today's Africa untainted by Africanist discourse.[1] Moreover, while Boyle, Dickinson, and Duggan have shown us how to produce metaconscious, historically grounded novels about the continent, the challenge remains for writers of nonfiction to either redefine travel literature or invent new methods of depicting Africa free from the distortions of Africanist discourse.

NOTES

1. Particularly in the light of recent events in Ethiopia, Thomas Keneally's *To Asmara* (1989) is an important book by a major author that de-

serves recognition. Keneally's unmitigated partisanship for the Eritrean People's Liberation Front, to whom he dedicates the book, is rare in outside writing about Africa. Moreover, to a great extent the work eshews Africanist conventions and consistently attributes events in Ethiopia and the behavior of its people to identifiable political causes. Although it certainly has been influenced by the expatriate tradition and at times becomes bogged down by the fictional editor's comments, the novel may mark the beginning of a post-Africanist era of outside writing about Africa.

Selected Bibliography

Abish, Walter. *Alphabetical Africa*. New York: New Directions, 1974.

Achebe, Chinua. "Image of Africa." *Massachusetts Review* 18 (Winter 1977): 782–94.

——— . *A Man of the People*. Garden City, N.Y.: Anchor, 1967.

——— . *Morning Yet on Creation Day*. London: Heinemann, 1975.

——— . *Things Fall Apart*. New York: Astor, 1959.

Adams, Percy. *Travelers and Travel Liars, 1660–1800*. 1962. New York: Dover, 1980.

Angelou, Maya. *All God's Children Need Traveling Shoes*. New York: Random, l986.

Ballard, J. G. *The Day of Creation*. New York: Farrar, 1988.

"Back to the Bush in Zaire." Editorial. *New York Times* 20 Nov. 1991: A26.

Barthes, Roland. *S/Z*. Trans. Richard Miller. New York: Hill, 1974.

Bellow, Saul. *Henderson the Rain King*. 1959. In *The Portable Saul Bellow*. New York: Penguin, 1977.

Birmingham, David, and Phyllis M. Martin, eds. *The History of Central Africa*. Vol. 2. London: Longman, 1983.

Bloom, Harold, ed. *John Updike: Modern Critical Views*. New York: Chelsea, 1987.

Boardman, Gwen R. *Graham Greene: The Aesthetics of Exploration*. Gainesville, University of Florida Press, 1971.

Bowles, Paul. *The Sheltering Sky*. 1949. New York: Ecco, 1978.

Boyd, William. *A Good Man in Africa*. New York: Penguin, 1982.

——— . *An Ice-Cream War*. New York: Penguin, 1983.

——— . *On the Yankee Station*. New York: Penguin, 1982.

Boyle, T. Coraghessan. *Water Music*. 1981. New York: Penguin, 1983.

Brantlinger, Patrick. *Rule of Darkness*. Ithaca: Cornell University Press, 1988.

Brent, Peter. *Black Nile: Mungo Park and the Search for the Niger*. London: Gordon, 1977.

Brooks, Gwendolyn. *Report from Part One*. Detroit: Broadside, 1972.

Burroughs, Edgar Rice. *Tarzan of the Apes.* 1912. New York: Ballantine, 1977.

Cary, Joyce. *Mister Johnson.* 1939. New York: Time, 1962.

Chapman, Abraham, ed. *Black Voices.* New York: New American Library, 1968.

——— . *New Black Voices.* New York: New American Library, 1972.

Chatwin, Bruce. *The Viceroy of Ouidah.* 1980. New York: Penguin, 1988.

Clark, John Pepper. *The Example of Shakespeare.* Evanston, Ill.: Northwestern University Press, 1970.

Clayton, John Jacob. *Saul Bellow: In Defense of Man.* 2d ed. Bloomington: Indiana University Press, 1979.

Churchill, Winston. *My African Journey.* 1909. *The Collected Works.* Vol. 1. Centenary Limited Edition. London: The Library of Imperial History, 1973.

Conrad, Joseph. *Great Short Works of Joseph Conrad.* New York: Harper, 1966.

——— . *Heart of Darkness and The Secret Sharer.* New York: New American Library, 1950.

——— . *Heart of Darkness.* 3d ed. Ed. Robert Kimbrough. New York: Norton, 1987.

——— . *Lord Jim.* 1900. New York: Bantam, 1958.

Crace, Jim. *Continent.* New York: Harper, 1987.

Cunard, Nancy, ed. *Negro: An Anthology.* 1933. New York: Ungar, 1970.

Curtin, Philip. *Africa and the West.* Madison: University of Wisconsin Press, 1972.

Curtin, Philip, et al. *African History.* Boston: Little, Brown, 1978.

Dickinson, Peter. *Tefuga.* New York: Pantheon, 1986.

Dinesen, Isak. *Out of Africa and Shadows on the Grass.* New York: Vintage, 1985.

Duggan, William. *The Great Thirst.* New York: Dell, 1985.

——— . *Lovers of the African Night.* New York: Delacorte, 1987.

Fabian, Johannes. *Time and the Other.* New York: Columbia University Press, 1983.

Fage, J. D. and Roland Oliver, eds. *The Cambridge History of Africa.* Vols 2–5. New York: Cambridge University Press, 1981.

Fanon, Frantz. *Black Skin, White Masks.* 1952. Trans. Charles Law. New York: Grove, 1982.

——— . *The Wretched of the Earth.* 1963. Trans. Constance Farrington. New York: Grove, 1968.

Fields, Karen. *Revival and Rebellion in Colonial Central Africa.* Princeton, N.J.: Princeton University Press, 1985.

Forster, E. M. *A Passage to India.* New York: Harcourt, 1924.

Foucault, Michel. *The Archaeology of Knowledge and The Discourse on Language.* Trans. A. M. Sheridan Smith. New York: Pantheon, 1972.

——— . *Language, Counter–Memory, Practice.* Ed. Donald F. Bouchard. Ithaca, N.Y.: Cornell University Press, 1977.

Fox, James. *White Mischief.* New York: Vintage, 1982.

Fussell, Paul. *Abroad.* New York: Oxford University Press, 1980.

Gardner, Brian. *On to Kilimanjaro.* New York: MacFadden, 1964.

Gates, Henry Louis, Jr. *Figures in Black.* New York: Oxford University Press, 1989.

———, ed. *"Race," Writing, and Difference.* Chicago: University of Chicago Press, 1986.

Gellhorn, Martha. *Travels with Myself and Another.* New York: Dodd, 1979.

———. *The View from the Ground.* New York: Atlantic Monthly, 1988.

———. *The Weather in Africa.* New York: Avon, 1981.

Gibb, H. A. R. *Mohammedanism.* London: Oxford University Press, 1949.

Gibbon, Edward. "The Decline and Fall of the Roman Empire." *Encylcopedia Britannica.* 1952.

Gide, Andre. *Travels in the Congo.* 1927. Trans. Dorothy Bussy. New York: Penguin, 1986.

Goonetilleke, D. C. R. A. *Developing Countries in British Fiction.* Totowa, N.J.: Rowman, 1977.

Gordimer, Nadine. *A Guest of Honour.* New York: Penguin, 1973.

Gorer, Geoffrey. *Africa Dances.* New York: Knopf, 1935.

Gould, David J. *Bureaucratic Corruption and Underdevelopment in the Third World: The Case of Zaire.* New York: Pergamon, 1980.

Gramont, Sanche de (Ted Morgan). *The Strong Brown God: The Story of the Niger River.* Boston: Houghton, 1976.

Gray, John. *Park, A Fantastic Story.* 1932. Manchester: Carcanet, 1984.

Greene, Barbara. *Land Benighted.* London: Geoffrey Bles, 1938.

Greene, Graham. *A Burnt-Out Case.* 1961. New York: Penguin, 1977.

———. *The Heart of the Matter.* 1948. New York: Penguin, 1978.

———. *Journey without Maps.* 1936. New York: Penguin, 1978.

———. *In Search of a Character.* 1961. New York: Penguin, 1968.

———. *A Sort of Life.* New York: Pocket, 1973.

———. *Ways of Escape.* New York: Simon, 1980.

Haley, Alex. *Roots.* New York: Dell, 1977.

Halverson, Marianne. *Under African Sun.* Chicago: University of Chicago Press, 1987.

Hammond, Dorothy and Alta Jablow. *The Myth of Africa.* New York: Library of Social Science, 1977.

Hansberry, Lorraine. *Les Blancs. The Collected Last Plays.* 1972. New York: New American Library, 1983.

Hargreaves, Alec G. "European Identity and the Colonial Frontier." *Journal of European Studies* 12 (1982): 167–79.

Harrison, William. *Africana.* New York: Morrow, 1977.

———. *Burton and Speke.* New York: St. Martin's, 1982.

Hemingway, Ernest. *Green Hills of Africa.* New York: Scribner's, 1935.

Hoagland, Edward. *African Calliope.* New York: Random, 1979.

Holtsmark, Erling. *Edgar Rice Burroughs.* Boston: Twayne, 1986.

———. *Tarzan and Tradition.* Westport, Conn.: Greenwood, 1981.

Hone, Joseph. *Africa of the Heart*. New York: Beech Tree, 1986.

Howe, Susanne. *Novels of Empire*. New York: Columbia University Press, 1949.

Hughes, Robert. *The Fatal Shore: The Epic of Australia's Founding*. 1986. New York: Vintage, 1988.

Hunt, George W., SJ. *John Updike and the Three Great Secret Things: Sex, Religion, and Art*. Grand Rapids, Mich.: Eerdmans, 1980.

Huxley, Elspeth. *The Flame Trees of Thika*. 1959. New York: Penguin, 1962.

———. *The Mottled Lizard*. 1962. New York: Penguin, 1981.

———. *Out in the Midday Sun*. 1985. New York: Penguin, 1987.

Hyland, Paul. *The Black Heart: A Voyage through Central Africa*. 1988. New York: Paragon, 1990.

Ingalls, Rachel. *Binstead's Safari*. New York: Simon, 1983.

Jacobs, Sylvia. *Black Americans and the Missionary Movement in Africa*. Westport, Conn.: Greenwood, 1982.

JanMohammed, Abdul. "The Economy of Manichean Allegory: The Fuction of Racial Difference in Colonialist Literature." *Critical Inquiry* 12 (Autumn 1985): 59–87.

———. *Manichean Aesthetics*. Amherst: University of Massachusetts Press, 1983.

Kabbani, Rana. *Europe's Myths of Orient*. Bloomington: Indiana University Press, 1986.

Karp, David. *The Day of the Monkey*. New York: Vanguard, 1955.

Keneally, Thomas. *To Asmara*. New York: Warner, 1989.

Kiernan, V. G. "Europe in the Colonial Mirror." *History of European Ideas* 1 (1980): 39–59.

Killam, G. D. *Africa in English Fiction 1874–1939*. Ibadan, Nigeria: Ibadan University Press, 1968.

———. "Introduction." Margaret Laurence. *This Side Jordan*. Toronto: McClelland, 1976, ix–xviii.

Laurence, Margaret. *Long Drums and Cannons: Nigerian Dramatists and Novelists*. New York: Praeger, 1969.

———. *New Wind in a Dry Land*. New York: Knopf, 1964.

———. *This Side Jordan*. New York: St. Martin's, 1960.

———. *The Tomorrow-Tamer*. New York: Knopf, 1964.

Leedom-Ackerman, Joanne. *The Dark Path to the Green River*. Dallas: Saybrook, 1987.

Lessing, Doris. *The Grass Is Singing*. 1950. New York: Ballantine, 1964.

Lloyd, Christopher. *The Search for the Niger*. London: Collins, 1973.

Macnaughton, William R., ed. *Critical Essays on John Updike*. Boston: G. K. Hall, 1982.

Mahood, M. M. *The Colonial Encounter*. Totowa, N.J.: Rowman, 1977.

Maja-Pearce, Adewale. "The Naipauls on Africa: An African View." *Journal of Commonwealth Literature* 20 (1985): 111–17.

Mannoni, Octave. *Prospero and Caliban: The Psychology of Colonization.* 2d. ed. Trans. Pamela Powesland. New York: Praeger, 1966.

Markham, Beryl. *West with the Night.* 1942. San Francisco: North Point, 1983.

Martin, Phyllis and P. O'Meara. *Africa.* Bloomington: Indiana University Press: 1977.

Mazrui, Ali. *The Africans.* Boston: Little, Brown, 1986.

McLeod, M. D. *The Asante.* London: Trustees of the British Museum, 1981.

Meyers, Jeffrey. *Fiction and the Colonial Experience.* Totowa, N.J.: Rowman, 1973.

Miller, Christopher. *Blank Darkness: Africanist Discourse in French.* Chicago: University of Chicago Press, 1985.

Mirzi, Sarah and Margaret Strobel, eds. *Three Swahili Women.* Bloomington, Indiana University Press, 1989.

Monsarrat, Nicholas. *The Tribe That Lost Its Head.* New York: William Sloane, 1956.

Moorhead, Alan. *No Room in the Ark.* New York: Harper, 1957.

Mphahlele, Ezekiel. *The African Image.* Rev. ed. New York: Praeger, 1974.

Mudimbe, V. Y. *The Invention of Africa: Gnosis, Philosophy, and the Order of Knowledge.* Bloomington: Indiana University Press, 1988.

Naipaul, Shiva. *North of South.* New York: Penguin, 1980.

Naipaul, V. S. *A Bend in the River.* New York: Vintage, 1980.

——— . *A Congo Diary.* Los Angeles: Sylvester, 1980.

——— . *Finding the Center.* 1984. New York: Vintage, 1986.

——— . *In a Free State.* 1971. New York: Vintage, 1984.

——— . *The Return of Eva Peron.* New York: Vintage, 1981.

Newman, Judie. *Saul Bellow and History.* New York: St. Martin's, 1984.

Ngugi wa Thiong'o. *Homecoming: Essays on African and Caribbean Literature, Culture, and Politics.* New York: Lawrence Hill, 1973.

——— . *Writers in Politics.* London: Heinemann, 1981.

Niane, D. T. *Sundiata: An Epic of Old Mali.* Trans. G. D. Pickett. Harlow, Essex: Longman, 1979.

Nicholson, Michael. *Across the Limpopo.* London: Robson, 1986.

Nietzsche, Friedrich. *The Genealogy of Morals and The Birth of Tragedy.* Trans. Francis Golffing. Garden City, N.Y.: Anchor, 1956.

Nkosi, Lewis. *Tasks and Masks: Themes and Styles of African Literature.* Harlow, Essex: Longman, 1981.

Nkrumah, Kwame. *Neo-Colonialism: The Last Stage of Imperialism.* London: Nelson, 1965.

Noble, Kenneth. "Once a Colonial Jewel, a City Hurtles Backward." *New York Times* 15 November 1991: A4.

Nurse, Derek and Thomas Spear. *The Swahili.* Philadelphia: University of Pennsylvania Press, 1985.

Nzongola-Ntalaja, ed. *The Crisis of Zaire: Myths and Realities.* Trenton, N.J.: Africa World, 1986.

Park, Mungo. *Travels.* 1815. New York: Dutton, 1954.

Paton, Alan. *Cry, the Beloved Country.* New York: Scribner's, 1948.

Prescott, Linda. "Past and Present Darkness: Sources for V. S. Naipaul's *A Bend in the River.*" *Modern Fiction Studies* 30 (Autumn 1984): 547–59.

Raban, Jonathan. *Foreign Land.* New York: Penguin, 1986.

Robeson, Eslanda G. *African Journey.* New York: John Day, 1945.

Rodrigues, Eusebio L. "Bellow's Africa." *American Literature* 43 (May 1971): 242–56.

———. *Quest for the Human: An Exploration of Saul Bellow's Fiction.* Lewisburg, Pa.: Bucknell University Press, 1981.

Roussel, Raymond. *Impressions of Africa.* 1910. Trans. Lindy Foord and Rayner Heppenstall. Berkeley: University of California Press, 1967.

Ruark, Robert. *Something of Value.* Garden City, N.Y.: Doubleday, 1955.

Rush, Norman. *Whites.* New York: MacMillan, 1987.

Said, Edward. *Orientalism.* New York: Vintage, 1979.

———. "Orientalism Reconsidered." *Cultural Critique* 1 (Fall 1985): 89–107.

———. "Representing the Colonized." *Critical Inquiry* 15 (Winter 1989): 205–25.

———. *The World, the Text, and the Critic.* Cambridge: Harvard University Press, 1983.

Scheub, Harold. *African Images.* New York: McGraw, 1972.

Smith, Grahame. *The Achievement of Graham Greene.* Totowa, N.J.: Barnes, 1986.

Smith, William Gardner. *Return to Black America.* Engelwood Cliffs, N.J.: Prentice, 1970.

Soyinka, Wole. *Myth, Literature, and the African World.* New York: Cambridge University Press, 1976.

Stanley, Henry M. *Through the Dark Continent.* 2 Vols. New York: Harper, 1879.

Stein, Gertrude. *The Autobiography of Alice B. Toklas.* 1933. New York: Vintage, 1961.

Thelwell, Michael. *Duties, Pleasures, and Conflicts: Essays in Struggle.* Amherst: University of Massachusetts Press, 1987.

Theroux, Paul. *Fong and the Indians.* Boston: Houghton, 1968.

———. *Girls at Play.* Boston: Houghton 1969.

———. *Jungle Lovers.* Boston: Houghton, 1971.

———. *Sunrise with Seamonsters.* Boston: Houghton, 1985.

———. "Updike in Africa." *Bookviews* 2 (Dec. 1978): 36–37.

———. "When the Peace Corps Was Young." *New York Times* 25 Feb. 1986, natl ed.: 31.

Thomas, Maria. *Antonia Saw the Oryx First.* New York: Soho, 1987.

———. *Come to Africa and Save Your Marriage.* New York: Soho, 1987.

Thompson, Era Bell. *Africa: Land of My Fathers.* Garden City, N.Y.: Doubleday, 1954.

Thompson, Robert Farris. *Flash of the Spirit: African and Afro-American Art and Philosophy*. New York: Random, 1983.

Thornburn, David, and Howard Eiland, eds. *John Updike: A Collection of Critical Essays*. Engelwood Cliffs, N.J.: Prentice, 1979.

Torgovnick, Marianna. *Gone Primitive: Savage Intellects, Modern Lives*. Chicago: University of Chicago Press, 1990.

Twain, Mark. *King Leopold's Soliloquy*. 1905. Berlin: Seven Seas, 1961.

Updike, John. *The Coup*. New York: Fawcett, 1978.

——— . *Picked-Up Pieces*. New York: Knopf, 1975.

——— . *Rabbit Redux*. New York, Fawcett, 1971.

Uya, Okon Edet. *Black Brotherhood*. Lexington, Mass.: Heath, 1971.

Vansina, Jan. *Oral Tradition: A Study in Historical Methodology*. Trans. H. M. Wright. Chicago: Aldine, 1965.

——— . *Oral Tradition as History*. Madison: University of Wisconsin Press, 1985.

Walker, Alice. *The Color Purple*. 1982. New York: Pocket, 1985.

Watt, Ian. *Conrad in the Nineteenth Century*. Berkeley: University of California Press, 1979.

Waugh, Evelyn. *Black Mischief*. 1932. Boston: Little, Brown, 1977.

——— . *Remote People*. 1931. London: Duckworth, 1986.

——— . *Scoop*. 1938. New York: Penguin, 1943.

——— . *A Tourist in Africa*. 1960. Boston: Little, Brown, 1986.

——— . *Waugh in Abyssinia*. Boston: Little, Brown, 1938.

——— . *When the Going Was Good*. London: Duckworth, 1946.

Weisbord, Robert G., ed. *Ebony Kinship*. Westport, Conn.: Greenwood, 1973.

Williams, John A. *Jacob's Ladder*. New York: Thunder's Mouth, 1987.

——— . *The Man Who Cried I Am*. Boston: Little, Brown, 1967.

Wilson, Jonathan. *On Bellow's Planet*. Rutherford, N.J.: Farleigh Dickinson University Press, 1985.

Winternitz, Helen. *East along the Equator*. New York: Atlantic Monthly, 1987.

Wishaw, J. "Life of Mungo Park." Mungo Park. *Travels in the Interior Districts of Africa Volume II: Last Journey, Life*. New ed. London: Murray, 1817.

Woodcock, George, ed. *The Canadian Novel in the Twentieth Century*. Toronto: McClelland, 1975.

Wright, Richard. *Black Power*. New York: Harper, 1954.

Young, Crawford and Thomas Turner. *The Rise and Decline of the Zairian State*. Madison: University of Wisconsin Press, 1985.

Index